About the author

Christopher Portway was born in Essex in 1923. After leaving school he joined the Army and fought in the Second World War. Captured in Normandy, he later escaped from three prison camps in Eastern Europe.

He is married to the girl from Czechoslovakia whom he first met while on the run from the Germans in that country. After 1945, he repeated attempts to reach Anna, though her home was subsequently sealed off behind the Iron Curtain. On one such attempt, Christopher was caught after cutting his way through the electrified fences and crawling over a minefield, to be awarded 104 years in jail. He now has two children; a son and a daughter.

Christopher is a member of the British Guild of Travel Writers and a Fellow of the Royal Geographical Society, as well as being a recipient of a Winston Churchill Award for biography and travel. He is a frequent contributor to various magazine and newspapers and is the author of seventeen books.

Books by the same author

Non-fiction:

Journey to Dana
The Pregnant Unicorn
Corner Seat
Double Circuit
Journey Along the Andes
The Great Railway Adventure
The Great Travelling Adventure
Czechmate
Indian Odyssey
A Kenyan Adventure
Pedal for Your Life
A Good Pair of Legs

Fiction:

All Exits Barred
Lost Vengeance
The Tirana Assignment
as John October *The Anarchy Pedlars*

Contents

Introduction   7

1   Covert Rail Travel in Nazi-occupied and
Communist-dominated Europe   11

2   By Direct Orient Express and Taurus Express to the Orient   33

3   Trans-Siberian Express: London to Vladivostok   61

4   Trans-Mongolia and Trans-North Korea to China   89

5   Round and About the Balkans: Recollections from a
String of Trans-Balkan Rail Journeys   121

6   Mediterranean Circuit: Trans-North Africa and the Orient   157

7   Trans-Asia   185

8   Round and About India by Rail   209

9   Trans-East Africa   235

10   Trans-Andes   255

11   Trains Galore   285
   Scottish By-lines   285
   Going Irish   292
   Rails to the Arctic   305
   Making Tracks in North-East Europe   312
   Trans-North America   331
   On the *Viceroy Special* in Sri Lanka   348
   Riding on the Luxury Trains of South Africa   358

Epilogue   376

References   377

Acknowledgements

I extend my sincere thanks to the multitude of individuals, companies and organisations for the support and help given to me over the decades covered by this book. There are far too many for full individual listing so I will only mention a few involved in the more recent events narrated. These include Regent Holidays Ltd and, in particular, Mr Neil Taylor; Indian Railways and, in particular, Dr Dandapani; Aer Lingus; the Polish National Tourist Office in London and, in particular, Krystyna Rees; South African Airways, and Rovos Rail in South Africa.

I also wish to thank Oxford Illustrated Press (Haynes Publishing) and Impact Books for allowing me to adapt extracts from three of my earlier books, as well as Thomas Cook for not only keeping me regularly supplied with their *European Timetable* and *Overseas Timetable* but also – in the case of Thomas Cook Publishing – for granting permission to reproduce portions of their excellent *Thomas Cook Rail Map of Britain and Ireland* and the *Thomas Cook Rail Map of Europe*.

And finally, thanks to my long-suffering publisher and, in particular, Elizabeth Kershaw.

Please note that since undertaking the journeys narrated in this book, bus connections have replaced sections of rail route in some instances.

Introduction

Railway travel is very much what you make of it. Go with the right attitude and it can be fun: go because you have to and the journey becomes no more than a chore to be borne. Commuters catching the same suburban local five days a week can hardly be expected to raise intense enchantment. Yet for some the train can be a vehicle to adventure. In between can be found a category of person who loves trains simply for the railway's sake and there is the occasional eccentric, like me, who finds in world train travel something of the challenge for which, it is alleged, medieval knights on white chargers were constantly searching.

To travel by train, particularly to a destination far removed from one's own environment, can still evoke a quickening of the pulse unmatched by that of transportation on the ubiquitous aeroplane or the humble coach. And this in spite of the withdrawal of now-thought-to-be-glamorous steam locomotion, the nationalisation and subsequent re-privatisation of the railway, not to mention the series of serious accidents that took place at the tail-end of the last century. It was not all that long ago that journeys around the world could only be accomplished by train. Today, however, the passenger train in some countries, notably North America, is in decline, though in others there is a heartening rebirth with new techniques, rolling stock and equipment to match. In South Africa, Japan, India, much of Europe, and even Britain where it all began, railways continue to hold their own.

On a long-distance train as nowhere else one's compartment becomes an observation post of life. Outside there is the ever-changing scenario of the world; inside one is amongst people who can become friends, or occasionally enemies, but from whom much knowledge and understanding of the world can be gleaned. One can stroll in the corridor, visit the bar, eat in the restaurant car. One can stop – or stop off – in towns and cities, cross borders and frontiers, all the while being accepted to membership of an

exclusive club. Journey's end can produce a warm feeling of accomplishment.

It took me years to discover that my destiny lay with the railway. Yet over those years a sizeable percentage of the most memorable events of my life were enacted on a train, close to a railway and, more often than not, were directly caused by my interest in and involvement with both. This notwithstanding, I am no true 'railway buff'. I am abysmally ignorant of how the wheels go round and, to me, a 4–8–4 could be a calibre of bullet. I suppose my introduction to the railway game was made during my childhood when I possessed a substantial clockwork model railway layout, though my interest was retarded by economy that denied me electric equipment. From my Hornbill assemblage I graduated, as a 1940 schoolboy in Herefordshire, to playing dangerous cat-and-mouse games in Kerrie Tunnel on the long-defunct Ross to Monmouth line; a kind of lethal musical chairs with oncoming trains as the music and tunnel safety slots as the chairs – a pastime that earned me a well-deserved thrashing. And one of my proudest accomplishments as a 17-year-old soldier recruit was that of effecting a ride from London to Carlisle and back on the same penny platform ticket!

But it was the demands and vicissitudes of the Second World War as well as events resulting from the post-war Stalinist era in East Europe that set me, in earnest, upon my quest for travelling the world by train in addition to my two feet. Someone once called me the Don Quixote of the trains, and certainly jousting with railway authority – or any authority come to that – has never lost its appeal.

I will detail later some of the more hairy rail involvement this 1944 to 1960 period inflicted upon me, but with the reasoning that led to them behind me I could respond to the bidding of the world's railways for no other purpose than for the pleasure of riding the trains and allowing them to show me the world under more pleasurable, if not always comfortable, circumstances. And

it is the more adventurous and interesting of these that form the core of this book. Some are made on famed expresses crossing the vast expanses of the then Soviet Union, India and North America; others find me on dirty little trains in Asia and South America. One moment I am sweating it out in Pakistan's Baluchistan Desert, the next courting altitude sickness riding the world's highest railway line in Peru. My fellow travellers are a pot-pourri of the globe: companionable Turks, garrulous Armenians, inquisitive Russians, suspicious Albanians, smiling Ugandans, polite Indians, not-so-polite Syrians, 'don't look now but I think we're being followed' East Germans. My corner seat is a plush roomette on America's Amtrak, a broken-down third-class wagon on Algerian Railways, and standing room only on India's Frontier Mail. Off the train I am being robbed in Kabul, arrested in Kampala, berated in Khabarovsk and reprimanded in Pyongyang. The incidents are mine but the main ingredients of track routes and trains that run them are, in the main, available to all. With a few exceptions the journeys narrated can be repeated, with variations, by anyone in the mind to do so.

The division between experience and adventure is ill defined. One man's experience can be another's adventure. Not all my recorded rail journeys involve, or lead to, high adventure. Some are little more than worthwhile train rides plus a little incident that fortuitously came my way. The wider subject of interesting rail routes covered could fill a further book and in this category how can one fail to do less than mention the tourist-neglected Chinese lines between Beijing and Sinkiang, the Royal Thai State Railway's Northern Express that carried me between Bangkok and the northern city of Chiang-mai via the jungles and paddy-fields of Thailand, and, nearer home, the super-efficient railways of Switzerland curving through picture-postcard Alpine scenery? Only in Cuba was I inexplicably denied a ride on a train in a country that possessed a railway – even following a personal request for permission to do so from the Castro family.

The World Commuter

As Ludovic Kennedy writes in his book *Railway Journeys*:

The sweetest pleasure of any long rail journey lies in its anticipation. I have never eyed any long-distance train I was about to board without wondering, as the old hymn says of Heaven:

What joys await us there?
What radiancy of glory?
What bliss beyond compare? [1]

Covert Rail Travel in Nazi-Occupied and Communist-dominated Europe

I'll start with the impossible rail journeys. With both a hot and a cold war no longer afflicting Europe, the circumstances of my journeys narrated in this chapter are those that cannot be repeated by anyone crazy enough to want to follow in my wake. However, the incidents described might raise a modicum of interest and possibly a smile or two, so I will get them off my chest.

Having the misfortune, at the tender age of 19, to be taken prisoner early in the 1944 Normandy Campaign of the Second World War, my German captors saw fit to despatch me to work as a slave labourer in a Silesian coal mine of the then Greater German Reich. This in itself involved virtually my first long-distance rail journey; one of nightmarish proportions as 50 and more of us soldier-captives, herded into cattle trucks, waterless, foodless and with barely space to sit, were jolted spasmodically for days across war-torn Europe under constant machine gun and rocket attack from the airforces of our own side. So desperate were we with thirst that a few of us prized up some floorboards of the wagon with the objective of attempting a semi-suicidal escape, but were forced to desist by the others who feared even worse treatment by our captors.

Once at the work camp, not being over-enthusiastic about coalmining as an occupation even at the best of times – and these decidedly weren't – I, together with one Gordon Primrose of a Scottish regiment, decided to abscond and make our way, by fair means or foul, to the nearest potential liberating army. This was the Soviet Red Army: our own, possibly more congenial, Allied forces being unattainable the far side of Germany proper. Escape had been a high priority intention for me ever since my capture

by the 12th SS Panzer Division in Normandy; I'd even tried getting out of the lavatory window on a passenger train taking me and others under armed escort from the headquarters of Stalag V111B on the Polish-Czech border to the Silesian coal mine, but had been rumbled and hauled unceremoniously back by an irate guard. Now came my first planned and prepared escape and evasion attempt commencing with the initial week-long clandestine hike across enemy territory, which I have detailed in earlier books so I will not go into this painful peregrination here.[2] Suffice to say that Gordon and I found ourselves, weak with hunger and fatigue, unable to progress further on foot. Thus we turned to the potential offerings of the railway.

Outside the now Polish town of Chrzanow, lying on a rail route to Crakow and our intended initial destination, we became fired with the idea of obtaining an unscheduled and illegal lift further eastwards by goods train. The prison cage from whence we had absented ourselves boasted no refinements such as maps, compasses and the complete escaper's survival outfit, so we were having to acquire the basic necessities of life on the run through simple robbery from isolated German farmhouses.

Chrzanow possessed a sizeable railway freight yard which might well have served as a jumping-off point but it was too well guarded, while in all probability we would not have been able to understand or rely upon the despatch and destination notes which might or might not be clipped to the sides of any wagons the yard was likely to contain. We therefore felt compelled to look for a stretch of track outside the town that fitted the circumstances of the situation; in other words a spot where we could lie in wait for a goods train going eastwards that was suitably remote and sheltered, with the topography raising a gradient and need for a curve of the line both to slow the train and foil vigilance from hostile personnel already aboard it. Freight trains, we were aware, sometimes carried armed guards as a precaution against sabotage. These were usually placed at the rear and with the locomotive crew up front. It was

imperative that such personnel remained ignorant of what we were attempting to do in the middle.

It took two whole days to locate a site that held the minimum of geographical requirements we had designated as vital for our proposal to jump a suitable train. A spruce forest provided adequate shelter from view, if not from the rain that fell during the night, and a curve of the line appeared sharp enough to conceal our movements from observation from both ends of the train. Under the dripping foliage we waited until dusk improved our chances of not being spotted when we emerged from hiding.

We had already taken cover from passing trains – passenger and freight, noting their speed and composition – that rumbled by in both directions and now, as we crouched in a hollow, another heavy-goods jangled into view. An overworked locomotive engulfed in a sweat of steam headed a long line of wagons that rattled and jerked against each other as if the driver was applying his air-brakes. We could see the driver and his mate leaning out of the cab and surmised that some obstruction ahead was causing a speed reduction. The pace of the train was perfect for our purpose but the thing was going the wrong way, damn it. I cursed our luck but then it came to me that the obstruction, if indeed there was one, might work for trains coming from the opposite direction too; those that had already been slowed but had not yet had time to pick up speed. We watched the brake van disappear into the damp murk.

Darkness was not complete when the sound of a train from the direction of Chrzanow lured us from cover, our hearts thumping against our ribs. A headlamp projected a yellow antenna ahead of another large locomotive, its stack belching spark-infested brown smoke. We lay flat for a few seconds to allow the engine to pass, then sprinted for the track, confident that the darkness would be intense enough to hide our running figures. Crouching close against the passing wagons, eyes peeled for hand-holds projecting from the dark mass of the high-sided coal trucks looming above

us, we jog-trotted alongside the train trying to avoid too close a contact with the cruel and menacing iron wheels.

My eyes were also trying to watch for signal cables and other lineside impediments. Behind me I heard Gordon pounding at my heels, swearing with the exertion. A lever on a wagon caught my attention and I lunged for it, clutching the cold metal, holding on and hoping it wouldn't give way. Dragged along the ballast, I envisaged a terrible fear that my legs might become enmeshed in those grinding, relentless wheels. Attempting to swing them outwards and into the air at the same time, my other hand fastened upon another protrusion. My feet dropped again, the toes of my boots bumping along the ballast, but with my two hands firmly anchored I was able to draw myself upwards, though the effort cost every ounce of my remaining strength. A red mist curtained my eyes as I fought to raise my body to the flank of the wagon, my right foot searching desperately for a toehold above the wheels. And then it was all over as, with a final heave, I reached the couplings between the two wagons.

Gordon was already atop the high side of the rear one and was working his way along its rim to join me. For a moment I cogitated upon the falseness of movies where the hero nips smartly up into such a train as this to a musical accompaniment from an invisible philharmonic orchestra. My hollow laugh was lost on Gordon as we turned our attention to the interior of the truck. To our dismay it was empty, bare of anything except a scattering of coal-begrimed sacks; a barren floor surrounded by four cold, damp walls.

Trying to stand up against the swaying motion we explored our new domain. There were enough sacks to superficially conceal our forms in the event of a cursory examination by railway staff, but that was all. We shook the coal dust out of some of the bags and gingerly sat down on them. The train rolled on making no effort to increase speed.

It was pitch black outside now; only the sparks from the locomotive made dancing illumination up ahead. By climbing

the walls of the truck we observed our progress over open country, but this told us nothing of where we were going. Chinks of light from passing houses occasionally slashed the night.

Abruptly the train screeched to a halt, the wagon couplings reverberating. No town showed, but we covered ourselves in sacks nevertheless in case of an inspection. Then came the wheezing thump of the locomotive and the sounds of a shouted exchange followed by a prolonged banshee whistle. The train jerked into motion again . . . but in the opposite direction.

We flung the sacks aside in exasperation, our faces smeared with coaldust. The train rolled on, still quite slowly, and we debated whether or not to bale out. But after the struggle to board it, the inability to believe that our efforts might have been in vain ensured that we stayed put. Maybe they were shunting the wagons on to another line? Perhaps there was a junction this side of Chrzanow after all? By the time we had exhausted the unlikely possibilities, our minds were made up for us when the train picked up speed, blocking any attempt to leave.

A glow ahead intensified, indicating a return to Chrzanow so we took cover once more, but the train never slackened pace for an instant as we rattled over a complex of points and crossovers, roared through the station, lights stabbing the darkness, and out into the open countryside again. The cold night air whipped our faces as we clung to the sides of what had now become our new prison. Which line had we taken? The question arose for, with Chrzanow passed, going at this pace would have us back in the Katowice coalmining region within an hour. We might as well drop off at the gates of our hated mine and give ourselves up. Bleak despair engulfed us.

An hour passed and the train sped on but no urban lights or pit workings showed. Maybe we *had* taken another line? We blundered through one biggish town, but though aglow with subdued light we were unable to make out its name.

It must have been in the very early hours when the train began to slow with ponderous deliberation. Still there was no industry to be seen, just as there were no stars in the sky. The faint outline of houses drew nearer the tracks. We waited, clutching the wet sacks, uncertain what action to take.

With a final hiss of steam we drew to a halt in a siding. Dawn bruised the sky and a handful of early-morning workers were going about their business, indistinct figures moving in the semi-darkness. Furtively we clambered out of the wagon and dropped to the ground. Checking that nobody was near, we ran to the fence that bordered the yard, clambered over it and melted into a deserted back street.

A lane led away from the village and we took it, having no desire to be seen at this hour of the morning. Clear of the last house we lay down, shivering and apprehensive, on a low mound of stalks and twigs amongst a patch of undergrowth. That we slept for a while was a measure of our exhaustion.

It was the cold that woke us, that and the noise of people on the road. Broad daylight showed us our surroundings in rude clarity; flat agricultural terrain similar to that through which we had been passing the last ten days. Jumping about to restore a sluggish circulation, we surveyed the methods open to us of retracing our steps, for plainly we had allowed ourselves to be transported deeper into enemy territory. The very fact that a train had brought us this far raised the notion that a train might be induced to take us back. And to make sure that we knew where we were going on this occasion, a *passenger* train offered a much more positive means of doing so. Walking was now completely out of the question as we were fast starving to death, while jumping goods trains was getting us no more than from a frying pan into a fire. We thought we had adequate funds – the rewards of our earlier farmhouse robberies – to finance such a project if the neighbouring township could raise a station as it had a goods yard. Neither of us much

cared for the idea of loitering around such establishments (anathema to escaped prisoners) but we concluded that a small one would be unlikely to raise all that number of authoritative nasties.

Straightaway we went to work tidying ourselves up as best we could, removing the coal dust from neck, face and our stolen attire with the help of roadside puddles. If we were going to travel in style we would have to appear a little less like the fugitives we were.

By mid-morning we had re-entered the township and located the station. Signposts showed Breslau (the Polish Wroclaw) and Opole on their westward-pointing arms, the former as something under 100 kilometres, so at least we had some idea of where we were. The station held more positive, even heart-warming, promise with Crakow as a direct eastbound destination; a train going there was scheduled for shortly after midday. Having elicited all the information we could want except for the fare, we slunk out of the station and out of town into the concealing countryside to await our further rendezvous with the railway.

My knowledge of and fluency in the German language is probably worse than anybody who professes to the very minimum of linguistic ability, with the possible exception of my partner-in-crime, Gordon, though his Scottish accent together with a smattering of Gaelic offers certain similar guttural overtones. While waiting for our Crakow-bound train in the concealing thicket we practised our lines, repeating to ourselves over and over again the German phrase we intended using at the station ticket-office window. '*Eine Fahrkarte erster Klasse nach Krakau, bitte,*' – 'A first-class ticket to Crakow, please,' – and the reason we chose to travel first class was two-fold. Not only did '*Erster*' trip easier off the tongue than the German equivalents to 'second' and 'third', but by travelling first class we hoped to raise a little more respect from a universally class-conscious authority and any minion of

that authority to whom we were likely to be subjected. Close to midday, under a weak sunshine, we made our way back to the station.

Our timing was perfect and, in company with half a dozen members of the commuting public, we lined up at the ticket-office exhibiting what we hoped was an air of nonchalance.

At the grilled window Gordon, clearing his throat, spoke the magic formula and received a hard look from a scowling German lady behind the grill. But with the scowl came a ticket and before she could tender the change from the sheaf of *reichmark* notes handed to her I swiftly added '*Ich auch*,' – 'I too,' – and the deed was done. On the platform a train indicator announced the next service as the *personenzug* to Strumien, though where Strumien was we had no idea. But it was plainly the destination of everyone else, for when the two-coach train arrived it scooped up all and sundry, leaving us loitering in the empty station – just the occurrence we had hoped to avoid. To hide our nervousness we stalked around the two platforms and so came upon a stall in the main hall that sold frankfurter-type sausages. Before I could intervene, Gordon had purchased half the stock.

Seldom has food had such impact. The sausages may have been horse or dog-meat, but it went down a treat. We tried not to show our intense hunger in case it drew attention, but within ten minutes we had scoffed the lot as we sat on a bench and munched away.

An hour and a half went by before our train steamed in 70 minutes late. It was a four-coach so-called *Schnellzug* and only a single section of one coach was reserved for first-class ticket-holders. We piled into one of the four compartments and settled ourselves, side by side, adjacent to the corridor and facing the engine.

The train gathered speed to bound along the single track over the flat terrain across which we had ridden the previous day. By a little stretch of the imagination it could have been the homely

countryside of rural Essex; small fields, woods and rural villages with un-Essex-like onion-domed churches. Gordon broke into a laugh and I too felt strangely light-headed.

The door slid open and we stopped laughing. The ticket-inspector stood in the opening staring at us questioningly. His *'Fahrkarte, bitte,'* was laced with sarcasm and impending wrath as if we had been caught in a higher class of travel than that for which our tickets were validated. The man was short and tubby but authoritative in his *Reichsbahn* uniform, and was plainly taken aback when we produced the appropriate tickets. Slamming the door he moved on, shaking his head, and we sighed with relief though at the same time hoping he wasn't going to air his misgivings to more potent authority.

Over the next hour came a number of halts at stations. Few people joined the train; equally few alighted, and none invaded our exalted portion of the coach. We stopped for longer periods at a larger, busier town. Its name was Oswiecim, one we'd seen indicated on signposts while on our excruciating walk several days earlier. People, soldiers displaying the double lightning-strike of the SS on their uniforms amongst them, joined the train, but again we were left in peace. At the time we did not realise the significance of the town's name which, in German, is Auschwitz.

The ticket-inspector padded down the corridor at intervals, glaring disapprovingly through the glass as he went by but taking no further action. The train bowled on, rocking from side to side.

A further prolonged halt occurred at another largish town and here our luck faded. While we were attempting to see its name, two officers, a naval lieutenant and a *Wehrmacht* captain entered, stowed their briefcases on the rack and sat down opposite us. We feigned sleep for all we were worth.

I felt the newcomers' eyes resting upon us, sizing up our un-first-class looks and attire. It was a hard penetrating gaze, loaded with query and, though I shifted my position thus proclaiming a

doze rather than deep slumber, I knew I was weakening, unable to ignore the stare, which I had glimpsed through my fingers.

Just for a moment I opened my eyes wider and was caught. The captain nodded and smiled, seemingly eager to chat. I nodded back, whereupon he enquired, in German, of our nationality. We were ready for this one so I mumbled '*Ungarish*,' a nationality we had 'borrowed' for just such an event, it being unlikely that anyone hereabouts could speak or understand Hungarian. Gordon too had abruptly 'awakened' and proceeded to enter the conversational gambit. The two Germans were handsome young fellows putting me in mind, for some reason, of fresh-faced American university students.

'I've never been to Budapest, more's the pity. A lovely city I believe,' observed the captain. I felt this needed more than a nod in reply so launched, in halting German and supported by Gordon, into a description of Bristol having not, at that time, been to the Hungarian capital. Unfortunately Gordon had Glasgow as his yardstick, which didn't help. Our German was atrocious and words of English kept intruding. But our military companions appeared satisfied.

The Navy now entered the exchange.

'What do you do?' I heard the word '*arbeit*' so caught on.

'We work in a hospital,' I said quickly, before Gordon could come up with something sardonic.

'In Crakow?' I nodded, hoping he wasn't going to ask which hospital. We'd only hit upon that occupation because it was comfortably vague, intimated useful war-work, and '*Krankenhaus*' and '*Lazaret*' – both meaning 'hospital' – were German words we both knew. I tried explaining that we had been working on a farm in the country over the weekend, but got bogged down through lack of the right words and also because I suddenly realised that I didn't know when the weekend was.

Gordon fortuitously interrupted. '*Fahren sie nach Krakau?*'

The two men nodded and mentioned some barracks or office of which we had never heard but pretended we had.

I began to wonder and worry about our proximity to Crakow. At all costs we'd have to leave the train before the station which would be a big one – a *Hauptbahnhof* – lousy with police, Gestapo, military *gendarmerie* and other abominations. I stared out of the window in an effort to pick out telltale signs of an imminent conurbation, but the terrain remained obstinately rural.

The captain rose to his feet, took down his briefcase from the rack and sat down again. He then opened the case with a snapping of catches and produced a bunch of black grapes in the manner of a conjurer producing a rabbit from a top hat. Grapes were a rarity in wartime Greater Germany even for privileged German officers, and they assuredly were for the likes of us. Breaking the bunch into four parts he distributed largess to everyone.

'*Vielen Dank,*' gushed Gordon and I with unfettered enthusiasm, pondering upon what the two would think if they knew they were bestowing comfort on the enemy. Gordon began wolfing down his portion, stalks, pips and all so I kicked him surreptitiously, trying to indicate that we should eat in a manner befitting a first-class ticket-holder.

'*Funf Minuten nach Krakau,*' vouchsafed the lieutenant, thereby helpfully supplying the answer to what I wanted to know. Outside, the countryside began to sprout a rash of houses.

I mumbled something about being late for work as an excuse to leave the compartment and, with Gordon at my heels, slid open the door.

'*Vielen Dank und auf Wiedersehen,*' we enthused, flashing our brightest smiles. We moved to the exit at the head of the coach, hoping nobody else would be in a hurry to alight and so be witness to our flight.

The corridor remained empty, giving us a clear and unobserved chance to make an unorthodox departure, which we proposed to

effect as soon as the speed of the train permitted it. The ticket-inspector was nowhere in sight.

The brakes came on with a squeal and we felt the slowing motion of the train. I unfastened the door, leaning out of the window, my eyes scanning the ground for an obstacle-free landing pad. At any moment passengers would commence issuing from their compartments.

Gingerly I climbed down on to the top outside step, hanging on to the handrail and restraining the door from swinging too wide. The wind was fresh in my face. I spied a heap of clinker and cinders – the spot where a locomotive had had its boiler raked out – coming up.

'Here we go!' I whispered urgently to Gordon who was breathing down my neck, and jumped.

I landed with a crunch, Gordon virtually on top of me, and together we rolled away from the moving train. The clinker was sharp, scouring my hands as well as my back even through the clothing I wore. Hardly had we risen to our feet when we heard voices further down the track and beheld a knot of passengers from an adjacent coach who had effected a similar exit. I wondered what their reasons were for doing so; simple ticket-evasion or perhaps they too were allergic to heavily-watched railway stations. I remembered we were now in Poland proper.

We climbed over a substantial fence and found ourselves amidst rows of lorries. Beneath the buck of the nearest vehicle we took stock of our surroundings and new situation.

The fact that we had landed ourselves in a German military vehicle depot was, I suppose, just our bad luck; good fortune couldn't be on our side all the time. But things still went our way as, concealed under our lorry, we awaited nightfall while sentries patrolled the yard. And luck was still with us as we finally made our getaway by climbing another fence at a point as far away as possible from the sentry-guarded entrance gate and venturing out into the dark suburbs of Poland's third city.

But our rail journeying by courtesy of the Deutsche Reichsbahn had reached its conclusion, so it remains only for me to add that the end of our fortnight of freedom came with our apprehension for a) breaking the curfew, and b) being caught in the act of robbing a bakery by a tolerant *Wehrmacht* patrol (who could have legitimately shot us on sight). With commendable misgivings our new captors, following a respite for us all to consume mouthfuls of newly-baked bread by a sympathetic baker, led us into the city centre to be handed over to the Gestapo. There followed several days of their traditional hospitality in the basement of their grizzly headquarters before, bruised and battered, we were transferred by closed truck in the middle of the night to the even grizzlier transit cage of the nearest holding unit which, as our declining luck would have it, was that of the death camp of Auschwitz-Birkenau. Thereafter, and into 1945, I was to be witness to unspeakable horrors.

Fast forward from 1944 to the early 1950s. The cold war which followed hard on the heels of the hot one produced, for me, a crop of instances of rail-related travel that might be worthy of mention while on the subject of train-riding and rail involvement in currently unrepeatable circumstances.

During a second escape attempt from German captivity, this time in early 1945 Czechoslovakia, I had been concealed and sustained by a Czech family, of which the second of three daughters became the most regular deliverer of food to my bolthole. To cut a long story short, the lady in question has since become my wife, though because of the scourge of Communism that had descended upon Eastern Europe in the meantime, it was 12 years before we were able to tie the knot. And it was during those dozen years that, having declared my own personal war against the whole Cominform, I made repeated and often highly illegal attempts to breach the fanatically-guarded Iron Curtain border that cut Europe into two opposing worlds. These activities

of mine were for the express purpose of effecting trysts with the said girl, because there was no other way we could meet. A number of these breaches and attempted breaches were made with the help of the railway; only one, executed in 1951 when the hand of Stalin lay heavy on the land of Czechoslovakia, was achieved solely on foot when I not only succeeded in cutting my way through a treble-electrified fence and negotiating a minefield, but also getting myself caught and sentenced to a 104-year prison sentence.

My first rail assault on the guarded border was by way of Bavaria's Nuremberg and aboard a segment of the Orient Express which I undertook more as a reconnaissance than a serious means of illegally entering the country. Visaless, I was, as expected, removed from the Prague-bound train at the Czech border town of Cheb some twelve kilometres inside Czech territory. Reprimanded and held for some ten hours by the immigration officials, I was then put aboard the subsequent westbound express. This was not, by any means, a wasted exercise for I had kept my eyes and ears open and learnt much about the details of the border restrictions and formalities, not least from its soldier guardians themselves, to add to the store resulting from my earlier researches.

I considered it vital for the continued relationship that, in addition to our fragile correspondence – often broken by Czech censorship – Anna and I should physically meet, however briefly, once in a while, otherwise the budding romance would wither and die. Therefore I planned the subsequent intended foray by the same method and I communicated secretly to her, in the hope that she could be at Cheb station for my second arrival. I had proved it possible to reach it so, unless my earlier unbidden arrival had altered the pattern of control on both sides of the border, the way still lay open. Anyway there was only one means of finding out.

Everything went almost clinically according to plan. Though I was told by the Bavarian authorities at the West German border

station of Schirnding to leave the train for my own good on account of not possessing a Czech visa, I had slunk back on to the coach when nobody was looking. An hour later the virtually empty express, delayed by Czech border guards at the actual fenced border for the customary search for 'spies' (this to maintain the pretence that the fences were there to act as a barrier against 'Western Imperialism' rather than curbing illegal emigration by their own people), drew into Cheb station.

My mind was a whirlwind of expectation and emotion as I scanned the multiple platforms. All at once I caught sight of her, a lone figure I knew to be Anna. She stood beneath an iron bridge and I wondered, for an instant, if she'd experienced difficulties getting to the platform serving a train from the West; indeed, even reaching a town situated in a border zone. As the train drew to a halt our eyes met and I had the door open. Seconds later we stood on the platform in each other's arms.

Unaccustomed to there being anyone from the West aboard the two coaches of the train, authority was slow to react. Though watched woodenly by two of the quartet of Tommy gun-toting soldiers who had ridden the exterior of the coaches for the purpose of ensuring that nobody left the train between the border and the town (a scheme I had in mind), Anna and I were able to converse and impart our sweet nothings before the vultures awoke to the situation and descended upon us. An officer of the border guard was the first to reach us. He seemed nonplussed as we unwound ourselves from each another.

'You're supposed to remain on the train,' he barked in German. He turned to Anna and a fierce exchange of Czech ensued. She interrupted the flow to explain to me.

'He says I'm not allowed to be on this platform or talking to you.'

With no other passengers to 'process', a group of officials went through my bag and visaless passport like a dose of salts. We were led to the same immigration office to which I'd been taken

previously, and given a further dressing down for carrying out an illegal meeting. Our individual statements were laboriously typed and then Anna was removed from the room.

The formalities completed, I managed to persuade the officer to give me a few more minutes with Anna. At first he refused point-blank, but gradually relented. At heart he was a reasonable man.

'You can have the few minutes before her train leaves for Prague,' he conceded, and led me out of the office.

The Orient Express still waited. It had moved to another platform and eight more coaches were added, thus giving it a little more dignity. These were filling up with citizens en route to the Czech capital or towns along the line. Ignoring my escort, I walked briskly along the train staring in through the windows. Most of the second-class coaches were full and there was an overflow of passengers in the corridors.

Anna was in the fifth coach. A soldier stood ostentatiously outside her window. Ignoring him too, I rapped on the glass and Anna swiftly left her seat to emerge on the platform smiling happily.

'I've come to say goodbye, but on stolen time,' I explained, and her smile faded.

Our prolonged farewells were witnessed by a throng of passengers in the corridor who had learnt of the renegade Englishman in their midst. They crowded to the window closest to us, offering words of encouragement and sympathy. A whistle shrilled and there was a banging of doors. Anna slipped back into the train and I watched it slide out of the station.

For the rest of the day and well into the night I was held in detention before being put aboard the next westbound express to be returned from whence I had come.

A total of 14 minutes together with one's girlfriend might seem poor return for a journey in excess of a thousand miles. But it

was worth it. So much so that, over an Easter weekend the following year, I set off yet again to repeat the performance. My baggage consisted of not much more than a toothbrush and an engagement ring.

Though the subject of our becoming husband and wife had featured in our more recent correspondence, I was aware that I had not actually put the question to Anna. And it came to me that the munitions of our battle to be together might be enhanced if we were officially engaged to be married; 'girlfriend' has a far less permanent ring to it than 'fiancée'. Yet simply to write the question and obtain a written reply would have made disappointing impact. Being old-fashioned at heart, I felt the occasion should be marked in the time-honoured fashion, as is the right of lovers everywhere.

For my well-meaning but inconvenient Bavarian antagonists at Schirnding, who were becoming stricter with visaless passengers attempting to go east, I had evolved a new tactic. By locking myself in the through-coach toilet of the Orient Express and placing a '*Kaput*' (out of order) notice on the door, I hoped to avoid their attentions. And it worked.

At the actual border of the Czech Republic nothing had changed. The repressive apparatus of the multiple fences stood stark and terrible in the early afternoon sunshine, the ploughed strip and mined zone of death running like a poisonous serpent through wood and meadow killing all that lay athwart its path. White insulators, like obscene growths, mottled the posts that carried the barbed-wire curtain. I shivered as I looked upon it, wondering how I had managed to pluck up the courage to cut my way through such an obstacle two years earlier. Again I appeared to be the only passenger in the reduced train and I maintained a low profile, pretending to doze, in case my increasingly familiar features should be recognised by the soldiers who searched it.

Approaching Cheb it was as if I were watching a film for the umpteenth time. Hanging out of the window I frantically scoured the platforms for the girl I had come to ask to be my wife. But the

concourses were empty; not a soul in evidence except for a soldier by a water-tower and a group of railwaymen at the head of the furthest platform. My heart was pounding wildly and despair raged within me. So she had been prevented from keeping the appointment. I'd given her the wrong date. She's not been able to understand my disguised instructions. A host of explanations surged into my mind as I leapt on to the platform, the momentum of the still-moving train carrying me towards the foot-bridge; from its shadows a figure detached itself, and I was in the arms of Anna.

I suppose it was a hopeless quest, but the notion of leaving the station unobserved had lain at the back of my mind. And we nearly made it. The immigration people obviously thought they were dealing with the usual empty train and had not bothered to leave their offices following a cursory glance at the coaches. I had tendered my ticket to the railway official at the barrier and we were on the verge of passing through when the policeman just inside the barrier laid a hand on my arm. A knot of passengers from another train flowed around us, thinned and dissolved. We stood alone, naked before authority.

Taken to the administrative building, we found ourselves before the same officer that had been on duty on the previous occasion that I had come this way. Recognition was instantaneous and mutual. The film was running again; the same old bits were showing on the screen.

'You again!' he all but bellowed. 'I presume you do have permission this time, but you can't just wander out of the station.'

He held out his hand for my lame passport. Its shortcomings again revealed, he was really quite nice about things. I told him I'd come to see my fiancée.

'How long have you been engaged?' he asked.

'About eight minutes,' I said. Already I had asked Anna to marry me, had been accepted and had slipped the engagement ring on to her finger under the noses of the soldiery.

This time the officer allowed us to be alone together for another ten minutes. He glanced at his watch.

'She must return to Prague on the express. I'm sorry.'

Once more under escort we walked back to the train, but the soldier with us insisted upon Anna going aboard the coach. I stood by the window and she came to it, stretching out her hand for me to hold. The whistle blew and our hands were dragged apart as the train moved away and I was left staring after a receding coach, a small arm forlornly waving from it.

Locked in a small unlit room adjoining the police office to await the usual enforced deportation, I was already planning the next move in the saga.

Thereafter my railway journeying took me all over Western, Northern and Central Europe as I made repeated attempts to forge reunions with Anna. Some were successful such as the occasion when the Czech embassy in Oslo – unlike those of Helsinki, Stockholm and Copenhagen – omitted to check their 'black book' of undesirables which included my name and *persona non grata* classification awarded me following my imprisonment in 1951. This oversight granted me a 48-hour transit visa which, combined with a 24-hour extension I had wangled in Prague, won me an idyllic three days and nights with Anna. Others were a failure: witness my attempt to meet her on the Austro–Czech border I had planned to travel to by train from Linz, when Austria was still under four-power jurisdiction. And here it was the Soviet zone, though it was agents of the American CIA who scotched the project.

I scored a victory, however, by joining a group tour run by a politically-biased company in London whose left-wing participants were covered by a group visa in which my name did not appear, and this gave me a whole fortnight with my fiancée. My most spectacular failure was, assuredly, following Soviet-permitted attendance at the first post-war Leipzig Industrial Fair

in the then so-called German Democratic Republic. On the assumption that East German officialdom would be unable to read yet still be impressed by my flowery and stamp-decorated Soviet visa, which was actually only valid for the environs of the city of Leipzig, I managed to travel by train to Bad Schandau, close to the Czech border which I surmised (wrongly) would be a 'soft' one and therefore not too difficult to negotiate. Though again I possessed no Czech visa, I managed to board the Berlin–Prague Express by dodging the German passport control but was given away by a pig of a ticket-inspector.

Arrested, I was handed over to a Russian captain at the town's Soviet *Kommandatura* who handed me back to the People's Police. With them I was taken by a one-coach special train almost up to the border, here marked by the wide River Elbe, and for two days was held by them at their border headquarters. On my return, under armed escort, to the special police-run train to take me back to Bad Schandau for my deportation back to the West, I attempted to make a run for it, knowing that Anna was waiting for me at the Czech border post barely a kilometre away, and was within a hair's breadth of being shot for my pains.

One final railway-associated failure I should perhaps mention is that which occurred in Hungary in 1955. On another group tour I managed to join I had noticed, while on the train between Vienna and Budapest, that the steel cantilever railway bridge spanning the Danube near the town of Komáron – here the border between Hungary and Slovakia – was undergoing repair. Playing truant from the two-day sojourn in the Hungarian capital, I took myself by train back to Komáron, hid myself in the undergrowth close to the bridge and, at dusk, climbed the scaffolding to inch my way along this and the girders of the span beneath the rail tracks. Trains passed above me just inches from my rust-dust covered form as I progressed slowly towards the Slovak bank of the river twinkling below me. The Judas this time was a Danube barge

captain who, spying my silhouette against the starlit sky, shouted a warning to the border guards on the bridge parapet. The thud of their running feet above me resulted in my swift turnabout and successful return-crawl in record time, beating my pursuers to the shore and ground-level by a small margin.

Further 'border-bashing' attempts by me involved no railway participation and, anyway, by 1957 the Czech government were getting so fed up with my antics, and the bad publicity they produced, that it finally granted Anna an exit visa and chucked her out of the country.

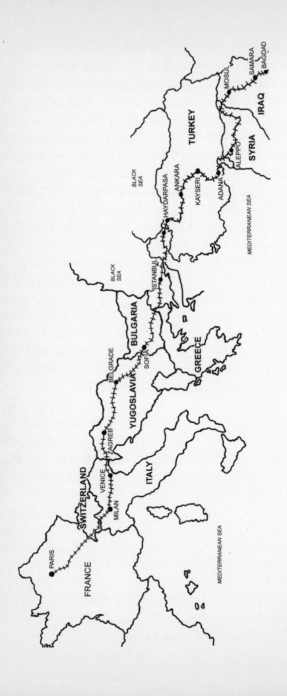

By Direct Orient Express and
Taurus Express to the Orient

My illegal dalliances with the railway over – well, more or less
over – I can turn to more productive railway journeying which is
the main object of this book. And there's no name that evokes
the subject better than that of the Direct Orient Express (once
the Simplon–Orient Express) now, alas, laid to rest with a fanfare
of trumpets at the end of 1977.

Once upon a time the very name of the Direct Orient Express
conjured visions of intrigue and adventure. Sadly, however, the
concluding years of this train were exceedingly dull ones. Only
in France was it an express at all. The expected skulduggery no
longer wrapped the train in its aura of romanticism; one had to
take along a sort of 'do-it-yourself adventure kit' if anything
remotely interesting was to be generated. Only once, for me, was
the famous express the vehicle that carried me to an adventure of
the cloak-and-dagger kind.

The train that skulked at a badly-lit platform in the Gare de
Lyon in Paris that late spring evening of 1969 bore those evocative
placenames: Paris–Lausanne–Milano–Venezia– Trieste–Zagreb–
Beograd–Sofija–Athens–Istanbul, which was all that signified to
me that this was indeed the famed express. It left, on time, at the
romantic hour of ten minutes before midnight, and was scheduled
to arrive 84 hours later in Istanbul.

The inaugural trip of the original Orient Express in 1883 was a
tremendous occasion, with many crowned heads of Europe and
Asia participating. At its zenith in the early 1900s, the great train
could accomplish the distance between Paris and Istanbul in 56
hours.

From Paris there were two departures for Istanbul, the route already mentioned and the other via Munich. The German section took three hours longer, and since a later departure time of 03.00 from Paris was frowned upon as an inconvenient hour for such a great express to leave from a great capital, a policy of an idling Swiss–Italian section until the two portions could connect in Yugoslavia was agreed upon by the Timetable Committee.

This body also had the onerous task of satisfying the various countries through which the Express passed. This took some doing since every capital along the route of such a showpiece train required it to arrive and depart at a suitable hour. Even the name 'Simplon–Orient' caused disagreement. Liked by the Bulgarians and Turks, it was eventually changed to 'Direct–Orient' and for this the Swiss, a big force in the railway world, were responsible.

In the context of route and timetable it must be remembered that the original Orient Express ran from Paris to Vienna, to connect with Danube ferries and newly-constructed railway lines towards Romania and the Balkans, and on to the powerful capital of the Ottoman Empire, Constantinople (now Istanbul). As its popularity grew, portions of the same train split at Vienna to serve Budapest and Bucharest. The line through the Alps was by way of the Semmering Pass but in 1906 the Simplon Tunnel was opened, so offering a more direct route to Turkey. Thus two entirely separate trains were introduced, the Turkish portion being named 'Simplon–Orient Express' and the original – boring through the Alps by way of the Arlberg Tunnel – the 'Arlberg–Orient Express'.

Italy was included in the route of the Direct Orient, as the Swiss insisted upon calling the Istanbul-bound train, in 1919 as a result of the defeat of Germany and Austria in the First World War. In the 'holier than thou' attitude taken by the Allies at the time of the Treaty of Versailles, the idea of a grand express of international repute crossing the tainted ground was repugnant. And with the opening of the Simplon Tunnel between Brig and

Domodossola, the way to Italy was assured. This well pleased the Italians who were building a gigantic showpiece station at Milan and wanted a prestigious train to grace it. Beyond lay a newly-created Yugoslavia with which France was anxious to establish friendly relations, so, supported by the Swiss and the Dutch, the Direct–Orient Express was born, offering sleeping- and dining-car service right through to Istanbul and also to Athens.

Since then, in spite of another war and the subsequent division of Europe, the ramifications of the Orient Express 'complex' spread to include Prague, as mentioned in the previous chapter, though today its only surviving service is that between Paris and Budapest.

I was whizzed through France at commendable speed, but at Vallorbe and the Swiss border my express faltered and shrank to a commuter's special, stopping at all stations and, sometimes, in between. The rock-infested greenery of Switzerland ended with the Simplon Tunnel and we came out the other side into a world of powdery white snow. But the pure whiteness soon lost its virginity as the train dropped down to the Lombardy plain and crept for comfort into the great soulless metropolis of Milan and its palatial station shivering in a cold blizzard.

Trieste, in contrast to Milan, was experiencing a foretaste of summer and as we entered the dry, sullen landscape the chirping of crickets defied the calendar. In sympathy the sea switched from green to blue.

It was with some trepidation that I watched the train zigzag up the steep incline to the Yugoslav frontier station of Cezana. Barely 18 months had passed since, at this very place, I had effected the Iron Curtain escape of my Czech brother-in-law. In doing so I had 'bent' any number of Yugoslav laws, so I had cause to wonder whether authority would catch up with me. If so, here was its chance to pounce. A variety of officials passed in and out of the almost empty train, but only one took close interest in me. Having

burrowed through my stamp-choked passport several times, he subjected me to a long hard stare. Maybe he'd seen my face somewhere before.

There is no room for sentiment in the communist mentality, and though only a light shade of pink, Yugoslavia had to debunk still further the remaining shreds of glory that clung to the Orient Express after its whistle-stop tour of Northern Italy. During the long wait at Cezana, a number of very local coaches and even a couple of cattle trucks had joined the train. We had sunk to the level of what the Germans would describe as a *Personenzug,* and had even to play second fiddle to the connection for Rijeka which left before us. I remembered it was the same with the Arlberg–Orient in Austria and Hungary some years before. In spite of then Russian sanctions, Austria had managed to electrify the line between Salzburg and Vienna, thus maintaining the standard of a train with the proud, if long-winded, title of the Swiss–Arlberg–Vienna–Orient Express. But what had crawled out of the capital's once down-at-heel East Station was a three-coach affair plus a couple of open trucks. Even then everything was searched and prodded with bayonets at the border town of Hegyeshalom – a similar charade to that on the West German-Czechoslovak border – before the debased express was allowed to proceed to Budapest.

But I digress.

From the balmy warmth of Trieste we plunged again into thick snow at Ljubljana. It lay, admittedly thawing, heavy upon the ground and in spite of a switch from electric to steam traction the Yugoslav Federal State Railway deemed it necessary to ration the central heating. I sat shivering in semi-darkness until the blaze of light that was Zagreb came into view.

Almost immediately my compartment was invaded by a squad of young soldiers, an arsenal of weapons and implements festooned about them. I gave up three of the four seats along which I had been reclining with little reluctance for it had been too cold for sleep. My new companions eyed me for a few moments,

discussing my probable nationality amongst themselves. I heard myself labelled German, American, French and Norwegian before the list foundered in a welter of Serbo-Croat. At least they had an answer for the lack of heat. A corporal with an indiarubber face produced a lemonade bottle of *slivovice* and passed it around. Each took a substantial swig, the last hesitatingly passing the bottle to me. The firewater bit into my entrails and I said *'Danke schoen'* and then 'Thank you'.

The corporal was the scholar. *'Engleski?'* he enquired, eager to prove his superior knowledge. I nodded and his face folded into a grin. Henceforth I became an honorary member of the Yugoslav Army. Two more bottles followed the first and the swigs became gulps. We held long incomprehensible conversations in which the occasional word that was universally understood became a signal for celebration and therefore more *slivovice*. When the heating came on an hour later it didn't really matter, for we were all dozing happily on each other's shoulders.

Uninterrupted sleep was effectively denied us, however, by the repeated incursions into the compartment of the ticket-inspector. A thin, lugubrious individual, he obviously held a low opinion of the Army and smelt a fish regarding the collective travel voucher held by the corporal.

For those of us who cared to look, dawn illuminated the most featureless section of the journey so far. Right up to Belgrade, the equally featureless capital, the flooded plain offered a dismal picture of a vast sea of mud. Dotted thinly across the landscape tiny villages, like islands, clung to almost impassable roads that were their only link with the outside world.

At Belgrade Central station my military companions departed, bestowing upon me much hand shaking and patting of my shoulders. The compartment became as empty as their lemonade bottles. Moving off again, the train gave me a circular tour of the city, an apparently necessary procedure when transferring from one platform to another.

Back in the station the status of my compartment rose with the entry of an Italian lady and a Yugoslav Airforce officer. They were entirely separate, but lost no time in remedying this state of affairs, even though both stoutly clung to their respective mother tongues. The officer wore a superbly creased uniform and a David Niven moustache, while the focal point of the lady was a red gash of a mouth soon to be firmly and permanently clamped round a cigarette. Plainly the uniform meant as much, if not more, than the budding acquaintanceship to the gallant captain, for a tremendous spring-cleaning operation was put in motion before the sea-green trousers were allowed to have contact with the seat. Flicking the sparse furnishings with a lace handkerchief, he next covered the seat with sheets of my discarded newspaper upon which I had previously deposited my feet. Various items of outer apparel were then carefully folded and deposited on the newly-polished rack before the lesser business of wooing could begin.

From the little snippets of Italian I could understand, the subject of his attentions appeared hardly inspired by the overtures. I watched the blue smokescreen ascend in thickening spirals all but obscuring the no-smoking notices, and coughed pointedly. The officer noticed my stare of disapproval and offered me a peppermint, the first of many from an endless supply.

Whenever he could discern his new girlfriend through the fog he would dash off an ode in Serbo-Croat. She responded with no great show of enthusiasm and eventually it got through to him that she was suffering from the cold. With exaggerated chivalry the captain threw up his hands in comprehension and zealously wrapped his overcoat around her knees. I watched his eyes trying to avoid the sight of an immaculate sleeve trailing in the dirt. But the gesture was in vain. The train rattled into Niš and in Niš lay his duty. Despairingly he swept up his coat, threw me a last peppermint, and fled.

Approaching the legendary Dragoman Pass the railway has to bore a way through the northern buttress of the Balkan

Mountains. The pass itself, a winding chasm in which the single track and the flooded tributary of the Nisova River become almost one, was curtained by a blizzard. At Dimitrovgrad the Bulgarian customs had their pound of flesh, and by the simple expedient of turning our bags upside down were able to effect their examination of the contents. Italian female and British male underwear lay strewn over the seats like a Women's Institute rummage sale.

I was still struggling to close my bag when the train slowed at the suburbs of Sofija. Here I was to break my journey, and though I held doubts concerning its likely attractions – doubts built upon experience of other Communist capitals – the city seemed worthy of a visit.

Accordingly I bade '*Arrivederci*' to my companion and for the first time in 50 hours left the train. At first I thought I'd made a mistake and alighted at the wrong station, so small and insignificant it was. Subsequently I learnt that the original main station had been destroyed in the war and nobody yet had seen fit to build a new one. Fighting my way through the Saturday night crowd that spilt dangerously over on to the tracks, I emerged at a tram terminus.

With no Bulgarian currency, lugging a heavy suitcase and with every notice and sign in an incomprehensible script, I would have had difficulty in locating the city centre even by public transport. And this mode of reaching it was out of the question, since every square inch of every tram in sight was occupied inside and out, while queues waited at the stops. So, in spite of the added impediment of a sleet storm, I walked.

I saw nothing en route that looked remotely like a hotel, but at a restaurant a kind waitress who spoke a word or two approximating to English confirmed that, in fact, I was on the right road. She also explained the system, common to much of continental Europe, by which one purchases tickets, singly or in blocks, at kiosks prior to boarding the vehicle. An element of trust is involved, since you clip your own ticket, but should a check

uncover a non-clipped ticket or ticketless passenger the penalties were severe, especially, it seemed, in Sofija. Having no particular desire to sample a Bulgarian jail I continued walking.

Suddenly to my joy I was in Vladimir Ilich Ulyanov Lenin Square – though the 'Little Father' seldom inspired this emotion in me – and immediately found myself in the centre of a gang-fight. Joy switched to alarm as a squad of pistol-wielding policemen waded into the knot of youths into which I had blundered. One of the contestants ran into me and sprawled headfirst over my suitcase with a policeman on top of him. Hastily I retired to safer regions.

My bleats for assistance in locating a hotel (for the Bulgarian script for even so international a word was incomprehensible to me) initially met with no response until, at about the fifth attempt, a group of people abruptly realised that there was a 'Britisher' in their midst. There was a rush to claim me. Following much gesticulating and airing of schoolbook English I was marched off inside a box of Sofijan citizenry, all talking at once. In spite of being classed as 'imperialist lackeys' by the Communist regime I was amazed how popular Brits appeared to be.

I had not intended to aim so high as the Grand Hotel into which imposing vestibule we trooped. With my squad of chaperones arrayed behind me, I enquired about rooms. Being outside the tourist season there were plenty, and upon learning the extremely reasonable rates I nearly surrendered without further ado. But my stubborn streak was showing and I had heard talk of a private accommodation service that existed in Bulgaria, as it did elsewhere in central and Eastern Europe. This would not only be cheaper but, more to the point, offer an insight into a Bulgarian home and way of life.

My further enquiries led me and my retinue round the corner to the still-open offices of 'Balkantouriste', the state tourism bureau.

'English!' exclaimed the female clerk, slightly taken aback by my nationality, 'I fear we can only offer you a German-speaking host.'

'That will do fine,' I replied with optimistic trust in my very limited German. And no sooner said than done, for there stood my allotted host at my elbow.

I'm quite sure that my escort would have come to blows over which of them was to accommodate me had they understood what was going on. As it was, a lot of bewildered muttering ensued as I paid the small service fee and, murdering the German language, my host and I escaped into the street. Even though I had managed to change some money at the bureau and was no longer a pauper in a strange land, my new friend insisted upon treating me to a taxi to his spick and span little flat off the broad 9th of September Street.

My host lived alone; his wife had died some years ago and he had retired from his job as a bank official a year later. He was a thin, slightly lugubrious man, though possessed of an infectious laugh. He had spent all his life in the city and he was immensely proud of it, a fact that I was soon to appreciate fully.

The two days that followed were full of interest as I was conducted around Sofija. Our first objective was the Alexander Nevsky Cathedral with its exquisite religious drawings, then the nauseating spectacle of Dimitrov's embalmed corpse in its see-through tomb. In quick succession came the Museum of the Revolution full of rusty machine guns and fragments of underground newspapers, the Archaeology Museum, the handsome Church of St Sophia and the finish of the People's Army long-distance relay race at the Liberation Memorial (to which liberation it commemorated I'm not sure, since Bulgaria was officially on the German side during the Second World War), where the exhausted runners were supposedly revitalised by the sight of fresh hoardings extolling the unbreakable bond that was

Bulgarian–Soviet friendship. One contestant was violently sick at the finishing line, but I think it was just exhaustion.

Only once did I bring up politics with my host. I asked him what he thought of his own army marching into Czechoslovakia in 1968. He was not the slightest abashed.

'The Czechs asked for trouble and got it,' he replied. Though he professed not to be a member of the Communist party, his sympathy was not at variance with it. I noticed another thing. Sofija was the only Communist capital I knew at this period where political slogans were still an accepted part of the landscape. But so were packed churches.

The second evening a lady friend joined me and my host for a meal in a Bulgarian folk restaurant that lay in the shadow of Sofija's mountain, Vitosha. It was plainly a popular nightspot, and we ate kebab and drank local wine out of mugs shaped like teapots while troupes of dancers pranced around to the rhythm of castanets and balalaikas. Next morning I attempted to climb Vitosha as an antidote to the excesses of the previous evening, but was defeated by drifts of soft snow.

For our midday meals we patronised the People's 'help yourself' restaurants that were a big draw to diners of all walks of life. The food was certainly cheap but exceedingly nasty. Consisting chiefly of various types of *wurst*, beans, shredded onions and soggy chips, it was served lukewarm on badly-washed plates. The beer, in unlabelled bottles, might have been what they washed them in.

For an hors d'œuvre we frequented a more classy establishment which specialised in home-baked bread consumed with a 'dip' of pepper. Too much of the latter and you blew your head off. The waiters were going around wearing masks, since hygiene was taken seriously in the larger Bulgarian towns at that time; food-store assistants and barbers invariably wore them likewise.

Struggling with a little-known language does not bode well for prolonged friendship and I think the feeling of relief was mutual when I was seen off on the evening train; the same portion

of the Orient Express I had left 48 hours earlier. My host had been immeasurably kind by giving me a home-from-home in his small domain, but the call of the open railroad was loud in my ears.

Ensconced in a corner seat my mind, activated by a kind of built-in thermostat, began sorting out the living habits peculiar to long-distance train travel. Hard experience had given me an insight into the art of sleeping on trains without the benefit of wagon-lit. Coaches varied; most second-class compartments catered for a complement of eight: four to each bench seat with an arm in the middle. Very occasionally it was only six. In general, numbers in a compartment seldom exceeded six for long, and by spreading oneself or giving an impression that you are holding a seat for a companion it is usually possible to discourage unwanted bodies when mass intrusion threatens. And it is surprising what can be done with a neighbouring empty seat. Padding the hard armrest in the corner or the middle of the bench seat with a jacket or coat for a pillow, some degree of comfort can be attained curled up like a cat. But I was a novice at these proceedings as the Orient Express shuffled towards the Greek and Turkish borders.

An impressive Russian-built diesel locomotive led us into Plovdiv and then stole away into the night as if ashamed of having soiled itself by hauling a train of such imperialist design that brandished such capitalistic placenames as Paris, Lausanne and Venice. Thereafter we were back to steam again.

Until the second city of Bulgaria, my travelling companions not only numbered the full complement of seven plus myself, but were the roughest bunch of cut-throats imaginable. The ticket-inspector, on seeing them, gave me a pitying glance. Making sure my wallet reposed close to my skin I prepared for the worst. Soon I was, once more, the object of curiosity and a merciless interrogation but again, upon learning of my nationality, I became exhibit number one and was treated with a deference that accorded

to my rarity. It was only the acrid smoke of seven stupefying cigarettes that caused me relief when Plovdiv emptied the compartment.

The builders of the main line out of Bulgaria could hardly be blamed for the convulsions of history that, in the course of a few years, made Edirne Russian, Turkish, Bulgarian, Turkish again, Greek and, once more, Turkish as it is now. Hence the line passed unnecessarily twice through a few dozen miles of Greece, and with no love lost between Greeks, Bulgarians and Turks, all three immigration authorities have a go at making life a misery with long passport and baggage inspections both going in and coming out of their slices of territory. A new line has since been constructed that bypasses Greek territory, thus slightly easing the lot of the traveller.

Dawn made amends for the petty quarrelling of man. Creeping up over the low hills came a gory football of a sun, dyeing the barren scrub-covered land in an unnatural orange tint. A profusion of wild snowdrops, crocuses and fluffy tumbleweed gleamed like fireflies through the crimson haze. Even in a state of semi-consciousness I had been able to tell when we were on Greek soil and not Turkish. The lullaby of the wheels had abruptly increased to a rapid tempo – like light infantry on the march – as we passed over short lengths of rail. Laid thus for easy manhandling instead of being welded and placed by track-layer, the remoter areas of Greece were the last strongholds of this old-fashioned method of railway construction. My latest companions, a trio of Yugoslav students, stirred and rose from various contortionist positions of sleep as the train crawled across the rolling downs of European Turkey. My portable electric razor went the rounds, for which service I was presented with a gratis breakfast.

The first hamlets marked by their white sentinel minarets speckled the countryside, each supplying a quota of villagers to welcome a train that went by three times a week. By midday we had reached the sea and, leaving the Istanbul International Airport

on our left, wound our way beneath the walls of the Topkapi Palace into mainland Europe's last outpost.

Istanbul. What can one say about this fabled city that nobody has said a thousand times before? But its magic was slow to filter through to me that warm and sunny afternoon. Maybe I was tired, but my first impressions as I strolled through the old part of the city were cynical and unkind. Take away the mosques and minarets and you have a vast slum stretching over seven hills and divided by an oily waterway. A loud, overcrowded slum hooting and yelling and flaunting its poverty.

And then as I walked the spell was woven, and through the dirt and squalor I perceived Istanbul in all its magnificence. The magic lies in the people; the slick leather-coated traffic police; the Bosphorus ferry-captains; the tough untidy soldiers; the voluble vendors of everything under the sun; the orange squeezers; the illegal money changers; the waiters, shop assistants, bazaar con-men, priests and the vast mosaic of humanity that *is* Istanbul. A city can be the loneliest of places, but loneliness is an emotion difficult to attain in the former Turkish capital.

For three days I explored its labyrinth of streets on foot and by taxi. It was in Istanbul that I made my acquaintance with that most practical and economic method of transportation, the *dolmus*, a community taxi plying a fixed route and collecting clients along the way. Wherever I went, friendly, smiling citizens, rich and poor, accosted me offering advice and greeting. Even the street vendors had a special quality about them, a transaction being of secondary importance to a complicated conversation with an out-of-season Englishman.

A voyage up the Bosphorus in one of the many ferries that hoot their way across the busy straits gave me, for a pittance, an insight into the growing spread of Istanbul, its suburbs now almost reaching the Black Sea: Uskudar, Galat-Besiktas, the double fortress of Rumeli Hisar and Anadolu Hisar, Beykoz and beyond.

The vessel's captain came over to me and, as we chatted while sipping small glass beakers of tea, I learnt of the respect and trust with which his profession is held throughout Turkey. It was raining when we returned to the ferry terminus by the imposing Galata Bridge, but the magic could not be doused.

The Turkish Railway of Europe and that of Asia are, to all intents and purposes, different rail systems. The Bosphorus ensures that the traveller ends his journey at Istanbul. He or she can then start another if so desired, but there is no such amenity as a through-coach, rail-ferry or even an attempt at a time-link between the two sections of railway. From Europe your journey ends at Sirkeci station and that's that. For Asia and the East the journey starts at Haydarpaa, a ten-minute *dolmus* ride and half an hour by ferry. *Thomas Cook's Overseas Timetable*, at that time, warned passengers in direct transit via Istanbul to allow up to eight hours for connection between trains. This seemed to me a gross exaggeration, but what this excellent publication didn't mention was the unbelievable laxity in timing of the Asian connection to Baghdad that I intended to catch. However, I had been told that the Taurus Express, my subsequent home on wheels, was invariably up to six hours late arriving at its termini of both Haydarpasa and Baghdad. However, for me on this journey time was not of the essence.

At least *I* reached Haydarpasa with two hours to spare before the scheduled departure time of the train. The station is an Istanbul landmark in its own right, though the giant building houses quite a small terminus. Grouped around it were a number of shops and markets, so I stocked up with fodder for the 2,500-kilometre ride ahead. Statistics showed that the mileage of the Turkish Railway totalled around five thousand miles. When compared with, say, Sweden which is equally mountainous, considerably smaller but with almost double the track mileage, it will be appreciated that the railway in Turkey is a mite thin on the ground. But what there

is constitutes a considerable engineering feat (in the Taurus Mountains there are 22 tunnels within just over 30 miles), in spite of the fact that much of the network was single track and non-electrified.

A history of the Turkish Railway becomes a study in politics. Construction began in 1888, when a German company secured permission to build the Anatolian Railway running between Haydarpasa and Ankara via Eskehir and, later, Konya. Following the state visit to Constaninople by Kaiser Wilhelm II, a convention was signed between the two countries granting the German Anatolian Railway an extension to Kuwait, on the Persian Gulf. This was but another concession in support of Germany's *Drang nach Osten* – 'Drive to the East' – that was the frustrated envy of politicians in Britain, France and Russia. But opinion in Britain at least was divided. Largely out of dislike for France and Russia, considerable support was given to the Germans and their plans to push the railway through to Baghdad by way of two routes. One was the old imperial route of the Romans through Angora (Ankara) and Shivas; the other followed the valley of the Meander River and over the enormous bulk of the Taurus Mountains into the plains of Mesopotamia.

The German line had got as far as Basra when the war came in 1914, and four years later Allenby's armies swept through much of the area capturing vast amounts of rolling stock and equipment. Thereafter the dream of economic conquest changes its nationality. But the British railway concept was more ambitious still. As well as the link with Baghdad, a line south through Beirut, Haifa and Gaza to Cairo was proposed. By 1930 the Paris–Baghdad route by the Orient and Taurus Expresses was a reality, and the timetables of the years before the outbreak of the Second World War involved the whole Eastern European and Middle Eastern complex.

Since then the realisation of the dream has withered with the growth of air travel and the post 1939–45 war situation in the Middle East. Turkey has taken over, one by one, the lines originally

built with European rather than Turkish money and, in support of her more modest dreams, has built lines linking the Anatolian routes with the Black Sea and the Iranian frontier. The Cook's Grand Tour for elegant ladies and dashing gentlemen was discreetly dropped from the agency's brochure, and the romance of a journey from Paris to Baghdad has become as faded as that of the destination boards on the Taurus coach sides.

Even so I was scandalised by the state of the present-day Taurus Express. Seldom have I seen a filthier train. The compartments were thick with grime and soot, the windows opaque with mud, the seatless toilets an affront to humanity. To cap my disgust I had my first dispute with a Turk, who demanded the equivalent of 50 pence for lifting my small bag of his own accord on to the train. He got 20 pence and a rude Anglo-Saxon instruction. Gingerly I parked myself in the cleanest corner seat I could find, weighed up the position of various head and arm rests, and prepared to endure 30 hours of suffering.

By the time we had moved out of the station I had with me in the compartment two Syrian youths and a quiet studious-looking Turk. I successfully discouraged a threatened invasion by three companions of the Syrians with a virtual mountain of baggage; I didn't much like the look of the ones already with me, and we glared at each other as if sparring for the first words of introduction as the suburbs of Istanbul melted into isolated villages and small towns.

Between Haydarpasa, Uskudar and Izmit the train made good time, outwardly giving a reasonable imitation of an international express. The thickly populated plateau followed by the Turkish naval base drew all eyes in the compartment and resulted in a general scramble to the window and the cessation of our hostility. Thereafter, my nationality revealed, I became again the mascot of the community and, one by one, their companions elsewhere on the train were invited into our midst for an 'interview'. Politics, the topical politics of the Arab–Israeli conflict, quickly became

the chief subject for discussion, our exchanges being carried out in a mixture of French and English.

There was no bitterness. For the Syrians the fact that Britain was, to them, backing the wrong horse, was simply reason for sorrow. Nor was there great hate. The Israelis of course had a right to live in peace, but not by stealing other people's land. I was forcibly reminded of a similar theme of three decades earlier. Hitler called it *Lebensraum*. Stolidly, as if uncomprehending, the studious Turk in the corner listened in silence to the tortuous debate. His countrymen had played it strictly neutral in that conflict too.

One cannot travel far in Turkey without bumping into a mountain. In spite of its twists and turns the railway line spanning the wild territory was unable to escape the inevitable, and by midday we were in the awesome grip of a million-year-old result of a volcanic convulsion. Through enormous clefts in the rock barriers we crawled, following a flooded river which had learnt the easiest route long before the railway. Hissing importantly, its pistons pounding, the big locomotive dragged its cargo at a walking pace up the severe inclines. Given the slightest encouragement it stopped at the smallest of stations to allow northbound trains to pass. There would follow a frantic competition between thirsty locomotive and soot-dappled passengers to take on water, the source being one and the same. Vendors of food disembarked at every halt to make room for others who boarded the train with replenished stocks.

Food plays an important part in a Turkish railway journey. In spite of a continuous cavalcade of vendors shouting their wares up and down the corridors, every traveller carries vast stocks of provisions. To my amazement, most of the bundles and boxes belonging to my Syrian and Turkish companions contained loaves of bread, fruit, homemade cake, joints of cooked meat and various bottles of liquid refreshment. I was pressed to join the mêlée as

Turk and Syrian pooled their resources and made swift inroads into them. As there was a restaurant car attached to the train I had purchased no more than the odd snack, so my own contribution was a minimal one of a couple of bars of chocolate and some Bulgarian cheese. But I was solemnly warned off the restaurant car. It's dirty, they said, and I could well believe it!

Occasionally our rations were supplemented by doubtful delicacies from the vendors. These ranged from kebab, the roasting of which was carried out on little portable homemade charcoal burners placed on the coach floor, to a kind of Turkish delight and a sweetmeat that looked like cotton wool. Bargaining was surprisingly infrequent, though my companions saw to it that in my few dealings with vendors I was not overcharged. One visitor to the compartment was a youth intent upon imparting the word of God. I suppose I looked a likely convert, for he loosed on to me an unending torrent from the Scriptures (or maybe the Koran). I nodded knowingly, not wishing to hurt the man's feelings, until my Syrian companions gleefully told him that I was unable to understand a word he was saying.

The most un-Turkish city in Turkey is its capital. True I only saw a bit of Ankara, and at night, but for a couple of hours I was able to wander in Ataturk Boulevard and Kizilay Square. It could have been Birmingham or Milan. The citadel and the Old Town in the north were hidden by the darkness, and an old woman in the baggy trousers of her country cousins drew stares as she waddled past the fashionable shops now closing for the night.

I arrived back at the station to discover that we had an uninvited guest in the compartment. He hadn't *come* in, I was told; he had *fallen* in. Drunk as the proverbial lord, my Syrian friends had propped him up in a corner seat – mine – retrieved his spectacles and pipe, and dusted him down. Promptly he rolled full-length over the seat and, finding this to his liking, settled down for the night. Indignant at what we thought might be a ruse to obtain a whole length of seat to himself, we pushed him back into the

corner from whence the whole performance was repeated. How long this would have gone on had the contingencies of nature not taken a hand, it was impossible to say. Suddenly he sat up and asked for the bathroom. We told him that this was not a royal train.

'Train?' he mumbled through his big drooping moustache as if he had never heard of such a phenomenon. 'What train?' We pushed him out into the corridor then drew the blinds and barricaded the door against his return. By this time Ankara was miles away. The poor devil was going to get a rude shock to go with his hangover in the morning. We never saw him again.

The morning brought a stupendous sight for us. Leaning out of the open window, bleary-eyed and risking the shower of smuts, I saw the railway making a beeline across the flat Anatolian plain straight for the enormous bulk of the Taurus Mountains. The dawn sun splashed the vivid whiteness of the peaks, dazzling the eye and reflecting upon the wisps of cloud that hung to their summits.

For the next seven hours halts were numerous, both scheduled and unscheduled. The stations were simply clearings where a double track could be laid to allow for trains to pass. Life for the few inhabitants revolved around the arrival and departure of trains, the children running amok amongst the shunting wagons.

I had made the acquaintance of the locomotive crew the previous late evening at a town at which a particularly long stop had been made, the couple readily accepting my offer of beer at the station bar. Consequently, I had been accorded the special privilege of being allowed to walk alongside the train for much-needed exercise when it reached a particularly steep mountainous section of track. And they were as good as their word. Near the highest point of the line the driver gave me two pre-arranged blasts on the whistle thus allowing me to leave the carriage, drop to the ground and stroll alongside the slow-moving train. Near

the top of the final rise another, but longer, blast of the whistle was signal for me to rejoin my coach, an arrangement that gave pleasure to me and considerable amusement to my fellow travellers.

Great blobs of pink and white blossom softened the sombre background of wild mountain scenery, but as we climbed towards the snowline this gradually gave way to barren rock. Herds of goats and, incongruously, the odd camel, were the only living things in the desolate region, while the occasional eagle soared above. The train crept at no more than walking pace for mile after mile through ravine and chasm, the locomotive wailing continuously. At first I thought that this might be a signal to me to avail myself of another trackside stroll, but thought better of it in case I was wrong and got left behind.

Upon reaching the small summit station an air of festivity infected both passengers and station staff as if reaching this point was cause for celebration. We halted here for a considerable time in spite of being already several hours behind schedule while, once the locomotive had received its fill of water, a knot of passengers including myself availed ourselves of the watering appliance for a sluice-down of our own bodies. The cold water and fresh air were great revivers and the bright sunshine mitigated the sense of exposure to the freezing temperature.

From here onwards the train became a hound unleashed. It pounded joyfully down the inclines, the locomotive hissing and snorting, pushing through a series of tunnels, filling everything with acrid smoke and emitting its banshee whistle. Being held up by signals was excuse for the most ear-splitting crescendo of sound it has ever been my misfortune to hear, with the mountains throwing the echoes back and forth, and the longer the signal remained at red the more prolonged and angry was the ear-splitting howl. I marvelled that such discord existed and that enough steam remained to drive the pistons before an unfortunate signalman

up the line, driven half-insane by the noise, allowed the train to proceed.

With black smoke, soot and showers of sparks pouring *in* through the window and charcoal smoke from our respective burners on the compartment floor trying to get *out* we paid dearly for our meals, and each time the train dived into a tunnel complex we were all but asphyxiated. I wondered what Turkish railway by-law we were breaking, but when the ticket-inspector passed upon his rounds his only action was to contribute culinary advice.

The peace of the Cilician Plain offered an abrupt contrast. The terrain fell flat on its back; the temperature switched to hot and humid. Our last halt before the city of Adana was at Yenice where everyone issued from the coaches on to the station forecourt for more washing and drinking purposes. Having not done so earlier, my companions stripped to the waist beneath the water appliance and scrubbed each other's backs, removing at least some of the ravages of travel and cookery. On the move again I watched the distant mountains behind us revert to their picture-postcard remoteness as we ground into Adana three hours late, a state of affairs that worried nobody.

Adana is the fourth largest town in Turkey, but you would never believe it; or at least I couldn't. It is a typical old Turkish town with some brash twentieth-century concrete structures thrust upon it. Narrow streets become quagmires when it rains, as I know to my cost from subsequent sojourns in the place. Whenever I come this way, as I have on several further occasions, it is to find myself marooned in Adana.

This time, however, I was to remain on a train that had become my home. And I was especially pleased to do so for, characteristically, it began to rain. By the time we were back in more mountains the downpour had become a deluge. Dry rivers became gushing torrents very quickly indeed, and I think it was the Aksit that was nearly the cause of our undoing. It was, no

doubt, normally a well-behaved little stream, but the rains had turned it into a crazed brown torrent flecked with the saliva of madness. It had burst its banks and threatened the bridge. We stopped and from the windows we watched the driver and his mate issue forth from the big locomotive. Gingerly they proceeded on to the trestle structure and, near the centre, inched forward like nervous skaters on thin ice, then jumped up and down as if testing the timbers. A discussion, punctuated with much gesticulation, appeared to produce a decision and, drenched, the two men returned to the train.

Slowly, slowly we crept over the bridge. Nobody dared breathe and children in the corridor were restrained from moving. White faces watched the engine reach the other side, then turned to peer fearfully down at the frothing avalanche of water tearing at the bridge supports. After five of the longest minutes I can remember we were over.

With the exception of the Turk and myself we were a fresh batch in the compartment. I felt like a senior prefect amongst an intake of new boys at school, and my strangeness again caused many enquiring glances of the 'how far have you come?', 'where are you going?' variety. My Syrians had, with a quick salute, melted into the alighting crowd, leaving me with another mixture of fellow travellers. But this time we had a lady amongst us, a young and not unattractive one at that, which could have caused problems had she been going further than Aleppo. The lady was Syrian, the men Kurds.

The new mountains into which we were entering were part of the Amanus range and a prelude to the plains of Syria. These uplands, glowing under the rain clouds, divided one country and way of life from another. Something about them reminded me of Scotland. But when did Fort William sprout mosques? No, this was Fezzipasa, the Turkish border station and a high-flying Turkish flag was there to prove it. A crowd of men hung about the platform, most wearing cloth caps and pre-1940 suits. I noticed this only

because I was becoming increasingly aware of Arab-dressed people in the stations.

Now the land was stilled and flat. A string of camels passed by going the other way. The unchanging East was with us and I never knew when it happened.

At Aleppo we were five hours late, yet the train remained a long and unexplained time in Syria's second city, making no impatient gestures of wanting to catch up the schedule. I think this was because the northbound Taurus meets its counterpart here and the drivers like to swap notes, the current political gags from Istanbul and Baghdad, and have a general chinwag. And the other train too seemed to be equally late. However, I was beginning to realise that the Taurus Express is *always* late; intending passengers check their timetables and simply add the hours it is invariably late arriving at their respective station. There is a kind of logic here I suppose, though I couldn't see it going down a bomb in clock-watching Europe.

In Aleppo it had been the citadel that impressed me the most on subsequent visits to the city. With the exception of the pyramids this must surely be the largest man-made object on Earth. Abraham may or may not have milked his cows on the summit, but his name is the one most bandied about throughout its turbulent history.

The *souks* of Aleppo are without equal in the Orient. Their stone vaults and passages reek of history as old as Saladin. Donkeys and heavily-laden horses come down the narrow passageways as they have for centuries, and at every turn there are marvels of colour and a variety of wares. These *souks* give to Aleppo an identity of its own that is neither Turkish nor Damascene, and the aggressiveness of the selling has no equal in all the Mediterranean lands.

Hardly had I switched my mind to things Syrian and taken in a desert that encroaches to the very doorstep of Aleppo when, blow me, we were back in Turkey again. And we were to remain

on Turkish soil, skirting the border all night. We – my new companions and I – were in a tangle of sleep at the second border village and authority was in no mood to inspect tiresome things like passports and visas. But the second Syrian border post was a different story. Furthermore it was the place I ran out of passport. I had often wondered what would happen when I arrived somewhere with a passport full to the brim with mauve ink. There had been occasions when the then Soviet Union had refused to place their visa opposite that of the United States, and once during the McCarthy era I had been denied entry to the United States solely because of the presence, within the pages, of a hammer and sickle emblem of someone's People's Republic. But I had never run out of passport space. Now I was to discover how Syrian authority would react to the situation. Nothing could be easier: they simply altered the dates and details of the cancelled visa, re-stamped it, charged me double and gave me a homily on the folly of not obtaining a new passport even though the validity of the present one had not expired.

More desert and we were at the Iraqi border where the train refused to move for an hour. And by the time we reached Mosul I had lost count of the hours we were late.

The *raison d'être* of Mosul is Nineveh, the older city that I could dimly see across the River Tigris. The capital of the Assyrian Empire was destroyed by the Medes in 612 BC, and nothing more was heard of it until the Sassanid period, when the existence of the town of Budh Ardashir is recorded. Mosul, meaning 'confluence' – that of the Wadi Khosar and the Tigris – first appears in AD 636, as the name of the town on the right bank. It grew to a great city in the Abbasid period, a centre of commerce and industry, with fine mosques, markets and palaces. It remained so under successive dynasties until the destructive Mongols, and later Tamerlane, came along to spoil things. Mosul never fully recovered from these blows, though its position in a fertile belt

of oil-bearing land and on a main caravan route from Aleppo to Persia assures it a certain significance.

Before 1918 it had a reputation for dirt, remarkable even in the Ottoman Empire, which is saying something. No doubt improvements have been made, but I was unable to judge for myself. The railway skirts the city and goes on an excursion round the corporation cemeteries. I stared a long time at the distant mosques and with a particular interest at one of them. The Great Mosque has taken a leaf out of Pisa's book and is supposed to lean to commercial advantage. But either the train was on the tilt or my Turkish friend's firewater was more potent than I thought, for every minaret in sight stood as straight as a soldier.

The Tigris led us out of Mosul. We had picked up two new recruits at the station, including a massive tribesman of the desert. He looked naked without his camel, though he was swathed in a voluminous *djellabah* over which, for good measure, he had wound a carpet not much smaller than the one covering my dining-room floor. It was a typically cool desert night, but it was hardly *that* cold.

'You going far?' I enquired tentatively.

None of the Kurds had spoken to me before, being content to smile and nod in a friendly fashion. However, here was an opportunity to transfer their friendly gestures into words by acting as interpreters, though none spoke more than a few words of English.

'He goes to Baghdad.' I was told.

'I go to Baghdad.'

This repeated information arrived in the form of a rumble from out of the belly of my sheikh opposite. He was afforded instant respect as a speaker of the English tongue and a traveller truly going far. The Kurds offered the information that they were going to a small town with an unpronounceable name, but as nobody had heard of it the pronouncement fell a bit flat.

We were diesel-hauled now and the train trotted along contentedly with no gradients to endure. Beside us ran the Tigris like a tame serpent, and at Samara we stopped at a station of some reckoning that had strayed from the town.

Our numbers down to four, our thoughts, in unison, turned to food and the ceremony of the unswaddling of the bundles and the positioning on the floor of the charcoal fires began. Soon we were feasting communally on joints of veal, pastries and a magnificent tart tenderly prepared, no doubt, by some unseen wifely hand in a forgotten village. A fresh bottle of the homemade liquid that could have been a by-product of petrol appeared from the Turkish quarter. It was shunned by some but not by me. It was night again and I had no desire to remain all that conscious. But at least there were no tunnels here or steam engine to cause near-asphyxiation during the culinary preparations.

I actually slept through that night to awake at my destination. I never even saw the suburbs of Baghdad before we ground into the Iraqi capital's grandiose West Station, which looks better from the outside than it does within.

Baghdad: city of the Arabian Nights, of bejewelled caliphs and veiled women, rich in lore and legend. A hot and dusty city, a city of beggars and evil-smelling bazaars, an insanitary metropolis harbouring a hybrid collection of unclean and underfed humanity packed in narrow adobe cells called tenements. I found a little of these descriptions on my first incursion into Baghdad though, as with Istanbul, its people are the jewels.

In Raschid Street I found the world: silk-clad sheikhs and slouching soldiers; Turks with bright headgear; Kurds in colourful faded robes; Assyrians and Armenians and an occasional American in slacks and a freshly-laundered shirt.

The heartbeat of Iraq is felt the loudest in Raschid Street. It is a populous bitumen thoroughfare which runs through the centre of the city, the whole of its length from the southern gate to the

northern, parallel to the Tigris, and is considered to be the Piccadilly Circus and Broadway of Baghdad, though I'm damned if I could find any resemblance.

I stayed the night in a hotel called Happiness, though it certainly wasn't mine. The European hotels were, I learnt, miles out of town, and anyway I was short of funds so one of the lowlier establishments would have to suffice. The proprietor had one eye and a gammy leg but a shrewd head for business.

'Two hundred fils,' he asked for the best room.

'I'm not buying the house,' I protested.

'A hundred and fifty.'

'Fifty.'

'A hundred.'

'Seventy-five and not a penny more.' I turned to walk out of the door.

'OK, OK, the room is yours. Come and have tea.'

So I joined his friends in a dingy backroom for a most entertaining hour with a delightful bunch of ruffians. I'd been told bad things about Iraqis, but it just goes to show how wrong people can be. And to reinforce this statement a complete stranger, next morning, invited me to lunch at his home. 'You'll find corpses hanging from lamp-posts,' insisted the pundits, but I found no such thing. Come to think of it, I didn't even notice a lamp-post.

I spent another day or two in Baghdad, but by the end of the first I was looking forward to the return journey. Where trains are concerned, the coming and going will always hold more attraction to me than the arrival.

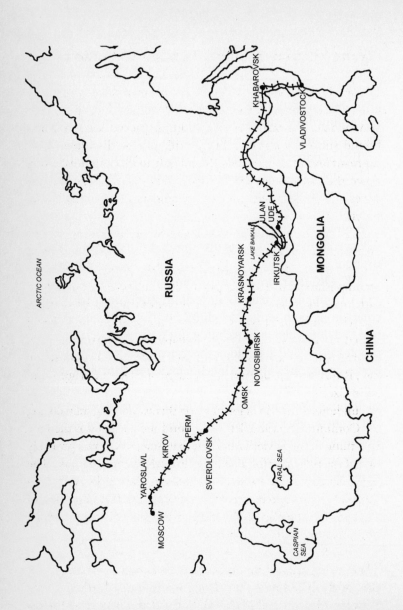

Trans-Siberian Express: London to Vladivostok

Engraved upon the heart of every Englishman there is a railway train. The etching may have worn a little thin with the passage of years and the frustrations of commuting on packed, late and strike-bound suburban services, but it still may be discerned. Our dormant love of trains stands second only to that of animals. Way down the list amongst the 'also rans', I've heard said, come our wives, our children and our cars – though not necessarily in that order!

Even so, nine days on the Trans-Siberian Express is not everybody's cup of tea. For me, however, it was a boyhood dream, the ultimate of railway journeys. Like most dreams, its accomplishment had to be pushed a little and paid for not only in cash but in kind. My family's holiday went to the altar of sacrifice, my wife – like most wives – seeing little amusement in being rattled across the world by train. Perhaps mine in particular since, on that first and subsequent journeys made on this astounding line, Russia was the dominating scourge of Eastern Europe – and she's Czech.

I undertook my trio of journeys on this astounding train during the Communist era and, let me say loud and clear, it was then the best thing in the Soviet Union. At that time, too, it was probably one of the most comfortable trains in both Europe and Asia. The wider Russian gauge ensured spaciousness, the coaches were kept spotlessly clean, and its timetable was strictly adhered to. Best of all, it was the one place in the whole of the Soviet Union in which one could live with its citizens.

There were, and still are, three trains that cover all or the greater part of the 5,778-mile line. There is the *Russia* hauling a train between Moscow and Vladivostok, the *Baikal* between Moscow

and Irkutsk (the chief city of Siberia) and the *Yenisei* to Krasnoyarsk. Vladivostok, however, is the end of the line and the logical terminus of the Trans-Siberian so, from the start, my shirt was on the *Russia* or, in the unromantic parlance of the then Soviet Railways, Train No. 2.

There was a snag, however: Vladivostok was off the tourist beat when I made my first Siberian crossing in 1970. And in the Soviet Union this meant 'out of bounds' with a vengeance. It was, and still is, a top naval base and is situated close to a then-disputed and touchy Chinese border. It was definitely a city where nosy tourists were not welcome. There were in fact only three places along the route of the Trans-Siberian Railway that Western visitors *could* visit. These were Novosibirsk, Irkutsk and Khabarovsk, the last 500 miles north of Vladivostok. A fourth place, the small port of Nakhodka, only 30 miles short, could be reached in transit should a traveller be going to Japan. But it was Vladivostok upon which I had set my sights, and I was determined to get there come hell or high water.

For me the journey had commenced at the Hook of Holland in a Russian through-coach on the East–West Express. Two Germanys and two Berlins, with each of their East and West zones and sectors competing for more prolonged and painful border controls, at least prepared me for the savage procedures at the Russian frontier. They didn't put down the welcome mat at Brest or any other crossing point either. Moscow was usually the second introduction to the Soviet Union and first impressions, particularly those of its hotels, were so awful that to climb aboard another train was a pleasure.

The organisation that controlled your every move in Russia was – and still is to a lesser extent – Intourist. At surveillance it was first class. At looking after the welfare and requirements of clients, it was a dead loss. They preferred their tourists in squads, of course; I was a loner and so one of the awkward brigade. In all towns and cities open to tourists they had their minions. They

met your train or your aeroplane and hunted you down however crowded the station or airport. To be fair, these minions were usually nice people working for an impossible organisation riddled with unbelievable bureaucracy. Its hotels varied. They fed you and lent you a bed to sleep on, but to obtain even these basic commodities you needed the patience of Job and a warped sense of humour. Nothing went smoothly. Things seldom worked, except the hotel telephones that were loud in their insistence on early waking calls you'd not ordered.

To crown all this I had a problem. The Soviet Embassy in London had seen fit to issue me with no more than a temporary visa, one just for Moscow only, and of seven days' validity. In the Russian capital I was supposed to have it replaced with a more comprehensive endorsement. But the embassy had reckoned without Intourist and its blind insistence to adhesion to the set programme. And my programme did not allow for detours to ministries for the purpose of rectifying lame visas. My bleats were ignored.

Moscow no doubt grows on you. It doesn't on me, despite subsequent visits. On this first occasion I just had time for a stroll in Red Square, a glimpse of the dead Lenin, an inspection of the statue-laden Metro, a visit to GUM (the city's main store) and the Bolshoi Theatre between endless formalities at the Bucharest Hotel and my reporting to the Jaroslav station next day.

Jaroslav station was even more of a madhouse than the Bucharest Hotel. Its platforms were awash with what I can only describe as nomads. Few appeared to be intending to travel anywhere; most seemed to have taken up permanent residence. Nowhere could I find any reference to the great Trans-Siberian Express, or even a Train No. 2. There were no officials to ask, so I went to a ticket window, put on a 'little boy lost' face and pointed to my soft-class ticket voucher.

Soft-class travel was compulsory for foreigners. The class of travel referred to the bunks: 'soft' indicated four sprung bunks in

a closed compartment; 'hard' described a more crowded wooden bunk-filled open coach. But since bedding was issued to both classes of passenger the texture of the bunks themselves was immaterial. The 'hards' were very much more communal, which could have been either advantageous or disadvantageous depending upon one's individual outlook. For me they were going to pay dividends.

Whatever impression the border people might give, a Russian will do anything to help a foreign stranger in distress. This one at the ticket window slammed down his shutter in the face of the person at the head of the queue, took me by the hand and led me to my train.

The Trans-Siberian Express is a window on Russia and the Russians. One can look out to see Russia and look in to see Russians. Both are fascinating. For me the supporting feature did not become immediately apparent. Word had to circulate that there was an Englishman on the train. In the meantime there was Russia.

My first companion in the compartment was, appropriately, a Russian. He spoke about as much French as I did, so we began chatting away understanding little even before we had drawn out of the station. Joining us just before departure was a young mother and, to my dismay, a toddler at what might be described as the messy stage of life. The little girl made straight for my neat pile of bedding and effected an introduction by leaking through her nappy, and the mother hardly improved matters when she used my towel to dry her.

The train slid so silently out of the station I never realised we were moving. The first excitement was Zagórz, the former Sergievo and the Canterbury of Russia, with the turnip-domes of its great monastery flashing gold in the sun. Jaroslav revealed the Volga, provoking adoration from my fellow travellers, but here it was no more than a wide muddy stream washing the backsides of factories. Kirov was but a noise in the night, while Sverdlovsk

(its name now reverted back to its original Yekaterinburg) gave an impression of being a great hulk of a city with chimneys like pencils scrawling rude words in the sky. A river called Chusovaya acted as the western border of both Siberia and Asia, while somewhere between Sverdlovsk and Perm came a rise in the dead-flat terrain which made me wonder where I'd got the idea that the Urals were mountains.

One cannot help but ponder upon the conception and history of this astounding line as train after train rumbled by in the opposite direction at intervals of very few minutes full of the sinews of life; and then death, for many were carrying the tools of war.

Czar Alexander III started things in 1890. Cost was no object, for the prime purpose was military. Sections of the line blossomed across the whole country and were put to use haphazardly. Haphazard, too, were the laying methods, much track having to be replaced in later years. In 1895 the western end of the line reached Irkutsk, capital of Siberia, but the great mass of water that was Lake Baikal baulked further progress. In 1898 the rails from east and west met near Chita, the link across Baikal being forged by a Newcastle-built ferry in summer and by temporary track laid directly across the ice-bound lake in winter. The dangerous winter schedules were finally safeguarded when a line was hacked through the granite mountains around the southern shore.

Luxury expresses never envisaged before (or since) went into regular service in 1903, in stark contrast to the trains of *teplushki* wagons carrying convicts to servitude. The wars of 1904 and 1914–18 suspended the luxury traffic, and during the latter the Trans-Siberian line fell into the hands of both Red and White armies as well as Semeonov's bandits, who used trains against one another almost as jousting knights of earlier conflicts. Communism brought miseries greater than those of war, and when Stalin died some fifteen million souls rotted in camps in Siberia and beyond.

Maybe they could find a spark of comfort from the railway; their predecessors had to walk those 5,000 terrible miles.

Now, life on the Trans-Siberian is refreshingly aimless. You wake up in the morning, your watch tells you it is eight o'clock, but you know it doesn't matter a hoot since, moving east, it will alter anyway and not just with the passage of time. Your berth – which can be adapted for sleeping at night and sitting by day – is commodious. There is no need to get up and no incentive or reason for doing so. You have little to look forward to and nothing to avoid. You sprawl on your seat, justifiably inert, seeing all there is to see without the slightest effort. Mostly there is nothing to look at, but there is no reason to stop looking. The one chore is (or was for me at any rate) that of making up one's own bed in company with the other occupants of the compartment. And this only, seemingly, because the female coach attendant was so busy polishing the brasswork and vacuum-cleaning the carpets that she simply had no time. Nobody was allowed off the train until she had rubbed down the handrails and doorknobs. The lavatories right along the train were a treat, and nobody nicked the soap or the paper.

As a break from monotony there was the restaurant car, full of noise and movement. The food was wholesome, though not of the variety indicated by the lengthy menu. Obtaining a meal takes time anywhere in Russia, but on the Trans-Siberian there is that commodity in abundance. I had purchased a certain number of food coupons in advance from Intourist, but found this to be a mistake, it being a more expensive way of doing things. Caviar is available from the restaurant car immediately following periodic stores replenishment at major stations, but it doesn't last long; thereafter it's back to bortsch, the staple Russian 'starter'.

Whether you wanted a meal or just a beer, a visit to the restaurant car was a social event. It was also the spawning ground for the invitations that started coming in on the second day out of Moscow. Sometimes, after stretching my legs along the tracks at

a wayside station, a Russian would be standing awkwardly by my compartment door, having noticed me in the restaurant car. The rigmarole of conversation in two utterly opposed tongues would commence until a few common basics made it understood that my presence was required in Compartment 14, Coach No. 8 or whatever. So I reported, as requested, to the designated venue, to be vigorously entertained there, often wined and dined and subjected to a multitude of questions on every conceivable subject, many requiring answers that would hardly please Soviet authority. Invariably there was someone who spoke a little English, German or French. Then the chain reaction would begin and one of the hosts would issue a subsequent invitation.

One, I remember, was for breakfast from a Red Army colonel. A true Red Army breakfast he had promised, and I was green enough to anticipate the equivalent of bacon and eggs. But it had consisted of tea tumblers of home-brewed neat vodka. Reluctant to let down the British Army, I knocked back the raw spirit until consciousness fled and I collapsed on the colonel's berth. The good man gave me a salute, covered me in his greatcoat and allowed me to sleep things off for the rest of the day.

Occasionally an exchange in the restaurant car would escalate into a general discussion, one of which ended in my lecturing all and sundry on the pros and cons of the Vietnam conflict. It was that evening that I met Peter.

In London I had attempted to obtain permission to visit Vladivostok. I had tried again in Moscow, and I was to try again in Novosibirsk, in Irkutsk and in Khabarovsk. But everybody was to make it abundantly plain that I could not visit Vladivostok. Nobody would offer any reasons beyond the unsatisfactory half-explanation that there were no Intourist 'facilities' in the city and that it was a naval base. Had authority not been so adamant about my going there, I might not have bothered. And then Peter, Peter the student from Komsomolsk, full of homemade brandy and a

sucker for my duty-free cigarettes, said he would get me a ticket for Vladivostok.

I had stopped off at Novosibirsk and taken a look at Academgorodok, the city of scientific establishments that Intourist fondly imagined to be a tourist attraction. Later I took time off from the railway at the much older and more historic Irkutsk, where I was enrolled into a clutch of East German package tourists. At least Irkutsk had more going for it than Novosibirsk, which was dreary in the extreme; a big, brawny, rolled-shirtsleeves kind of place with pavements that were death traps, full of holes, open drains, broken curbs and weed-infested paving stones. Only the enormous River Ob gave it any saving grace in my eyes.

Irkutsk, however, was a different story. Even Chekhov had some kind words to say about the place. In 1890 he wrote of it as 'A splendid town. Thoroughly cultured. A theatre, museum, municipal park with music [and] good hotels'. Since then it has grown into a city boasting a university, a library housed in a one-time Czarist governor's residence, and a lot of sedate nineteenth-century public buildings set amongst tree-lined, wide-pavemented streets of residential *izbas*: square wooden houses that were fast dying out elsewhere.

My hotel here would hardly have inspired Comrade Chekov, its charms (or lack of them) being on a similar gloomy plane to those in Novosibirsk. However, it did rise to a certain charm for me. Unable to accept the fact I was a lone tourist, the management insisted that I sit with an East German group at mealtimes. This was fine by me, especially as on the following day they invited me to join their excursion to Lake Baikal, so I did what I was bid. And when I came to pay my meals' bill at the end of my stay this was refused, the staff insisting that I belonged to the German group who were on an all-inclusive rate. Hence my meals were gratis and placed to the account of the German Democratic Republic which worried me not at all.

Except for the Caspian, which is described as a sea, Baikal is the largest lake in the world. It is 390 miles long and up to 50 miles wide. Eighteen hundred species of plant life, many of them unique, live in its crystal-clear waters, 5,500 feet deep. Fed by 333 rivers and emptied by one, the titanic Angara, it broods in a silence that is uncanny.

He who hasn't seen Baikal, they say, hasn't seen Siberia. Its uncharted bed is a graveyard of railway engines, trucks, lorries and motorcars, and amongst them the rotting skeletons of man. This jetsam is the legacy of those trains that failed to negotiate the lake's treacherous winter ice, and with their demise were born the stories which are woven into the legends of Baikal.

While sitting on its shore and ruminating upon these matters, I was accosted by a middle-aged Russian who bet me a bottle of vodka that I wouldn't take a dip. Again the honour of Great Britain was at stake so, stripping down to my underpants, I took the shortest dip in history: about two seconds, since the water was paralisingly cold. Having won the bet, we consumed the contents of the bottle my companion had with him – though since he drank faster than I, my victory was a doubtful one.

Next day I took myself to church in Irkutsk, an odd thing for me to do as I'm not much of a churchgoer. A police check was in progress at the door which was obviously putting off much of the potential congregation, so I felt a sense of perverse solidarity with the priest. The body of the church was heavily ornamental with paintings on the ceilings, while candelabras, icons and gold-painted effigies that left little space for a standing, largely peasant and middle-aged congregation of about thirty. The shawled old women and *tolstofka*-clad, peak-capped old men came straight out of a Tolstoy novel.

By Siberian standards Irkutsk is an old city. It was founded in 1652 and for a period was a staging post for exiles, including Trotsky, and headquarters of the gold-mining industry. My walkabout took me along streets bordered by the chocolate-

coloured single, and two-storey wooden houses, some of the pavements being the original raised sidewalks of timber planks. After the hideous modernity of Novosibirsk, Irkutsk was a town to explore with rapturous abandon.

Back on another Trans-Siberian Express, my dreams that night were of what I found at the bottom of Baikal, a nightmare that woke me up. I lay listening to the sounds of my train passing through the granite barrier along the southern shores of the lake. We were to be exclusively steam-hauled from Irkutsk onwards and the echoes of the mighty locomotive in cutting and tunnel made a satanic lullaby.

My estimation of Soviet towns, it might be noticed, did not rise very high. Nor, when in them, could I get much change out of their residents. Talking to strangers on a train provided no problems, but once off it one was shunned like the plague, simply on account of fear of the consequences from Soviet authority. Only in the anonymity of the railway carriage did Russians emerge from their shells to display the famed Russian hospitality.

The best season for Siberia is autumn. It is a world of trees: pine, cedar, larch and birch. They call it the *taiga*. It goes on unbroken for hundreds, indeed thousands, of miles. In the North, in the permafrost, a larch takes a century to grow. In the South are tiger-inhabited jungles. In between one could fit the United States with plenty of room to spare. The sun shining on the autumn colouring of the trees turns Siberia into a gigantic vat of burnished gold. Occasionally the sea of trees breaks into a storm of rock, as at Baikal and beyond Chita. The mountains of Mongolia and Manchuria show blue in the distance. Tiny churchless villages of square wooden *izbas* huddle together in clearings, fighting a battle for existence against the relentless *taiga*. Their loneliness has you by the throat. Perhaps this is another reason why Russians talk on trains.

Peter, who had joined the train I'm not sure where, told me of his hopes and fears for the future. A native of L'vov close to the Polish border in the Ukraine, he could hardly have found a destination further away and still remain within the Soviet sphere with Komsomolsk, the new city on the Amur River north-east of Khabarovsk. Founded in 1932 Komsomolsk was built on a site hacked out of dense forest by idealistic Communist Youth. Peter remained immensely proud of his home town and, though far too young to have known Polish rule, had a fervent love for things Polish.

After the third cigarette in my compartment he invited me to meet his friends in the more austere portion of the train. I had already explored some of the hard-class coaches, but this subsequent visit was more rewarding as, escorted by Peter, I had to go around shaking everybody by the hand and patting children's heads. Many of these people were emigrants with all their goods and chattels with them, and I could sense a strong community and pioneering spirit.

That evening Peter and I dined together, mostly on beer, in the restaurant car. Provisions were getting low with even less choice on the menu than usual. We were joined by an older man who bombarded me with questions again of the kind not likely to endear him to the regime.

Another night, another dawn. Again that incredible horizon of trees rose to circumscribe the sky. Everyone rises late on the Trans-Siberian. The samovars are stoked up, the first glasses of tea poured down sleepy throats, while yawning men and women in pyjamas or track-suits parade in the corridors to view the new countryside which has barely changed since yesterday. I was told half a dozen times by complete strangers that we were passing through such-and-such an *oblast* (county), or that in the night we had passed over so-and-so river. One can feel the immense pride Russians have for their giant country.

My compartment companions came and went. With me for several days was an engine driver de luxe. He was going right through to Vladivostok to take over a westbound express. A wonderful chap with a lined face and Stalin moustache, he was delighted at my interest in the workings of the line, and though we frequently became encumbered by misinterpretation, we had all the time in the world to iron out the sense of the discussion. The coach attendant treated him with great respect, bringing him – and me – copious glasses of tea, despite the fact that the engine driver barked at her unmercifully.

At Ulan Ude, capital of the then Buryat Autonomous Soviet Socialist Republic, I had joined the more hard-up members of the train community for a picnic breakfast in the station. A bunch of melancholy old women had installed a long bench loaded with home-grown or homemade wares amongst which were eggs, milk, yoghurt, gherkins, tomatoes, blueberries, pies, cakes and batter puddings; a far better selection of edibles than the restaurant car on the train could offer.

It was on this journey that I learnt to play chess. I never have been one for games of this sort, but because it is the Russian national game I felt obliged to accept the invitation to learn. I sat miserably moving pieces about the board, having them taken away with every move. By about the third game I began to get the general drift of the rules but was beaten hollow at every subsequent contest.

Over the second half of the journey, Peter was my most frequent visitor and companion. I had already put to him my Vladivostok problem and, giving him sight of my reduced cigarette hoard, again suggested that he might like to help. Yes, he would get me the ticket and the reservation at Khabarovsk for he, too, was alighting there. Khabarovsk was as far as I could officially go and no doubt there was an Intourist representative there to take me under his or her wing and to ensure that I *didn't* go further.

Peter would contact me at my hotel. He seemed to know which hotels were for Westerners; in order to keep us apart from the common herd at that time, Westerners were installed in segregated establishments. There would be no problem.

I slept well for the last full night before Khabarovsk. The landscape was as flat as a pancake with just a hint of strained-out mountains in the far distance. Around midday we crossed another mammoth river, probably the Bureya, a tributary of the great Amur which formed the border with Manchuria, only a short distance away. I noticed that each and every bridge was guarded by soldiers. Somewhere in the night we had passed out of Siberia into a region then called the Soviet Far East.

A furtive little man came into my compartment, which I now had all to myself, to offer me a string of anti-Soviet jokes of the 'what Lenin said to the bishop' variety. I couldn't understand any of them, but laughed politely. He was my last visitor. Though the train was not due at Khabarovsk until midnight, I was left severely alone thereafter as if by intention. I began to view the coach attendants with deep distrust, for it could only have been them who diverted further potential occupants of my compartment. Or was I imagining things?

Late in the afternoon, with a return of some hills and a beautiful autumnal gold glint on the trees, I was tempted to the rear of the train to take some final photographs. Hardly had I focused on a scene when the camera was knocked sideways and I received a severe castigation from a blue-uniformed policeman who had appeared from nowhere. And then I understood the reason for the shunning I was receiving. The line ran very close indeed to the Chinese border and, being a restricted zone, police patrols were on the train. And with authority came fear, or at least prudence. I stalked back to my compartment.

It was one o'clock in the morning when we crawled into Khabarovsk. For the first time since I had left Moscow I was glad to leave a Russian train.

Khabarovsk grows on you too. The growth, for me, stemmed mainly from the pretty woman from Intourist who, even at that late hour, had come to meet me. I was even dazzled into an apology for having kept her up so long, though it did occur to me that I hadn't asked her to do so. She was beautifully uncommunicative as we raced, in an official car, through the back streets of the city.

My hotel was the AMYP, or at least that's what the Cyrillic lettering meant to me. Actually it meant Amur, the name of the river. It being so late I was spared the agony of the reception formalities and bid my guide good-night, promising to be ready following breakfast later that morning for my compulsory tour of the local cable factory, seemingly the high spot of Khabarovsk. Hardly had I dumped my bag when I found myself being solicited by a weird, unshaven individual who barged into my room unannounced. His first request was for a cigarette; his second was less explicit, but it made clear that he had designs upon my person and that his bedroom was next door. With some difficulty and gentle force I got rid of him.

I was awoken by the telephone. Into my ear poured a torrent of girlish Russian in a questioning tone and I was about to answer '*Ya neponimayu,*' when I realised I *did* understand and changed it to '*Niet*'. The second call was an early call I'd not requested. I left the receiver off the hook and flung the bedclothes over my head. But I couldn't win. The last inmate of the room had left the radio on full volume and at five o'clock in the morning exalted rendering of the Soviet national anthem hit me. This set off my passionate neighbour who started banging excitedly on the wall.

That was not the end of my tribulations. Rising, sleepless, well in time for breakfast, I washed, dressed and made to open the door. It wouldn't budge. I tried and tried again to no avail and my hammering on it only set off the guest next door. So I did what any normal guest would do and phoned reception. Well, that's what I thought I did, and in the absence of any list of hotel internal numbers had dialled 100. In Khabarovsk it was the number for

the fire brigade. I heard the clanging of bells and shriek of a siren outside, but never realised it was anything to do with me until my door was smashed open by a couple of beefy steel-helmeted men wielding axes! Behind them a manager was wringing his hands, asking why I couldn't have simply rung reception.

As well as losing my sleep I also lost my breakfast, and was even a little late for my appointment with an irritated guide whose name I discovered was Jane. Thereafter things went a little better. She actually laughed when I told her of my all-night cabaret, and I was able to talk her out of the threatened cable factory tour with the promise that I would take her to the cinema where a French-language film was showing. Foreigners had immediate access to such popular movies as opposed to the locals, who were forced to reserve seats weeks in advance.

So in lieu of the Amur cable factory we went to the pictures, though Jane insisted on giving me the spiel on the former's production figures as a sop to her conscience. We also toured the city with Jane rabbiting on about Yerofei Khabarov, how he had erected a fort on the site of the city in 1652 and how, in 1858, the Russians settled there under Count Muraviev. We had a quick look at Yerofei's statue and then strolled along the banks of the broad Amur near to its confluence with its tributary, the Ussuri: two giant waterways rolling into one. And that was about the sum total of Khabarovsk's charms.

I would have bet little on the chances of my student friend keeping his appointment with me. And I would have been wrong, for there he was in the foyer of the hotel that evening. Together we took a tram to the station and, leaving me outside, he went in to undertake the promised deed, to emerge in due course waving both ticket and hard-class reservation. But the enormity of his actions had sapped his strength. I paid him the fare, gave him the rest of my cigarettes and shook his hand, whereupon he withdrew with an embarrassed smile and, I think, considerable relief.

Subsequent examination of the ticket revealed that it was valid only for a single journey to Vladivostok. This would mean applying for a return ticket and berth reservation, compulsory on long-distance journeys in the then USSR, in Vladivostok, an action that filled me with a certain amount of foreboding. The fewer people who knew that I was in forbidden territory, the better.

In the light of the *fait accompli* of the ticket, I made my plans. I had four days allotted to me in Khabarovsk, and one had already expired. I had time to reach Vladivostok, spend eight hours in the city, and return to Khabarovsk before my scheduled departure on the fifth day. Both the outward and return journeys would be made overnight, and I'd still be back for my last night in Khabarovsk. If all went well nobody would know that I'd been away.

My new train was again the *Russia*, the same eastbound Trans-Siberian Express as had brought me to Khabarovsk 24 hours earlier. I left my baggage in my bedroom, slunk out of the hotel at midnight and arrived at the station to see the great Express pull into its platform in a sweat of steam.

I found my more humble hard-class coach at the rear with some difficulty. The female attendant gave me an odd glance and twice checked my ticket. I thought she was going to start asking questions, but a scuffle at the other end of her domain sent her scurrying off. With still more difficulty I located my berth amongst the prostrate, snoring, smelly bodies sprawled everywhere. An old woman was sleeping noisily on the berth whose number corresponded with that on my reservation slip, but the one above was free. I clambered up amidst a chorus of grunts. As soon as the train moved the attendant appeared with my bedding which I spread awkwardly. I didn't bother to undress.

On the whole it was not a bad night, or what was left of it. From my vantage point on the top bunk I watched the coach come alive as daylight flooded its interior. Children's voices, in laughter and complaint, rose in volume as parental control lapsed and big

women contorted themselves replacing or tightening garments removed or loosened during the night.

I lay dozing until quite late. My bunk was too high for me to see out of the window and I did not want to draw attention to myself until it was necessary. The train was not scheduled to reach Vladivostok until 1.00 p.m., so I had the whole morning to lie low. Then the attendant began collecting bedding and I was forced to emerge.

There was a flurry of excitement as it flashed through the community that an Englishman had joined it. There was amazement, too, for tourists never travelled hard class. I tried to tell a hushed audience that this was no fault of the tourists and that their own organisation – Intourist – was to blame. I hoped they got the message, for the compulsory segregation in hotels and elsewhere was a source of considerable bitterness amongst simpler Russians. I *was* able to get through to them, however, that I would be in serious trouble if authority caught me on board this train, and received enthusiastic offers of help with my concealment should the need arise.

Thereafter I was invited to share in a score of breakfasts by the good folk around me and soon was replete with salami, hard-boiled egg, fish and cheese. Fussed over by old men and women of peasant stock, whose gnarled hands kept passing me more food whenever mine were empty, I felt a great affinity with these generous and kind-hearted people. Outside, the grey morning was increasing the sombreness of steeply rolling countryside. Uncultivated grasslands rising above the undulations were, in turn, overlooked by hills and a narrow road ran for miles alongside the railway. Later the hills became slag heaps, universally ugly, and some birch woods offered the illusion that we were back in Europe. Yet China was but five miles distant across that dew-laden grass.

We stopped at Nadejinskaya, the junction for Nakhodka, and amongst my fellow-passengers strolling on the platform – many

flaunting jazzy pyjama suits – I noticed that police were more in evidence than usual. They were infesting the train, too, so I kept firmly to my bunk resisting the temptation of exercise.

My new friends had the situation well in hand and seemed to know the ways of authority on the last leg of the journey. Soon after the train drew out of the station I was persuaded to lie flat on my berth while soft bundles of belongings were piled on top of me. My concealment was looked upon as a huge joke with everybody chuckling merrily as I disappeared under a mountain of pillows and private bedding. I never even saw the policeman that entered our section of the coach to inspect travel documents.

The few minutes it had fallen behind schedule the train made up in the last 30 miles and we drew into Vladivostok station exactly on time. I had been released from confinement and assured that there would be no further official intrusions. I felt a glow of satisfaction. With the last 500 miles from Khabarovsk I had, whatever happened next, accomplished my goal. I was nearly 6,000 miles east of Moscow, nearly 8,000 from home. I had reached the Pacific on the other side of the world and, except for the English Channel (not much wider than some of the Siberian rivers), it had all been done by train.

I left the train within the ranks of a detachment of soldiers and so managed to leave the sizeable station again without being seen by anyone who might have reason to question my presence. And once outside I made for what I hoped would be the city centre.

Vladivostok means 'Ruler of the East'. Count Muraviev, who had a hand in the colonising of Khabarovsk, selected the site for the port after the Treaty of Aigun in 1858, by which the district was ceded to Russia. In 1860 the first settlers arrived, and the port itself came into being 12 years later; to the discomfort of Japan, who had no great desire to have a Russian naval base on her doorstep. But Vladivostok is not only a naval port: its four-by-one-mile harbour, kept ice-free all the year round, is home to the

Russian whaling flotillas and her Far Eastern fishing fleet. The town itself is heavily industrialised.

It was also over-populated with soldiers as well as sailors, a fact I discovered hardly had I left its rambling station, as a battalion of fully-armed troops disgorged from a nearby barracks. The town, I discovered, was exceedingly awful. Even Novosibirsk was fairyland in comparison. Ports anywhere can rarely boast of exotic surroundings but those of Vladivostok, even with its backdrop of hills, were truly functional. Everywhere frowning buildings of flaking plaster and devoid of paint hemmed me in. Here and there a vase of flowers in a window tried to make amends amid an urbanity of despair.

I have never been able to hide a guilty conscience, and the one I bore as I skulked down those depressing streets was the most monumental ever. The fact irritated me, for I could not accept that I was doing wrong. 'Don't go and do anything silly,' had been the refrain from my loved ones as I left home, and here I was flouting the rules simply to satisfy a whim. In my heart I knew the source of the conscience.

I attempted to solve this a little in the knowledge that I had taken a few precautions. Hadn't I left my camera back in my Khabarovsk hotel? And didn't I look reasonably nondescript Russian in a pair of thick fawn slacks and a leather jacket? I had not shaved for a couple of days either. However, I still jumped at the sight of the expressionless little man standing in what was almost certainly Karl Marx Square. I had long realised the significance of the Lenin-style cloth cap and ill-fitting overcoat. Hadn't I, years before, cut my teeth in the secret police recognition game, both Nazi and Communist? And this specimen was no different. I sheered away but when I stopped to tie a shoelace, in the time-honoured fashion, he wasn't following. I began to suspect that the only person I was scaring was myself.

Suddenly I saw the sea. It was brown and lifeless, but the moment notched a small milestone in my life. I had seen the

Pacific before off California and elsewhere. I'd even swum in it amongst surroundings far more pleasant. But that glimpse between an unfinished building block and a sheaf of dockside cranes shone the brighter in my memory.

To approach the sea I had to walk along the harbour front. Shipping of every description jostled the docks, which hummed with activity. I watched deck swabbing on trawlers and whalers, and the unloading of crates from cargo vessels. All the while, in the background, the gaunt forms of destroyers and cruisers showed stark against the sky. Seamen and sailors, all speaking the language of the sea in spite of their contrasting dress, thronged the dockside. Soldiers, out of place in maritime territory, self-consciously lounged around a convoy of heavy lorries and I felt their eyes following me as I walked stiffly by. Red slogans announced 'Lenin – Our Teacher and Our Friend' from wooden hoardings. They alone shattered the illusion that this port could have been Portsmouth or Plymouth.

I partook of a meal in a stand-up buffet serving frankfurter-type sausage, cabbage and potato. It was a rough dock-area kind of establishment, but its exclusive supply of sausage and mash offered a minimum of likely chat. Late in the afternoon I walked around the corner of a back street into a funeral cortège. The double row of deliberate men in white shirts escorted an open coffin carried shoulder high. Behind them followed a gaggle of women with no apparent sense of the dignity of the occasion.

Some of those back streets housed families living in poverty, pure and simple. There was no other word for it. Yet many left-wing writers on Russia did not recognise that poverty exists in a Communist state as it does in a capitalist one, and it gave me no great pleasure to have proved them wrong. Here, perhaps, was another reason for the exclusion of tourists from Vladivostok.

With dusk I entered a bookshop to browse around the shelves, as I invariably do when at a loose end. Most of the literature was political and deadly dull. A man recognised me as English (so

much for my efforts to look otherwise) and behind the pages of a large volume he told me something of his years in both Hitler and Stalin camps, and my heart went out to him. Now he was a man without rights and without hope.

I left the bookshop to return to the station, even though there were hours to spare before my train left, but I had a gut feeling that attaining a ticket was going to be a hassle. And it was then that I realised that I *was* being followed. The man was a nondescript little fellow whom I'd noticed in the bookshop, and he dogged my footsteps in spite of the circuitous route I intentionally took. In a supermarket of half-empty food shelves I tried to lose him, to no avail. He must have been aware he'd been rumbled but made no attempt to conceal his actions; it was as if he didn't care.

My 'tail' was with me all the way back to the station, and I hoped the man didn't like walking for it was quite a distance. Before going to the ticket kiosks I visited the toilet and, in my confusion, entered the 'Ladies' whereupon a giant of a woman confronted me, spun me round like a top and ejected me with force back out of the door and straight into the arms of my tormentor! He gave me a sickly grin and retired while I went in search of the ticket-office. I never saw him again.

I had been prudent enough to obtain from my proletarian travelling companions on the earlier train a piece of paper on which had been written 'A single ticket to Khabarovsk, please,' and this I pushed at the face behind the grill of one of the kiosks. The face spoke words to the effect that I must obtain reservations from an office in town and pushed my paper back with an address scribbled on it.

A terrible vision arose within me that I would never get out of this unsavoury place, that my ghost would haunt it forever. Since my passport held an already out-of-date Soviet visa for Moscow only, and that I was 6,000 miles off course, meant I would be unable even to put up at a hotel.

Not bothering to note whether I was being followed or not, I raced back into the town and located the address I'd been given. The office seemed to be a department of the railway and, to my great relief, was still open. It was pillared, high-ceilinged and full of travel posters mostly of places unattainable to the average Russian. As I expected, no one spoke English. However, my request for a reservation was understood by a chubby individual in a shiny suit, but some sort of document seemed to be required to support the application. It was not a passport, and anyway this was the last document I wanted scrutinised. Instead he kept invoking the name of Intourist which didn't help for he must have known, as I knew, that there was no Intourist office in Vladivostok. Even so I showed him the correspondence I'd had with that organisation which at least took his mind off the passport. Then I had a brainwave and mumbled the word 'diplomat' without much conviction, not quite certain whether I was making things worse. From my wallet I withdrew and displayed my driving licence, regimental association membership card, RAC membership card and Barclay's credit card. Each came under scrutiny, the credit card scoring the highest points (could it have been the word 'Visa' that meant something?). Shrugs followed, but they were constructive shrugs, the kind that says 'What the hell, anyway'. Maybe it was near closing time and the man wanted to go home. Whatever the motivation, here came the capitulation and the issue of the train reservation, together with the indication that this would permit me to purchase a ticket back at the station. Thankfully, I fled.

On my way back I passed a cripple, horribly disfigured. On the man's jacket was a treble row of medal ribbons and I realised that he was one of the legion of maimed ex-servicemen who had fought for a country that, allegedly, exiled its broken ranks to places not visited by foreigners. To me this was perhaps the ugliest facet of the Soviet Union, and one that never reached the pages of the glib Intourist brochures.

The acquisition of my ticket produced no incidents and I
offered no argument when I perceived it to be for soft-class travel.
I still had two hours to wait before departure of the train, but in
the station I felt on safer ground. Hadn't I made a simple mistake
and come to Vladivostok instead of Nakhodka, and was now
waiting like a good citizen for the return train? A likely story
perhaps, but it sounded better here in the station than it would
have done in the vicinity of those battleships. Unwilling to take
any further risks I took refuge in a corner of a waiting-room
notwithstanding its clouds of pungent tobacco smoke.

The westbound Trans-Siberian Express left on time and my
empty compartment was a balm. The female coach attendant gave
me bedding and a funny look, though not an unfriendly one. I
thought ruefully of my £20-worth of bed that had been wasted in
my Khabarovsk hotel. But my dismal little excursion had not been
wasted. Maybe it had been cheap at the price.

Back at Khabarovsk, Intourist gave me what could almost be
described as a royal welcome. I was obviously the first foreign
tourist they had lost, and the return of the prodigal son had them
rushing over to my hotel full of the joys of spring. The hotel had
reported my absence, I was told, and the staff of the Intourist
office had been *most* concerned. What *had* I been doing? They
were in an unfortunate position. To have demanded a full
explanation would have put Intourist in a bad light. And as I wasn't
telling they could only jump to conclusions. My answers to their
questions were evasive in the extreme, giving the impression,
possibly, of shame, so they jumped to the wrong conclusion.
Firmly convinced that I had spent a couple of nights with a woman,
they next wanted to know who. I gave nothing away and made no
denials and as their concern was plainly centred upon some female
'deviationist' whose political thoughts I may have corrupted, so I
let them sweat. And anyway, hadn't Intourist been telling me how

prostitution no longer existed in the Soviet Union? Finally, I received a mild lecture on inconsiderateness.

The rest of the day I spent behaving myself in Khabarovsk. Next morning I flew west. I hadn't wanted to fly, but Intourist insisted. Back at Novosibirsk came a change of direction and I flew south across the barren corrugations of the Kirgiz Steppe to Alma Ata ('City of Apples') grovelling at the foot of the Tien Shan ('Mountains of Heaven') and on to Tashkent; a new Tashkent of modern concrete that had arisen following its last disastrous earthquake.

There is a perfectly adequate railway covering the southwards route but its trains – if there were any – were not for the likes of me. *Thomas Cook's Overseas Timetable* quoted the line under Table 877, but only the section from Tashkent north-west to Moscow could seemingly offer any sort of public service. The railway map showed a 2,000-mile stretch of line between Novosibirsk and Alma Ata without a single station marked. One, however, we must have flown over. It was Karagunda, where the penal camps were. I would have given much to have travelled that line. From Tashkent a short-haul monoplane made a poor substitute for the famed Golden Road, but the byways of history along the old Silk Routes were also barred so I had to make do with an air corridor to Samarkand.

And the impact of Samarkand was staggering. It spoke to one of Tamerlane and Ulag Beg. I spent my allotted hours amongst its fabulous treasures, even breaking the rules again by dodging a checkpoint and walking a mile or two along the Golden Road. They were putting down drainage pipes, which rather spoilt its romantic image.

Next I was shuddered on to the city of Emirs and carpets that is Bukhoro. And here, too, was history come alive as one wandered, deliciously oppressed by its grim Tower of Death and ghosts of generations past, along streets unchanged from the dawn of time.

From Bukhoro back to Tashkent and the long flight across the time zones of the incredible Kizil Kum and Kara Kum deserts, the swamps of the Murghab River, the ruins of Merv (the oldest of all cities) and the Aral and Caspian seas until a long-overdue night finally caught up to curtain a mind that was drunk with wonder. But the darkness could not blot out a city sitting squarely on the Volga. The atmosphere in the aircraft was heady with emotion as we passed above the twinkling lights. Few Russians had not lost a son, a husband or a dear friend at Stalingrad, and their blood-soaked land they loved the more for it.

From Kiev I managed to get back to my beloved railway again, and caught the Danubius Express, its route originating in Moscow and ending in Bucharest. A steady rain was falling to lay tears on the great black Ukrainian Plain that is likewise drenched in soldiers' blood, and is therefore the more terrible. Sad little villages swept by, their houses a contradiction of white paint, their tiny gardens tended almost as gestures of despair.

At Ungheni was the border with Romania, and the outgoing procedure from the Soviet Union was no less arduous than that at Brest. For me, it was worse. An irate personage with the starred epaulettes of an officer bore down on me in the station while I was changing my remaining roubles into Romanian lei. He waved a passport.

'Are you Mr Portway?' he demanded. I was surprised he had to ask.

'Do you realise your passport is out of order?' His voice with tinged with both anger and awe.

I said that the last place they had promised me an extension to my visa was Tashkent.

'*Tashkent!*' he shrilled, 'Where else have you been?'

I gave him the full list, carefully omitting Vladivostok.

The officer's face became a darker thundercloud as each city was reeled off.

'And now Ungheni,' he ended. 'Don't you know your visa was for *Moscow only*, and even that has expired?'

'Oh, *that*,' I replied merrily. 'Intourist never gave me time to get the thing altered.'

The man all but threw a fit. His voice rose as he recited the laws I had apparently broken.

I said nothing. If I had said anything it would have been rude.

I was to get to know Ungheni station rather well. For 18 hours I was forcibly tethered to it as my crimes finally caught up with me, even if they were the wrong crimes. My lame visa, of course, was the root of the trouble: Vladivostok never came up. Moscow had to be informed of my deficiencies, and I suspect that it was poor telephonic communication that was behind much of the delay. I spent a night in a border guards' hostel adjoining the station, listening to the lullaby of bogie-changing by an infernal machine that lifted coaches bodily into the air for the operation.

There was a myth going about at that time that the wider 5-foot gauge was evidence of traditional Russian suspicion of the outside world. Actually it was an American called Whistler – the one with the mother-in-law – who recommended the wider gauge. The strategic significance is negative, since it is easier for an invader to re-lay one rail on a broad-gauge track than it is to widen the gauge on standard-gauge track in the opposite direction. At daybreak I watched the bogie-switching operations with some interest. They had the job taped to a fine art, and the most numerous articles to be seen at Russian border stations are discarded bogies.

Having surrendered my passport I saw no reason why I shouldn't take a stroll around the town which, of course, lacked any worthwhile attractions. So I extended my walk westwards and came face to face with the physical border of the USSR: a conglomeration of electrified fences, watch-towers and a rash of concrete dragons' teeth. It all looked depressingly familiar. Across

the River Prut I could see Romania, its territory ending in a mine-laden riverbank.

Even the stroll cost me a reprimand, but I really dug in my heels when told I would have to pay for my overnight accommodation and meals. The cheek of it! After all, I didn't ask to stay in their damp barrack room. Refusing point blank the demands of the spotty-faced Intourist woman who had been summoned all the way from Odessa, we finally negotiated a compromise. I would surrender one refundable accommodation voucher and two meal vouchers if the Soviet authorities purchased my onward rail ticket to Bucharest. And, you know, they did just that!

They gave me the green light late in the afternoon. A soldier with an automatic rifle escorted me on to the Bucharest-bound express, proffered an unsmiling salute and waited pointedly in the corridor. The train belched and trundled out of the station. Close to the wire entanglements marking the frontier it stopped for the customary search. As we rolled towards the bridge, at the last moment, the soldier jumped off. Having forced me to remain on Soviet soil for 18 extra hours, its minions were determined to ensure that I no longer remained of my own free will. They needn't have worried.

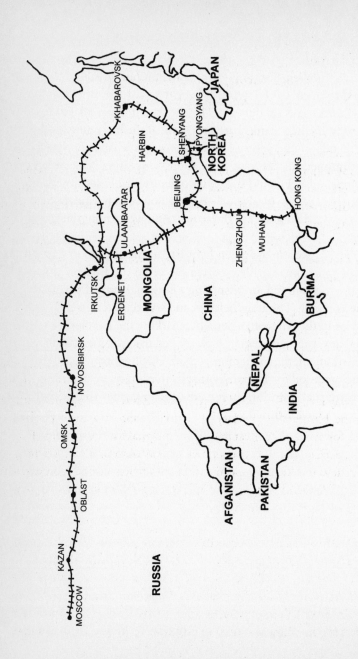

Trans-Mongolia and Trans-North Korea to China

Those eccentrics like me who find a certain bliss in being trundled by train across vast portions of the globe might consider a further couple of journeys I made during the 1980s. Both involved further traverses of the then Soviet Union. One, in 1984, deflecting southwards off the main Trans-Siberian line beyond Irkutsk to Mongolia and beyond to China; the other continuing from Ussurysk, the main line's junction which is within sight of Vladivostok – to North Korea and, again, China. This last I accomplished in 1989 shortly before the collapse of Communism in Russia and her transformation from a shackled USSR to an unruly Russian Federation. At a later date I was to fly to Mongolia for a less fleeting visit.

My UK point of departure in both cases was the revitalised Liverpool Street Station, once London's most depressing terminus. However, its rejuvenation did not do away with the railway lore-impregnated Great Eastern Hotel built upon the site of the Hospital of St Mary of Bethlem (abbreviated to Bedlam and for centuries the capital's chief hospital for the insane). This fact, perhaps more than any other, put my passion for long railway journeys into true perspective as my Harwich-bound train eased out of Platform 9 at the start of an even longer rail trek than that narrated in the previous chapter.

In 1984 my incarceration, which this time was the Baikal Express to Irkutsk, was to last but five days, which actually should have been four and a half had it not been for a serious derailment of a freight train on the Trans-Siberian main line that necessitated a multi-hour halt in a queue of other trains. This actually proved a blessing in disguise since, in addition to giving us passengers

opportunity for a stroll in the pleasant flower-strewn countryside under a surprisingly warm sun, it offered me a chance to befriend the locomotive crew who allowed me into the cab of the header locomotive. And there I was nicely installed drinking tea when the signals switched to green, fortuitously trapping me as the train moved off. The driver was visibly agitated about having a member of the public with him, particularly one from the despised West, and dropped me off with some relief at the subsequent station some 50 miles on. But like everyone else hereabouts, the crew enjoyed my duty-free cigarettes.

Reduced to a restaurant-car diet of macaroni, Russian champagne and, believe it or not, caviar, we crawled into Irkutsk nearly 14 hours late, leaving 8 hours or so remaining before my transfer to another train optimistically called the Irkutsk–Ulaanbaatar Express, though its hard-back seats, dirty blankets and still dirtier windows made a mockery of the title. In this anticlimax of a train we continued 450 kilometres along the main line as far as the junction of Ulan Ude, there to be connected to a rust-pink – more rust than pink – diesel unit of Mongolian Railways which hauled us in spasmodic fashion southwards along a non-electrified single track snaking into low hills of Sussex Downs-like overtones.

Why the Soviet Union should have had to bar the way into its subservient Mongolian satellite with the full paraphernalia of electrified fences swept at night by the blue-tinged beams of searchlights beats me, as did the five-hour attentions of Soviet authority in the corridors. The long dalliance at an end, the locomotive emitted a long shriek and, off the leash, we pranced merrily forward across a dawn-illuminated landscape of more rolling plains: the habitat of the wild camel, wild horse and the Gobi bear. Occasional lonely, windswept villages of hexagonal *gers*, or *yurts* as some call these typically Mongolian tents, drew my eye from the sheen of grass.

There was little to hold me on that first visit of mine to the Mongolian capital, Ulaanbaatar, though it is not an unpleasant little city. The usual segregation meant that I had to stay at the designated hotel for Westerners, in this case the Hotel Ulaanbaatar, the best, I supposed, in town. Three days of sightseeing included the excellent Natural History Museum displaying substantial dinosaur remains, the most amazing of which are the complete skeletons of two baby dinosaurs locked together in death, the jaws of one embedded in the pelvis of the other. Another day I was to spend at the Buddhist monastery of Gandang, the one lamasery permitted to function by the Communist regime in the whole of Buddhist Mongolia. Here I attended the Christian equivalent of matins, with saffron-robed lamas of all ages doing their thing to the accompaniment of drumbeats, conch shell squeals and a droning chant. Compulsory viewing included Bogdo Khan's modest palace and, of course, the Soviet Liberation Monument standing aloof from the town's bustle.

On my last day, breaking the restrictive rules again, I managed to leave the city by catching a local train from the main, and only, station, an edifice of handsome solid nineteenth-century railway-style architecture, intent upon going anywhere as long as it wasn't Ulaanbaatar. The result was Erdenet, a town that owes its existence to copper and other metals mined in the district. Here the populace, or at least all that I saw of it, were even more astonished to see a foreigner than were those in the capital or my probably forbidden bottom-class two-coach train. However, the hospitality was overwhelming and I was pressed to drink copious mugs of tea and *kumise* – fermented mare's milk (ugh!) – in company with assorted households all telling me how much they despised their government, their Russian occupiers and an upstart by the name of Sukhe-Bator. This last entry in the hate list referred to the leader of the 1921 revolution which resulted in the Sovietisation of their country, and who gave his name to Ulaanbaatar's frowning central square dominated by his statue. One elderly gentleman,

sporting a trilby and pyjamas, insisted that I drink a watery concoction with a kick like a mule for the purpose of toasting the regime's downfall, and join him in a dual performance of spitting on the floor with noisy eloquence.

As evening approached I sneaked back to the capital on the only train returning there, attempting to look Mongolian and avoiding anyone in uniform.

Mongolia's most famous son, Ghengis Khan, whose hordes conquered much of the then known world, was out of favour with the regime. Instead, Ulaanbaatar's official adoration was centred on the despised and more youthful Sukhe-Bator, a far lesser figure. And it is youth that typifies this city, whose name translates into 'Red Hero'. Two thirds of the population were reported to be under 35 years of age, and the state encouraged large families in direct contradiction to its Chinese neighbour; eight to ten children per family being the norm. With an increasing population, new homes were in constant demand and rows of cheap-jack flats were fast taking the place of the traditional, more attractive and highly practical *gers* that were much in evidence in fenced ghettos on the outskirts of town and in the countryside.

In unison with the USSR there was little worthwhile buying in the shops but, as I had found in Erdenet, the citizens were more open and outgoing to foreigners, unfazed by disapproving authority even in urban centres like Ulaanbaatar, the leafless bowl that was once a township named Urga that took over the capitalship from the city of Karakoram further west. Though its factories, colleges and apartment blocks were uniformly bleak the quality of life was, I was told, slowly improving. But it would be more than seven years before the fiery, excitable Mongolians could taste the first heady fruits, both sweet and bitter, of capitalism.

I digress at this point to narrate the occurrences of my second and longer Mongolian visit. This was in 1991 and I reached the capital, this time boringly by air from Irkutsk; though perhaps

not so boringly as all that, since Air Mongolia was, then at least, a most original airline. My Russian propeller-driven Antonov 24 that carried me provided no seats, let alone seat-belts; one just sat on the floor amongst the cargo or, if you chose, with the pilot who was quite happy to put his aircraft into a dive to low level should something below spark the interest of a passenger. And upon landing bumpily on the grass runway of Ulaanbaatar Airport, I was to find a very different state of affairs to those of my earlier sojourn.

It was immediately apparent that the novelty of foreigners to Mongolians had cooled; the city was virtually teeming with Germans and Japanese. Its topography had altered little except that additional to the glowering governmental edifices surrounding Sukhe-Bator Square was a shining pink stock exchange! But the Russian military had gone home, the new regime, though still Communist, was tolerating opposition parties, and the Buddhist religion was enthusiastically back in business. Strangely, the despised Sukhe remained untoppled on his pedestal in the square and, stranger still, my arrival coincided with a nationwide celebration of the 70th anniversary of his revolution: though this, it transpired, was simply on account of it being excuse for a party. And it was a party – actually a wedding reception – to which I was inveigled barely had I checked into my hotel.

It has to be said that such parties were a useful method of distracting Mongolian minds from the national economic crisis that was afflicting the country, its chief supplier of goods – Russia – demanding payment in an almost non-existent hard currency, as a result of which the Mongolian store cupboard was bare. Rarely had I seen emptier shops than those in Ulaanbaatar.

Back in the popularity polls was the country's favourite citizen, Genghis Khan, long pronounced by the old regime as a mass murderer (which assuredly he was) and therefore a non-person. Following his hordes' overrunning of huge chunks of territory, Genghis Junior, Ogadir, took over the reins and it was he who

founded the imperial capital Karakoram in the thirteenth century. After the rolling back of the Mongol Empire by China's Manchu rulers the victors divided the Mongol homeland into Inner Mongolia – today an integral part of China – and Outer Mongolia but, when in its turn the Manchu Empire collapsed in 1911, the latter declared its independence under the temporal and spiritual rule of the living Buddha's Bogdo Khan, leader of the Mongolian Lamaists. Independence, however, was short-lived and the ensuring years of turmoil brought Chinese forces, Czarist Russian troops and then the Soviet Army into the country, following which Sukhe-Bator arrived on the scene to form his People's Republic and subdue the lamas.

The only restrictions to movement around the country now were those imposed by an almost complete lack of metalled roads. Instead I found excruciating and unsignposted dirt tracks that multiplied at the whim of those humans and beasts that used them. Thus I was dependant upon the aeroplane and the bus for my travels outside of Ulaanbaatar since, except for the main line connecting Russia with China and a couple or so short branch lines (one of which – to Erdenet – I had already ridden), there were no rail services.

The Western Gobi made an obvious destination for the likes of me, and another dilapidated Antonov flew me there in little over an hour. In this semi-desert distances are vast; an endless terrain of eternally faraway hills and depressions of Sahara-like sand that look barren and empty but hide verdant valleys and gorges such as the valley of the Yol – a yol being a large vulture – and the valley of the dinosaurs where dinosaur eggs were found. Such valleys are now inhabited by heavily-coated yaks and adorned with all-year-round ice in their clefts. Westwards lay the grasslands and steppe where the famous horses and *hainags* – a cross between a yak and a cow – roam in great herds. In place of hotels or guesthouses are guest-*gers*, specklessly clean, warm and comfortable even if the sanitary facilities are a little primitive. In

both desert and steppe I found a wealth of wild flowers ranging from the homely dandelion and purple aster to carpets of edelweiss. Eagles, cranes, kites and Mongolian larks soared in the sky while marmots scurried between their burrows and the timid ibex and antelope haunted the rocky outcrops.

From my Gobi encampment of *gers*, in which I based myself for several days, I made a bumpy bus journey to the plains to take up temporary residence in another such encampment adjoining the township of Khujirt and its newly reinstated lamasery. Not far distant, too, was the much bigger lamasery of Erdenet Dzu at nearby Karakoram. Both were enthusiastically operative once more and in a fever of repairs after years of neglect. Everywhere in the country the lamaseries were rising again, as was the recruitment of young novices to play their part in the Buddhist act of worship deemed so vital to the nation's life. All that remains of the old capital of Karakoram is a stone turtle hunched on a sea of grass. Nearby is a valley containing a stone penis installed, so I was gleefully informed, to spoil the fun of younger lamas who regularly played truant with the village maidens.

Another destination I attained by bus was the northerly town of Bulgan, famous for its wrestling bouts. My arrival there coincided with the wrestling finals which formed part of the 70th anniversary of the revolution celebrations. The venue was grassland on the outskirts of town, and it was here where I met Dashiyin who was to offer me more of an insight into Mongolian life than I had hitherto found. I had approached him in an effort to ask about the wrestling bout now taking place.

He interrupted my enquiries to prance up and down, wave his arms and scream what sounded like obscenities. I turned my head to see what had caused the outburst of excitement shared by at least a thousand of Dashiyin's compatriots all bouncing about, waving and yelling as he was. The two half-naked giants on the stage were prostrate on the ground with the winner of the bout spread-eagled across his opponent, pinning down the flailing legs

and arms. Victory confirmed by the ring of colourfully-attired referees surrounding the battling couple, victor and vanquished rose, the former executing his own triumphal dance in acknowledgement of the sustained roar of the crowd.

Dashiyin (like many Mongolians, he prefers to use only one name) wore traditional dress: a graceful, ankle-length silk *del* lined with sheepskin, in spite of the heat of the day. Many in the crowd wore similar dress: their Sunday best. His headgear – on the occasions when it was on his head and not being thrown in the air – was a typical Mongolian felt helmet, purple in colour and rising to a point. His lined face was wreathed in smiles while his gnarled hands pummelled my shoulders as the ecstasy of the moment slowly subsided. Amazingly, he spoke a little English as he steered me towards a line of *gers* nearer the town. Outside his home we paused and I was ushered through a brightly-painted door that was the only solid item of the *ger's* exterior. I was seated in the place of honour – the centre of a row of five four-legged stools – while Dashiyin took his place on another. Behind me stood an orange chest of drawers upon which were arrayed a dozen family photographs. Around the felt-lined canvas walls were three brass-framed beds and some similar chests.

I had already learnt that the western side of a *ger* (by tradition all *gers* face southwards) holds the man's possessions, often including saddle and harness (since all rural Mongolians possess and ride horses), while a wife's chattels and the family pantry line the eastern side. I indicated the two further beds.

'Who do they belong to?' I asked, having learnt that he was a widower.

'They're for my two sons who live some miles from here,' replied Dashiyin. 'Since I am technically retired they look after the sheep, dividing their time with me here and wherever the pastures are. They are busy shearing this week and I should be with them to help, but we Mongolians love parties so I have stolen

today as a holiday to join the festivities. The privilege of an old man,' he added, giving me a guilty smile.

This exchange was a lot more complicated than I have made it sound, but I was able to pick up the gist of what he was telling me.

The roof flap was open to the bright blue sky. Through the flap poked a black stovepipe carrying away the smoke from the stove occupying the centre of the floorspace. Dashiyin seemingly carried out his own cooking when his sons or their wives were unable to be present. Outside the *ger* I had noticed a heap of dried dung which acted as fuel, wood being scarce here in spite of the woodlands to the north of Bulgan.

I was offered liberal helpings of *arul*, a hard yellow cheese, warm camel's milk and Mongol *arkhi*, a strong liquor similar to vodka made by distilling fermented mare's milk. It was served warm with melted yak butter. We toasted each other, talking animatedly, but sticking, by custom, to three topics: the weather, the animals and the family.

The weather was fine, and that's all there was to say about that, so we concentrated more interestingly on my host's herd of 600 sheep. His sheep had long been charted and systematised by government decree, as were all farm animals, and even people, in modern Mongolia. At the last official count the country had 591,500 camels, 1,985,400 horses, 2,397,100 head of cattle, 14,230,700 sheep and 4,566,700 goats. Dashiyin had all the statistics in his head and reeled them off parrot-fashion. Like the land itself, the animals were nationalised and controlled by the state through the Mongolian People's Revolutionary Party, until recently the only party. Already the present regime had accepted the need for opposition parties in government.

'So actually they are still not your sheep but the state's,' I suggested and received a non-committal shrug from my host.

I asked next how often Dashiyin's farming sons moved their portable *gers* in the summer months.

'About ten times,' he affirmed. 'Of course, it really depends upon the amount of grass in a specific area and how fast the sheep consume it.'

I switched the conversation to family matters again, and with a glance at the photographs on the nearest chest, asked the age of Dashiyin's offspring. I was told they were 22 and 24 years old respectively.

'Any grandchildren?'

The photographs offered a clue but the details were confirmed by Dashiyin.

'The eldest son has four, the youngest two. But neither have finished their quotas yet,' he concluded with a laugh. I remembered being informed how the previous regime encouraged large families and I presumed the new one was not averse to the idea either.

Mongolians are touchy about their ages so all I got in reply to my enquiry about his own was 'over 60' which could well have made him younger than my own, then, 67 years (and me with only two offspring!). As gently as I could I asked how his wife had died and was informed that she had expired four years earlier from an unidentifiable illness. Dashiyin brought from the chest a photograph of a care-worn but upright lady dressed in the traditional ankle-length *del*.

Acknowledging my interest in family matters he then told me a little about his life. He had started out as a shepherd at the age of nine, with a break for schooling and a period in the Army when he had fought the Japanese during the Second World War. Dashiyin broke off at this point to show me his European-style jacket bearing a double row of medal ribbons.

Upon learning that I, too, had fought in the same war, though against a different foe, he insisted on recharging my glass with *arkhi* and drinking to the downfall of enemies worldwide.

I told him that Ulaanbaatar was currently full of Japanese and German tourists, and he nodded knowingly before resuming his

life history. Gradually he had acquired his own flocks of sheep and now was one of the most respected farmers in the community.

The conversation turned to the subject of retirement. Someone had mentioned to me that there was an old people's home some ten kilometres outside the capital. When I referred to this Dashiyin had snorted.

'What are sons and daughters for?' he demanded. 'Not only do they look after the sheep, but also the old shepherd who once tended them. That's how we in this country bring up our families.' Maybe Britain could learn something from Mongolia.

I left this good man following a great bear-hug of a parting. I was to come to regard Dashiyin's friendship as the most valuable occurrence of my second Mongolian sojourn.

I now return to my first visit. There were in 1984, and still are today, just two trains a week crossing the whole of Mongolia between Russia and China, though currently there are two further services between Russia and Ulaanbaatar, and Ulaanbaatar and China. The Ulaanbaatar–Beijing train that carried me onwards again made no pretence of being an express; indeed, such was the interest generated in me by the territory through which we ambled, any faster speed would have been a shame. My preconceptions of the Gobi – evoked by the chronicles of Marco Polo – took a knock. Instead of the expected sandy wilderness I found myself looking upon an abundance of flora and fauna amongst verdant plains. Central Mongolia is dominated by the Hangai range and contains much of the country's richest grazing lands. Only near the southern border do the wind-eroded Gobi-Altai undulate into desert tracts of gravel.

That my new coach was Chinese instead of Russian or Mongolian was confirmed, if confirmation was necessary, by the flasks of jasmine tea supplied to each compartment. The furnishings included shaded lamps, soft seat backs, dainty coverlets and chintz curtains. The neighbouring coach was full of Chinese

refugees in the process of being thrown out of Mongolia. Their loathing of everything Mongolian and Russian did not preclude hospitality to the British representative next door, and I was to spend some fruitful hours helping them consume Mongolian vodka in return for arranging for some of their extensive baggage to be moved into my compartment. This transfer was made in the belief that Mongolian customs officers at the next border would be less severe where a Western tourist was present, a supposition that proved correct.

Erhlien is the Chinese border town, and here I put to use the long delay photographing, without restriction, the bogey-changing operations being carried out on our train's coaches, as China uses the standard-gauge track. Between Erhlien and Datong we were headed by a huge black QT-class steam locomotive, a product of the latter city that contained the last remaining steam locomotive factory in the world. And it was in and around Datong that I was to dally a further few days.

To the general public the city is renowned for the Yungang Buddhist Caves, the legacy of the northern Wei rulers who established their capital at Datong, and it was they who cut into the cliffs of Wuzhoushan mountain to form a series of caverns containing a cavalcade of 50,000 statues. I dutifully inspected some of these, though my chief interest lay in the locomotive factory of which I was given a private tour by one of the managers. In my enthusiasm I led him a merry dance through workshops, beneath half-built locomotives and over great mounds of spare parts, to be finally installed in the cab of a new QJ locomotive to accompany it on a trial run.

By a year or two I was only just in time. Soon the largest of the smoke-filled workshops and steam hammers of the Datong Steam Locomotive Plant would fall silent as, 112 years after the country became a wary host to its first railway line, the last factory in the world producing mainline steam engines ceased production. When trains were introduced to China in 1876, more than 50

years after the opening of the world's first public steam railway in Britain, their arrival was not received with national glee. Not only were the Chinese concerned that the railways might allow foreign aggressors into the interior of the country, but the mandarins in the Imperial Court worried that the rumblings of the engines would disturb the ancestral spirits in their graves. Over the next 70 years, in fact, only 22,000 kilometres of track were laid, and even that scattered network was effectively halved during the years of fighting that led up to the 'Liberation' of 1949.

Another day saw me cantering across the rolling steppes of the Inner Mongolian countryside on a game little Mongolian horse in the company of a squad of People's Liberation Army soldiers who subsequently entertained me in their slogan-embellished detachment *ger*.

From Datong I was to backtrack and detour to the Inner Mongolian capital, Huhehot, on a lesser train of more spartan amenities. And in Huhehot I was inveigled into attending a local horse show in which, at its conclusion, the military put on a display that involved a charge down the course, the riders standing on their saddles blazing away with machine carbines held in one hand, an event that would certainly liven up the rather staid proceedings back home in Hickstead. Afterwards I was invited to try standing on one of the horses, though even when stationary I found it none too easy to maintain balance.

The main line from Datong to Beijing is electric-powered and a new dawn found my train amongst the first mountains I had seen on my journey so far; not of great altitude but mountains all the same. The rock-bound fastness of the Tahaite Shan range, of which these uplands formed part, was made the more evocative by displaying portions of the Great Wall perambulating about their flanks. And it was these mountains reduced to mere hills that heralded a morning entry into Beijing.

On all my earlier and subsequent arrivals in the Chinese capital I have had to do the rounds of the tourist circuit, which basically

remains unchanged today. The Forbidden City, the Temple of Heaven, the Summer Palace, the Ming Tombs, the Fragrant Hills Park and, away from the city, the virtually rebuilt section of the Great Wall at Badaling. And so it was again on this occasion, my base being the institutional-like Friendship Hotel. I can't say I much like Beijing, and have always tried to avoid it on subsequent arrivals, invariably without success. There's something impersonal and unfinished pervading the whole great unwieldy metropolis; I feel as if I'm not in a city at all, but on a building site where one day a city might be created.

However, on this occasion I noticed something different in the city centre. It came to me in apparent trivia; girls wearing skirts and lipstick, free-enterprise markets awash with sacks of clothes, fruit and everything under the sun spilling over the pavements, women walking arm in arm, a couple kissing in public view. Compared to the Beijing frozen in the puritanism of Mao's regime, the last years of which had been when I was first there, all this was truly remarkable.

After another few days in the capital I could hardly wait to be on my way. Beijing's Central Station was the exit: a railway cathedral with twin clock towers giving it almost an air of nobility. In the early morning the concourse can be nearly empty, but all too soon it becomes a seething, living mass of humanity flowing in all directions. It was a wonder that I landed up at my Beijing–Guangzhou (Canton) Express without being swept elsewhere.

Ahead of me stretched a 2,300-kilometre, 26-hour journey via Zhengzhou and Wuhan, the first 9 hours of which I spent in bed if not in uninterrupted slumber. I rose the first morning to perceive a countryside I thought existed only in the fanciful minds of Chinese painters: fields of lotus flowers backed by impossible sharply-pointed hills. The train rumbled across gigantic lattice bridges spanning waterways of the calibre of the Yangtse and the Yellow River, the former reminding me of an earlier rail crossing made by way of Nanking's massive three-mile structure that took

ten years to build after Russia had withdrawn her labour, expertise and the blueprints. We passed through the dramatic valley of the Pah-Kiang and halts were made at huge towns with names of which I'd never heard.

Canton has become the less-pronounceable Guangzhou, and is one of the oldest cities in China. For my brief stay here I was put up at a cockroach-ridden hostelry of, to put it kindly, considerable originality; today the opulent White Swan Hotel, overlooking the port, has arisen to provide unoriginal standardised luxury. I made an excursion on the good ship *Kuo Lu*, more a floating bar than a vessel, on the busy Pearl River, its brown, effluent-streaked waters agitated with barges. Then, with Hong Kong not much more than two hours down the line, I caught my last train of the journey.

A long, frustrating delay at the final border, and we crossed the famous iron bridge to enter the so-called New Territories, and from there into the concentrated ranks of high-rise concrete of this stronghold of capitalism, the train drawing to a stop at the terminus of Kowloon.

I flew home a few days later on a Cathay Pacific 727 looking down, just for a couple of ruminative minutes, on a landscape over which I had travelled so much more hopefully and eventfully.

Hello Khabarovsk. Here we are again, the year being 1989 with the amazing contradictions of *Glasnost* materialising. Outwardly little had changed since my first trans-Siberian journey in 1970, but any city that draws me, stiff-legged, off a Trans-Siberian Express could, temporarily, become imbued with a certain charisma. My onward vehicle was to be a Vladivostok-bound train 48 hours later that was to arrive in Khabarovsk 9 hours behind schedule: that seemed to me to be the most tangible evidence of the new political toleration.

I had learnt that a single-track line had opened to foreigners that ran southwards from near Vladivostok, along the Soviet Pacific

coast. It continued through North Korea to, eventually, Beijing. In my capacity as a travel journalist I had succeeded in joining a small group of writers invited to the still fanatically hard-line Communist North Korea for the purpose of advising the authorities on tourism matters.

With a couple of days to spare in the Russian far-eastern city, I had little expectation of it other than it being the depressing place I had known previously. To my surprise, except for there being only watermelons in the shops, Khabarovsk wore a much more cheerful air than hitherto. The usually dour Intourist was almost skittish in its enthusiasm to show off the region, even to the extent of giving us a helicopter flight over the once top-secret Sakhalin Island close to Japan. With rotor-blades chopping the air over the autumn-tinted *taiga*, I was permitted to take photographs of the landscape below, something that was strictly taboo in earlier times.

The Russian Far East is Moscow's easternmost frontier. Sparsely populated but rich in resources, it is supposedly destined to become an improbable Shangri-La to the discerning foreign visitor, particularly its remote coast which, shortly, I was to look upon from ground level.

The main line southwards out of Khabarovsk is, of course, that of the Trans-Siberian Railway ending at Vladivostok. However, our late-arriving train was to drop our small party at the junction of Ussuriysk, where we were to transfer to a train consisting of just one battered old sleeper coach hauled, for some obscure reason, by two powerful diesel locomotives. The entire complement of the coach consisted of a dozen assorted North Koreans, the Egyptian military attaché to Pyongyang, our party of five, and two Russian conductors.

Actually, for most of the daylight hours the coach's complement was deficient of me. While waiting at Ussuriysk station I was idly taking an interest in the wheel-couplings of the leading diesel unit when the driver invited me into the cab. I needed no second invitation. From this exalted position as we moved southwards, I

looked upon the coastal scenery magnificent with gentle hills, picturesque bays and secret beaches: a developer's paradise. For a while the city of Vladivostok stood mistily in the background, but soon passed from view as we wound round its bay at a steady 25 kilometres an hour.

The driver and his mate shared their picnic lunch with me at their insistence, substantial hunks of bread and peppery-hot tomato ketchup. I was then given the go-ahead to drive the train on condition that I kept to a 20-kilometre-an-hour speed limit on the bends; a limit that was also enforced by warning noticeboards placed prior to each curve in the line. Feeling like a schoolboy again, I took over the controls while the crew sat at the back of the cab seemingly quite content with my abilities. Both had shaken their heads in puzzlement when informed that I was going to North Korea. 'They've got *Communists* there,' they insisted!

As we sped through the remote stations the railway men or women, standing stiffly to attention holding up their green flags, gaped in astonishment when they beheld the strange personage driving the train. Only as dusk fell did I relinquish control to return to my role as passenger.

The Russian border township is Hasan, a small urban centre of desolate appearance and of an emphatically sensitive situation since not only do the frontiers of Russia and North Korea meet here – the former just across a river – but China likewise. Our late arrival had caused us to miss the connection to Pyongyang, the North Korean capital, which was to involve us in an 18-hour wait in the sidings. And there being no restaurant car on our train, we issued forth into the depressing little town in search of fodder.

We found it in what appeared to be the only restaurant in town, a sort of workman's canteen where our bortsch and pasta was ladled out to us on dirty plates to be consumed at even dirtier tables. The clientele of the establishment were a rough-looking bunch who viewed us with open-mouthed amazement.

Hasan was in a fever of building construction, so with nothing worthwhile to see two of us took it upon ourselves to make a post-meal constitutional out of town and up the hill into the actual border zone. At first we were not aware of its proximity until we found ourselves strolling nonchalantly along high wire fences overlooked by manned watch-towers that divided the three countries. Nobody had mentioned the fact this was a forbidden area, though I bet they have now, for our casual arrival there, strewn with cameras, gave the Soviet border guards near apoplexy! A shout from the nearest watch-tower arrested our footsteps and an Asian NCO, who issued from a wooden building nearby, made threatening signs to us to accompany him to it. But we weren't having that so, making train noises and indicating from whence we had come, we turned our backs and moved resolutely away, intent upon returning to less tetchy regions, ignoring barks that could well have been 'Halt! Halt! Or I shoot!' from behind.

Our depleted train, forlorn and lonely, made a peaceful venue for that night's sleep. In the morning we 'lost' two hours by entering a new time zone once on the other side of the river, having undergone the rigorous procedure deemed vital for leaving the USSR. We resigned ourselves to the likelihood of undergoing further hours of North Korean ditto and were not disappointed. Our old wagon must have been the most thoroughly searched and prodded coach on any railway.

The North Korean border station here is Tumengan. A huge portrait of the late Kim Il Sung, together with the more profound of his utterances engraved on wall and banner, proclaimed our entry into the Stalinist state, a display of the personality cult I was to discover encompassing the whole country, even on the highest mountain tops where it is carved for posterity: a graffiti dauber's dream. We left Tumengan a fully-fledged train again, replete with half a dozen passenger coaches.

A second night in our sleeper was enlivened by a compartment party which most of the complement of the coach attended. The

remnants of our duty-free alcoholic beverages were consumed in an atmosphere of considerable gaiety with one of our number, a steam loco buff, leaping to his feet with cries of ecstasy every time a steam-hauled train hove into sight. The Egyptian military attaché, loudly proclaiming himself a strict Moslem and a fervent Communist, was the heaviest consumer of my scotch as well as being an avid reader of my out-of-date *Daily Telegraph*. At Yonghung our train veered away from a forbidden and heavily fenced coast to rumble through the mountains of the country's northern hinterland.

Pyongyang station, a cross between a cathedral and an opera house, its marbled platforms and plush interior denied the rank and file – who have to wait for their trains outside – gave me a taste of the new city that had risen from the ashes of the Korean War. It is something straight out of a Jules Verne fantasy. The wide, empty boulevards thrust between ranks of architectural creations of a futuristic design; statuary of the grandiose awfulness of the Stalin era and gigantic pavilions that are museums, ministries and sports complexes. For a supposedly bankrupt nation its mighty Kim Il Sung (who else!) Stadium alone could pay its national debt. A metro, with station decoration that rivals, if not surpasses, those of central Moscow, competes with a woefully inadequate bus service. An Arch of Triumph (again to you know who) twice the size of its Paris counterpart and a then unfinished, 105-storey pyramid-like hotel with its top floors already lost in cloud, are further examples of overwhelmingly exaggerated construction. Neat blue-uniformed traffic policewomen swivelled doll-like on their podiums, directing the odd car or lorry.

That North Korea was, and remains, a repressive state there was little doubt. A multitude of checkpoints on the roads severely reduced inter-provincial travel, and I was told that permission had to be obtained to go from one region to another. This, together with an overwhelming preponderance of police and soldiery, and an eastern and western seaboard (including miles of idyllic beach)

barred by electrified fences, was explained away by the need for 'vigilance,' a once-favourite East Bloc term. South Korea, flaunting its new-found capitalism, was of course the *bête noir*, and the hate both governments expressed against each other was vitriolic. But all things are relative, and it has to be remembered that Korea has long been embroiled in conflict. In fact the country has spent the better part of its 4,000 years being invaded, crushed, subjugated, colonised and trampled upon by Chinese, Russian, Mongol, Manchu and Japanese neighbours. The North's invasion of the South in 1950 (the North have it that it was the other way round) led to the latest debacle, the country being virtually laid waste by American aerial bombardment from which it was still recovering. In spite of a much-vaunted agricultural mechanisation programme and the then alleged prosperity of the people, I saw little evidence of either though it is a fact that North Korea is a land with no income tax, rent or rates plus free education and health services.

Throughout our 11-day stay we travelled everywhere by minibus on concrete roads, impressive to look at but excruciating to ride upon. One of the excursions was to the one-time village of Panmunjom on the 38th-parallel, there to look upon what is still perhaps the most ruthless and tense border on Earth. Before us lay an immense fence topped by coils of razor wire and bolstered by trip lines and electrified cables. Notices warned of minefields and all around were searchlights, ground sensors, watch-towers and the furtive movement of patrols. Under heavily armed escort I was permitted to enter the conference room which is the focal point of the 151-mile DMZ, or Demarcation Zone, where representatives of North and South Korea can express their hate without recourse to bullets. By walking round the conference table I was, for a moment, inside South Korea. And standing within a foot of the white demarcation line between the two halves of the country I could almost touch the United States Army colonel, standing on the other side, to whom I was forbidden to speak or smile, while that worthy colonel repeatedly took close-up

photographs of me standing between my two North Korean military guards. I suppose I'm now blacklisted in Seoul, if not the United States!

Other, less stressful, visits were made to the Dolomite-like mountains and here, with the dawn mists curling around their flanks, it was easy to see why Korea has long been known as the 'Land of the Morning Calm'. The exquisitely beautiful Diamond Mountains make for tranquil pilgrimages for anyone who finds rapture in hill walking, with waterfalls and lakes such as the one called Chon on Mount Paekdu adding to the attraction. Mount Myohyang is a place of pilgrimage too; alas part political, since at its base stands an ornate hall containing chamber after chamber of Kim Il Sung's gifts from a supposedly grateful world, including a miner's lamp from Britain's Arthur Scargill. On another occasion we toured the huge eight-kilometre long West Sea Barrage and industrial Nampo where I managed another ride in the cab of a steam locomotive, the dirtiest and most ill-maintained specimen I have ever seen.

North Korean towns, other than Pyongyang, I found depressingly modern with only here and there a historic gateway, vivid with colour, some but reproductions. However, the country is littered with ancient sites such as the remarkable tombs associated with the Koryo, Kogwayo and Shilla monarchs guarded by attendant stone sentinels.

Our base for these carefully orchestrated excursions was a large barracks of a hotel in the capital producing, for the few meals we had in it, an unappetising cuisine of semi-European dishes. Only when we were served meals elsewhere did we get to sample local dishes including Korean delicacies such as mouth-burning *kimchi*, *hoc* (raw fish) and, to drink, adder wine – not wine at all but firewater from a bottle containing the spirit-preserved carcass of the said snake which is supposed to encourage the imbiber to drink at one sitting the whole contents before the carcass can decompose!

Permitted to explore Pyongyang on our own, we were able to obtain an idea of living conditions in the capital. The shops were reasonably well stocked at the time I was there, but the 3-tier system of pricing I found obnoxious, with holders of hard currency coming off best in many supermarkets. Shoppers holding East European rouble-based money had to pay more than double for their goods, while the unfortunate rank and file were forced to cough up most of all for their basic foodstuffs. Meat was rationed, though rice and vegetables were cheap at any price. I spent an hour or two in the Historical Museum learning how Comrade Kim single-handedly won the Second World War, took a look at his humble birthplace treated as a shrine, and was invited into a kindergarten to listen to the sickening glorification of him in a form of childish musical worship. We were shown the interior of a private dwelling but assuredly it was a carefully selected one, the occupants primed to reply to our questions without compromising the party line. We were also taken to a funfair on the outskirts; a kind of Alton Towers of Pyongyang, equipped with the most expensive gadgetry imaginable. This excursion was presumably to show how much the populace were enjoying themselves under so beneficial a rule.

I managed to obtain a better idea of conditions on our last day in the country while in Wonsan, a town on the east coast of pleasanter aspect than the others. While strolling alone through the town I chanced upon a group of ex-service pensioners exercising in the recreational park. A dozen elderly ladies and gentlemen had formed a circle and were prancing happily hand in hand to the methodical beat of a drum wielded by a matron of equally advanced years. One of the dancers caught sight of me, noticed my beard and my then 66-years-worn face and promptly drew me into the ring, there to set me undertaking a little prancing myself to the general approval of everybody. The average age, it transpired, was 77 which made me a youngster.

Breaking for a rest I was able to obtain glimpse into their lives in spite of the handicap of our differing tongues. They made quite clear the fact that they had no complaints, a revelation that I'm quite certain was in no way dictated by prudence. Yes, there were shortcomings to be borne, but these were being energetically dealt with by their 'Great Leader' – virtually a compulsory term of address here – who had their welfare as a primary consideration.

Two of the male members of my new-found friends were Army veterans of the Korean War, the row of medal ribbons displayed – another custom in this part of the world – on their jackets proclaiming the fact. I asked them about their experiences in that conflict and, in a flurry of gesticulations and conversation in opposing languages, succeeded in gaining the gist of their stories.

One of the veterans – his name sounded like Jung – had been in action against our Commonwealth Division which included the Gloucester Regiment, though not in the famous Gloster Hill battle where their enemy were Chinese. He was full of admiration for the tenacity, courage and efficiency of the British Army, though somewhat contemptuous of the backing both in provisions and fire-power that Western armies insist upon as a prelude to combat. The Korean soldier, he affirmed, expected no more than a handful of rice; the actual ration being three bowls a day plus a little soya-bean soup and boiled cabbage, though he seldom enjoyed such largess. His pay then had been microscopic; even a general got no more than the equivalent of 20 pence a day.

Another ex-soldier, Paik – my prancing partner – broke in to say that both then and now military service was not a popular option. Every North Korean male had to undergo three years of military service during which period he was not permitted to remove his uniform except in bath or bed, which to me partly explained the numbers of soldiers I saw everywhere either on or off duty. But once caught up in the military machine most men, and not a few women who enlisted voluntarily, liked it.

In both Jung's and Paik's cases they had been conscripted into the Army at the outbreak of hostilities and had no idea when, if ever, they would be released; a call-up then was regarded as a life sentence or, more to the point, a death sentence. But once in they both agreed that they had committed all for their country.

'We had no air cover like you and the Americans,' pointed out Jung without the slightest degree of bitterness. 'We had a certain amount of artillery and armoured support but usually it was simply a matter of going straight in, in waves, with the bayonet. The Americans didn't like that,' he added with a recollective grin. I could well believe it.

Turning the tortuous conversation away from military matters I asked the others what their average meals were at home. Rice, they affirmed, continued to be the staple diet; it was cheap even on their pay or pension. But vegetables too were cheap, as I'd already seen, as was fruit. 'And meat?' I enquired. The ladies made wry faces. Again I knew meat to be rationed but wanted to know what they thought about this restriction, though all I got for my pains was a diatribe on how the Great Leader was ensuring that his subjects lived on a healthy diet. Assuredly they wouldn't suffer from obesity.

Hastily I steered the conversation away from the threat of politics and enquired about wages. Before retirement, they told me, each was earning something under a hundred wan a month which, with no income tax or other reductions, allowed them to save from 20 to 30 wan a month which produced about four per cent interest in the banks. I tried to equate these figures to the prices I had seen in the shops and supermarkets of Pyongyang, but it made little sense.

Living conditions, mine and theirs, came up next. They all lived, it appeared, in the modern but poorly-built blocks of high-rise apartments I had seen in the suburbs of the town. None had been institutionalised, though homes for the aged were in existence. Didn't they miss the individuality of the picturesque little one-

storey houses with solid roofs, wide eaves and tall chimneys that made a pleasant feature of the countryside and even in the towns where the high-rises had not swept them away?

'No,' claimed most of them without much conviction.

'Well, yes,' replied a bolder spirit, a haggard-faced man who had not previously taken much part in the exchanges. He missed the countryside where he'd lived much of his life, he told me, and hadn't much liked being resettled. But with his dependants gone he understood the reasons and accepted it with good grace. Hadn't the Great Leader their interests at heart and so on and so forth? I marvelled dazedly at the influence one man could wield over people, even those possessed of the wisdom of age, who looked upon Kim Il Sung and his kin as God in a godless and brainwashed society.

Our complicated exchanges had gone on for a considerable time, and I felt it appropriate to withdraw to let the good folk continue with their romping session. Jung and Paik and several of the ladies, with tears of frustration in their eyes, attempted to tell me how welcome I would be in their homes but . . . They stabbed the air with raised hands to indicate implacable rules and regulations that had to be obeyed. I felt sad more than angry.

As I made my farewells I thought of my day's excursion to the one-time village called Panmunjon and the hate-crazed death zone and killing ground it represents. Somehow it made my afternoon with the pensioners of Wonsan that much more unreal, even ethereal.

We left North Korea on the Pyongyang–Beijing Express, crossing the Yalu River into China's Manchuria with a lot less rumpus than one General Douglas MacArthur had aroused five decades earlier. And at the Chinese border town of Dandong, the other side of the impressive girder bridge that carries both railway and road over the wide river, we stayed for a couple of days prior to joining a rail tour of Manchuria at the invitation of Chinese Railways.

Called Dongbei by the Chinese, Manchuria is characterised by a bitter winter climate, enormous rivers, rich soil and untold mineral resources. Sparsely populated, it is nonetheless the industrial heart of China; a region few foreigners reach, though its history is not unknown to the West.

Dandong, from where we commenced the new journey, was formerly Andong and, after the stifling hand of state nationalisation in North Korea, it was a refreshingly alive city, its endless open-air markets joyous with free enterprise. During our stay in the city I not only explored these markets but also took a boat ride down the Yalu River and made futile efforts to remove the wrinkles in my rhinoceros-hide with a speciality face cream called *Ganoderma* for which the town is known.

A four-hour train ride brought us to Shenyang, China's fourth largest city, the one-time Mukden of 1905 Russo-Japanese War fame and the power base for the Manchu conquest of China. With a population of nearly six million it is a brute of a conurbation, entirely devoid of beauty, and with not a single building that I could find of architectural merit. It produces iron and steel, tractors and chemicals, coal and petrochemicals, and could have fitted without being noticed into Birmingham's former Black Country at the turn of the last century or one of Pittsburgh's outlying mining areas. We were taken on a tour of the town, which only confirmed my opinion that it was the ugliest I have ever seen. The streets seemed to have been laid out with rulers, then scored with tramlines and edged with jerry-built shopfronts displaying dusty posters and very few goods. Yet I found its teeming streets, as well as the surrounding region backed by an industrial landscape, full of interest.

A local train carried us on a branch line to the town of Fushun, 60 kilometres distant. Here is not only the largest open-cast mine in the world, a sight worth seeing for itself for its great depth and circumference, but the Japanese war criminals' prison in which Pi Yi – the last Emperor – was accommodated. Although part of

the prison was still in use as such, a visitor could explore a neighbouring labyrinth of spacious cells at will, a quite fascinating experience as one goes from one to the other in a dingy but quite bearable environment. Pi Yi's cell was by no means cramped or wretched; the window looked out on the prison gardens that he tended during the final years of his life. For his sins, particularly as the Chinese viewed them, I would have thought those years would have been far less bearable. The wartime Japanese occupation and its attendant bestiality is not forgotten here, and the macabre open mass grave of 3,000 local victims was enthusiastically displayed to all, including contingents of excited schoolchildren.

I hardly expected that we would be allowed to see the still operational prison hiding behind a high brick wall topped by coils of razor wire, but my curiosity was tempered by the knowledge that, some years earlier while on another journalistic tour, I had spent the best part of a day inside Shanghai Central Prison, a very much larger institution in which were incarcerated murderers, rapists and embezzlers, the latter two categories of crime carrying the death sentence. The building had been constructed by the British early last century, then used by the Japanese and after them the Chinese Nationalists, so it bore a long history of detention. Four thousand men and women lived their lives here, the cellblocks and workhouses arrayed on all sides in palisades of blank concrete and barred windows, their world. I watched, with mixed feelings, the blue-clad squads of convicts exercising like robots in the yards, sitting at long rows of workhouse benches sewing, trimming and ironing beneath red banners proclaiming the benevolence of the People's Republic. None raised his head or smiled; all remained silent and expressionless. To me they all looked alike, as if they weren't human at all. I was allowed to speak to one of them, a murderer 'in' for life. He had become an artist and painter and was currently producing a portrait of Mao Zedong for no reason other than he found the face inspirational.

Or so he told me in soft monosyllables, his sad eyes flickering between me, the interpreter and the wardens accompanying me. I was happy to leave.

Northwards now on the main Harbin-bound line, and we found ourselves in the province of Heilongjiang where most of the passenger and freight rail traffic was hauled by those gigantic black QJs, a dying breed even here in this last bastion of steam. The province also likes to present itself as a winter sports location though its facilities, as Europeans know them, were non-existent. However, the basics were in place in the guise of mountains, forests and a volcanic landscape which, in winter, is covered in snow. On a more prosaic level, timber is an industry that is emphatically on show in its raw form at smaller towns of the likes of Langxiang and Nancha, to which the provincial tourist authority insisted we go to see.

This part of Manchuria is home to an assortment of minority peoples which include Manchus, Koreans, Moslems, Huis, Mongolians, Sibos, Owenkis and Kirkus, some living in autonomous towns and counties, maintaining their own language, traditions and cultures. I was told that no restrictions were placed upon these minorities while, additionally, each family was permitted to raise as many children as they wished, again in direct contradiction to the one-child-per-family edict that was imposed upon the main Chinese Han population.

Our interest in railways in general and steam engines in particular had us being raced around marshalling yards whenever any were on the itinerary. Here we met drivers, firemen and railway workers in abundance who, after momentary astonishment at the sight of Europeans, became immensely friendly. The spectacle of rows of great black locomotives bathed in a sweat of steam outside the sheds had our cameras working overtime while we toured their domains. We were also invited to ride the narrow-gauge, steam-hauled timber-carrying trains of

the logging camps around Langxiang and watch the logging operations in the nearby forests.

Our accommodation on these jaunts was vested in government guest houses of simple but adequate comfort, albeit sometimes lacking in hot water and bath plugs. A great deal more was lacking, however, in one of the simple village dwellings, probably typical of this rural backwater, into which I was invited one morning before breakfast. It was brick-built and single-storied; what we would call semi-detached. A wall down the centre of the building divided it into two separate 'houses', each one subdivided by a partition allowing two rooms per house. In one room stood a stove made of brick on which the cooking took place. The other room was the living and sleeping space, across one side of which were raised brick and cement 'beds', and since the flues of the stove ran beneath one bed I suppose you could say that the house was equipped with central heating. The 'beds' were covered with bamboo matting while above a row of cupboards and chests there were piles of brightly-coloured cotton quilts. The cupboard between the beds contained the family's decorative possessions; here a cheap non-operational alarm clock, a couple of china mugs and a small framed photograph or two. For wall decoration there were pictures torn from magazines, including one of Chairman Mao. The rooms were specklessly clean but over everything hung that sweet and sour smell I found everywhere inside Chinese buildings. I was pressed by the man of the house, a timber worker of rough but kindly countenance, to a dose of the local firewater while his wife, hesitant and withdrawn, stood awkwardly in the kitchen doorway. I felt an interloper in a century long gone by.

The Manchurian capital is Harbin, to whence we travelled next. The city is situated in the so-called Land of the Black Dragon, bounded in the north by the Black Dragon River that borders Siberia and which, in Russia, is the Amur. More rail sheds were put at our disposal here prior to us being marched briskly round

the lively park running alongside Harbin's own river, the Songhuajiang, a tributary of the huge Black Dragon.

The city's architecture holds European overtones, a legacy of the once-occupying Russians, and includes onion-domed churches. In the summer months the citizens swim in and sail on the river, while in winter, when it freezes over, they go ice-skating or ice-sailing, though neither of these activities was in evidence when we were there.

Harbin was the limit of our northbound tour; thereafter it was ever southwards back towards Shenyang on the main line though we fitted in another side-detour to Benxi, an obscure town of one and a half million souls. The high spot was a voyage on electricity-powered boats through the celebrated water caves beneath the spectacular roofs of illuminated stalactites. All very Disney-like but, unlike Disneyland, these caverns and geographical features were real. A less picturesque goal was the vast Tan Shan Steelworks, with the emphasis on its marshalling yards where some of us took tea with a gang of workers in their canteen.

Second time around I found Shenyang a mite more appealing, and I take back the harshest of my earlier comments following exploration of one of its vaunted attractions, the Manchu Imperial Palace, a mini Forbidden City where Emperor Shunzhi was crowned before setting off to cross the Great Wall in 1644. At least its series of vividly-coloured pavilions within a leisure park subtracts a little from the dourness of the metropolis.

At the turn of the nineteenth-century Shenyang was occupied by the Russians as part of their 'railway colonisation', and it remains an important rail centre with six major lines converging on it, including freight lines from Anshan's great steelworks. Industrial output of the city rivals that of Shanghai, and it has recently become the site of the new Stock Exchange. Opposite the station stood the largest Mao statue ever; it zoomed out of Red Flag Square, a giant epoxy-resin figure flanked by vociferous

peasants, soldiers and workers. I'm told it's still there: no doubt almost a collector's item today, and the last word on the personality cult and the follies of the Cultural Revolution.

Before continuing to Beijing – one just can't escape the capital – we made a further side-trip directly southwards to Dalian, the former Port Arthur, situated at the tip of the Liaoning Peninsula jutting out into the East China Sea. We had earned a sleeper coach for the near six-hour overnight run, and arrived there reasonably fresh in the early morning. We were to find yet another vast city of some five million plus, this one combining shipbuilding with seaside pleasures along an indented, cliff-edged coast – though the beach and pleasure facilities were hardly on the scale of, say, Bournemouth or my own Brighton. The city itself was remarkably clean and orderly with wide avenues and solid, handsome buildings contrasting strongly with the hideousness of Shenyang.

And so eventually to my *bête noir*, Beijing, a 24-hour rail run with a change of train back at Shenyang. My ultimate destination was Ürümqi, capital of the Sinkiang province in China's far south, and though I could have got there by train on a 30-hour journey, authority deemed otherwise. For once I didn't argue.

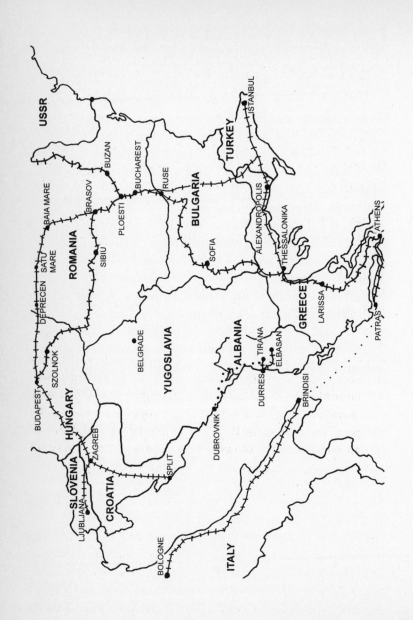

Round and about the Balkans: Recollections from a String of Trans-Balkan Rail Journeys

Following my two rail journeys through the Balkans made during the Communist era, the first of which I have briefly narrated in the first part of Chapter 2, I felt it time to observe how things had changed a quarter of a century later. So, in 1995, I more or less made the same circuit; rather more than less, since I included Northern and Eastern Germany, the north-west tip of Poland, the then newly-designated Czech Republic, the breakaway Slovakia and European Turkey. And with the fragmentation of Yugoslavia two of its then provinces, Croatia and Slovenia, had become independent nations too. Though the railway map of this part of the world has barely changed in those 25 years, the conditions of travel and those of the places en route are, today, very different.

I intentionally set out on the new circuit with no set itinerary in mind. I would go where I fancied and as the whim dictated. My customary minimal amount of baggage included just four vital items: a passport, a toothbrush, a copy of *Thomas Cook's European Timetable* and the Rail-Europe interrail pass valid for one month, which basically allows free travel on very nearly every rail system in Europe as well as one or two outside it.

My departure point was Harwich, using initially the P&O Stena Line Harwich–Hook cruise liner-type ferry which, in company with other cross-channel services, offers reduced fares for interrail pass-holders. And once through The Netherlands I made for Lübeck, simply on account of the fact that I'd never been there before. By way of Amersfoort, Osnabrück and Hamburg I reached this lovely old Hanseatic city to find it endowed with as much charm and charisma as I expected; its towers and spires and, in

particular, the massive Holstentor, a fortress-cum-city gate, giving the place an almost mythical appearance. I spent a night in the centrally situated youth hostel before catching a local train to Travemünde, Lübeck's Baltic seaside resort just up the line. It's a port too; one from which regular ferries serve Denmark.

I debated whether to continue northwards to Scandinavia or turn eastwards, tossed a coin and it came down eastwards. Thus a train, the 14.59 from Lübeck, carried me none too hurriedly to Rostock, and from there to Stralsund, Hanseatic cities all, with restoration following 40 years of Communism and neglect in full swing. Both cities, like Lübeck, have their neighbouring seaside resorts-cum-ferry terminals; Rostock with Warnemünde's acres of sandy Baltic beaches, and picturesque Stralsund, its neighbouring Isle of Rugen replete with gleaming chalkstone cliffs, gentle hills and a tremendous diversity of plant and animal life.

Crossing the one-time zonal border east of Lübeck invariably gives me the creeps, even now, having had, as already intimated, personal experience of traversing and attempting to traverse, legally and illegally, the former Iron Curtain which lay, fanatically guarded, along a line from the Baltic to the Adriatic. My mind slithered back to some moments of terror I experienced nearly half a century gone by:

The wire parted with a twang and I froze in terror. I was lying on my back beneath the triple electrified fence, inexpertly wielding a pair of rubber-handled wire-cutters by the dazzling light of a row of arc lamps.

The year was 1951 when the hand of Stalin lay across the lands of Eastern Europe and the Iron Curtain divided East and West. Here on the Bavaria-Czechoslovakian border my mission that late summer night was to effect a tryst with the girl in the East and, all conventional means of achieving this end exhausted, the wire-cutters were my last resort.

With the parting of the first strand I knew that in the nearest watch-tower a red light would be flashing to alert the Czech guardians of the

border, and my calculations, based upon months of research, gave me a
maximum of six minutes to effect my breakthrough without interruption.

If I live to tell the tale these would probably be the most frightening
minutes of my life.

The paraphernalia of fences and watch-towers is no more than a
bleak memory for those who live in close proximity to the
demarcation line; crossing it today has no meaning with the two
Germanys reunited. On this latest journey one could tell when
the train entered the former German Democratic Republic by
the general dilapidation of the towns and villages along the way.

My choice of accommodation was that offered by the Youth
Hostel Association as not only was this inexpensive but the
network of hostels was comprehensive and, in early spring,
unlikely to be overbooked. Such a hostel existed in Rostock, but
instead I fell for a '*zimmer frei*' sign outside the station which
resulted in a more expensive but essentially homely night in a
private house hosted by a pleasant German couple. Most of the
town's edifices of architectural merit were wrapped in scaffolding,
but those of Stralsund, situated within a ring of small lakes, were
ebulliently on full display.

The town's splendid construction and an almost Scandinavian
ambience, resulting from two centuries of Swedish rule, is striking,
with gigantic churches – the *Marienkirche* and *Nikolaikirche* in
particular – of overpowering Gothic bulk, and a city hall with a
frontage of painted spires more remarkable than beautiful. But
beauty there is in the narrow streets and along the old wall, broken
by stone arches, which once encircled the town.

Being close to the Polish border I could not resist a short detour
to and stopover at Szczecin (more pronounceably Stettin) simply
on account of my noticing a train about to leave for that city from
a junction on the southbound line to Berlin. Though I go to
Poland quite frequently and know many of its cities, I had never
set eyes on this north-western Polish port.

What I found was a handsome port-city, seldom visited by British tourists in spite of living costs being considerably lower than in neighbouring Germany or even more touristy Polish centres. In it I put up once more in a hostel, a perfectly adequate one costing all of £3 a night. Yet another Hanseatic city, but one minus the more visible attractions of those along the German Baltic coast, Szczecin has had a cruel history ending with almost total destruction in 1945 as the Red Army advanced westwards towards Berlin. The most sizeable of its monuments is the castle, home to the Pomeranian dukes and, later, that of Prussian aristocracy. A short walk south brings one to the town hall, one of the city's finest edifices; its surrounding old buildings were razed to the ground in 1945 and never rebuilt, leaving the town hall itself standing conspicuously on its own. The daylight hours I spent in the city were mostly filled by exploring the streets and witnessing life in a Polish workaday town that, incidentally, is the birthplace of Catherine the Great of Russia.

Back in Germany the tracks converged on Berlin, so to Berlin I went, the first time I had been there since the removal of its greatest tourist attraction – The Wall. An April blizzard was sweeping the city so, to keep warm while awaiting a nightime connection further south, I rode the suburban network of the *S-Bahn* for which the interrail pass is also valid. This gave me brief glimpses of many of Berlin's more dramatic edifices before landing me up at Potsdam for a brisk toddle around Frederick the Great's well-known summer residence of hardly bungalow proportions.

Continuing south, one can't pass by Prague without a pause. The Czech capital is arguably the most beautiful city on Earth, and a cold but sunny day sparked fire from its myriad domes and towers of burnished gold bordering the River Vltava. It is a city that has had much to do with my destiny, and it heads a country I have looked upon over the years in its Nazi-occupied agony, its Communist discontent and, from 1989, its joyous autonomy.

Thereafter, having decided that I wanted to keep going south, I headed for the Balkans without further dalliance, leaving from Prague's down-at-heel second station, Holesovice, on a train bound for Budapest. It was listed as an express, but you could have fooled me. A more superior conveyance would have been the *Csardas* but the timing was inconvenient. Not that 02.30 was all that convenient either, particularly since the train was more than an hour late. However, a night in the company of the city's down-and-outs who use the station as a dosshouse gave me an insight into a slice of Prague's low life. The individuals I met were an amusing bunch who insisted on sharing their firewater and bench seats with me, and though we all got ejected from the station forecourt several times by the police, we repeatedly crept back as soon as they had departed.

The rural delights of Moravia were hidden by the darkness, but as I had but recently hiked across the Czech Republic's second province I was not unaware of its charms. And Slovakia – no longer a province but a fully-fledged state – I likewise had visited a number of times, including a traverse of its eastern portions by bicycle. Dawn illuminated the new country's capital, Bratislava, more of a provincial town than a capital.

Which countries actually constitute part of the Balkans? I had always harboured a vague notion that Hungary formed part of the so-called Balkan Peninsula, but a Hungarian doctor in my compartment indignantly corrected my supposition. The very idea! The *Encyclopaedia Britannica* is a little vague on the subject, merely expounding the fact that the name has been given to the most easterly of the three southern prolongations of the European continent. It states that 'Balkan' is a Turkish word for 'mountain' though in modern usage it is applied only to a particular mountain belt lying south of the lower Danube.

However, Balkan or not, Hungary's capital greeted me with a fine warm morning and a Keleti terminus undergoing restoration. Mid-morning was a good time to arrive in Budapest since it gave

me plenty of time to stretch cramped limbs by walking the three miles or so across the city centre to the second of three main rail stations, Deli in Buda. Even under Communism Budapest had been a comparatively hedonistic city; its citizens never lacking in *joie de vivre* and the ability to eat and drink well. Three years earlier I had cycled through the city during the morning rush hour (not to be recommended) to find it, as it is now, fully Westernised with prices to match if you don't know the dodges. Perhaps not quite up to the standard of Prague, Budapest is nevertheless high on the list of most beautiful cities.

Via the shores of Lake Balaton, shores today almost completely blockaded by small resorts, camping/caravan sites and private villas in contrast to the 1960s when I could remember only a few rural villages being in evidence, my new train trundled me into Croatia which, like Slovakia, had recently blossomed into statehood.

It was midnight before we reached Zagreb following stop-start progress and a prolonged halt at the border. The city's youth hostel was fortuitously quite close to the station and, more to the point, still open though the doors were closed for the night behind me.

I spent the day strolling through this very walkable capital, a capital, like Bratislava, abruptly pitched into a national one from its provincial heyday and still unsure as to how it went about the transformation. Zagreb is not a particularly picturesque town; nor is it as pompous as some capitals go, but it is workaday handsome and is endowed with busy markets and pleasant half-hidden squares. With Croatia I was, presumably, firmly in the Balkans since the old Yugoslavia assuredly formed part of it.

A further night in the hostel, and by the following midday I was aboard another train, this one purporting to go to Split on the Dalmatian coast. Croatia boasts the largest proportion of this indented, island-strewn coastline of any country on the coast's eastern flank, and I can wholeheartedly recommend to any intending holidaymaker the so-called 'Croatian Riviera' centred by Roman Pula. But I had my sights on another Roman coastal

city: that of Split, where I hadn't been for years. The line was open, I was told, even though it ran close to and over the Bosnian border where civil war was raging. And a consumptive diesel-hauled train of just two coaches proved the line by reaching Split after an eight-hour crawl.

There is no line accompanying the fabled coast beyond Split, but a daily ferry plies between Rijeka and Dubrovnik, calling at Zadar and Split, and I was in half a mind to catch it. But I knew Dubrovnik well; in fact, when post-war Yugoslavia first opened its doors to Western tourists at the end of the 1940s I was the first to cross beneath the raised frontier pole and the first Western guest to stay full-board at one of Dubrovnik's top hotels for the then equivalent of 65 pence! And beyond Dubrovnik and the rock-bound fastness of Montenegro lay Albania. A strong recollection arose of a visit, no, two visits I made to that then forbidding country some twoscore and more years earlier while again in transit through the Balkan lands:

Having traversed the then Soviet Union from Moscow to Vladivostok on the longest line in the world, I suppose it was a kind of reaction and a logical step to follow this with a ride on the shortest rail network; that of Albania.

For over two decades the small country had been 'out in the cold', suffering under a hard-line Communist regime that tolerated few Western visitors. Not surprisingly, the two million Albanians who resided in their native land (there are another two million outside it) had lost much faith in human nature. With many of their former friends suddenly pronounced enemies and everybody liable to be labelled 'spy', 'deviationist', 'imperialist' or 'revisionist', it was not surprising that any stranger was looked upon with the gravest suspicion or even open hostility.

The country (its proper name is Shqiperia – 'Land of Eagles') is no larger than Wales, and much of it barren rock. The railway, unconnected to the European system, was little more than 120 miles in length – though since completion of the extensions to Vlora and Ballsh, under construction

when I was first there, another dozen miles or so have been added. A foreigner stands out like a yeti in Oxford Street while every visitor, upon arrival, has the 'riot act' read to them in support of the instruction not to stray from the fold or transgress the myriad prohibitions. Given these circumstances individual travel around the country presented a sizeable problem. I found the bicycle to be one answer. The sight of a middle-aged English gentleman sedately riding a heavy 1940-framed bicycle was a disarming one, and on the various excursions I made on my hired steed I was never stopped by authority once.

The train provided a better vehicle, for on this you can get right amongst the people. Railways, as I have already made clear, are great levellers of values; none more so, perhaps, than Albanian Rail which had second- and third-class trains, never a mixed one (today this is reduced to single-class trains). Months prior to my visit I had written to both the Albanian Ministry of Communications in Tiranë, the capital, and to the State Railway offices for permission to ride the railway, but no replies were forthcoming. Not even a plea to a People's Government was going to get me a simple train ticket. And on arrival at the border with Montenegro my worst fears were realised. Amongst the list of prohibitions, transgression of which was punishable by execution, was unauthorised travel by foreigners on the state railway. But this carried no more than a 25-year jail sentence as the punishment; at least there was a chance of staying alive if I were caught.

So I joined the queue for a third-class ticket at the dingy station at Durrës. My destination on this first occasion was Tiranë, some 30 miles distant. At the ticket-window, heavily screened, I said 'Tiranë' in what I hoped was the local inflection and tendered a soggy 10-lek note. The crush was so great that even had the overworked girl behind the grill noticed my foreignness there was no time to do anything about it. I felt a little glow of achievement when my ticket, together with some change, materialised through the window.

No policeman guarded the barrier, and the train that waited at the single platform could have earned a fortune in a transport museum. The Czech diesel locomotive was fine but the things it hauled – little oblong boxes on wheels – were pure Keystone. But at least I got a seat.

Mariánské Lázně. The author and his wife, Anna, on a return trip in 1969.

Trans-Siberia Express and Peking Express.
Both trains halted by an accident on the line, west of Irkutsk, USSR.

Trans-Siberia Express, USSR. The author and his fellow passengers.

Ulaanbaator–Peking Express. Mongolia.

Steam Locomotive. Namp'o, North Korea.

Students at work in the Children's Palace. Shanghai, China.

Bogey changing at the Mongolia–China border.

The city of Ürümqi. Xinjiang autonomous region, China.

Boiler assembly shop. Datong Locomotive Works, China.

The author's train crew. Hedjaz Jordan railway.

The citadel in the Valley of the Tombs. Tadmur (Palmyra), Syria.

A memorial tablet at the Buchenwald Concentration Camp. Weimar, Germany.

Avenue of the Sphinxes. Karnak Temple, Egypt.

That first journey was disappointing. There was little opportunity for conversation if only for the disturbing fact that one of my fellow travellers was a policeman. All eyes were on my Western-made shoes and blond Anglo-Saxon hair, but the looks were friendly and the smiles seemed to infer 'Thank you for being one of us'.

Tiranë station stands surrounded on three sides by open fields. It hardly wore the aura of a terminus for a capital city and no nameplates graced its two short platforms. I enquired, with some doubt, if this was in fact Tiranë, and received a shake of the head so stayed in my seat while everybody else alighted. Then I remembered that, in the topsy-turvy world of Albania, a shake means yes, a nod no.

Tiranë matches its station. In the vast Skanderbeg Square the lonely policeman on a pedestal went through the motions of directing a non-existent stream of traffic while whistling indignantly at pedestrians daring to cross within sight of the slowest distant ox-cart. Skanderbeg, the Albanian national hero, horsed and armoured, glared down in bronze disbelief from the hub of the square while, in lesser positions astride a broad empty highway to nowhere, Joseph Stalin and Vladimir Ilich Ulyanov Lenin stared at one another in granite disapproval.

The minaret of a one-time Turkish mosque that had been turned into a museum held its own against an impressive façade of concrete that fronted the People's Palace of Culture. This contained an opera house, a theatre and a number of shops with little to sell beyond Chinese toilet paper. 'Glory to the People's Republic of Albania' read the giant slogan on its flat roof, hardly an original statement for a country where glorification and the personality cult (of President Enver Hoxha) proliferated on walls and mountainsides.

These were the high spots of a dusty unkempt Balkan town of 190,000 citizens. From it I returned to Durrës by a second-class train of slightly superior rolling stock even though a Saturday afternoon crowd bound for the superb Durrës beaches ensured a sardine-like occupation of the corridor. I nearly missed the train by virtue of another of those head-shaking episodes which had me initially ensconced in another waiting train bound for Lesh in the opposite direction. My new companions comprised a jovial throng

who, after the first fever of curiosity, accepted me as one of themselves. We discoursed in schoolboy French on the subject of English literature and Mr Edward Heath.

'You got away with it the first time; you'll never do it again,' pronounced the pundits back at my beachside hotel, and at Durrës station a couple of days later they were nearly right.

No Saturday crowds masked my ticket acquisition this time and the face behind the grill surveyed my un-Albanian features morosely. '*Ausweis*,' barked the face and I passed over my passport, a plea of ignorance of the regulations ready on my lips. Together with the passport was my sheaf of copy letters to the Ministry of Communications to confuse the issue. Slamming shut the partition, my tormentor emerged in search of a policeman and found the one I had carefully dodged upon entering the station. Together they scrutinised my credentials, pronounced them fit and, to my amazement, I was handed my ticket for the Durrës–Tiranë–Elbasan flyer.

There were six and a half in my compartment: the half was a baby boy asleep on the lap of a swarthy Tosk. A word about Tosks and Gegs, the 'English' and 'Scots' of Albania. The line of demarcation is the Shkumbini River, dividing two peoples with different dialects, customs, behaviour and social structure. The orthodox Tosks are more easygoing than the Moslem Gegs, though the communist line was that there is no difference and that only enemies of the state wished to differentiate so as to sow the seeds of discord. My neighbour may have been either by geography, but was a gynaecologist by profession, or so she informed me in good French laced with a dash of German. We conversed at length, our exchanges being laboriously translated into Albanian for the benefit of the other travellers. Surprisingly she openly displayed a dislike of things Albanian; an opinion that appeared to have taken root following a sojourn in Paris. She gave me to understand there was nothing of interest in Elbasan, a fact I had amply confirmed for myself while on an officially-sponsored coach visit the previous day.

This uninspiring central Albanian town was for me, however, notable as the one place where I met a really dissatisfied Albanian. He sidled up to me in the main street and asked point blank in English if I would undertake

to get him out of the country. A policeman, disapproving of the contact, waved the man away, so saving me from a reply. Albania, so far as I knew, was the one Communist state in Europe where unauthorised emigration was punishable by death.

My timetable gave me a choice of six minutes or five hours in Elbasan. I chose six minutes, so raced round the back of the ramshackle station to buy a ticket. In doing so I encountered the charge of the light brigade of locals intent upon acquiring a seat on the same train and I was swept, ticketless, back to the platform.

Eventually my plaintive cries of 'Billeti? Billeti?' were heeded and a youth came to my assistance. Together we counter-attacked against the flow and arrived at the hole in the wall through which tickets were issued. With about 80 seconds to go before the train left, there was no nonsense about passports and, escorted by my saviour, I dashed for the rear coach and found cramped standing space in the corridor. The train thereupon delayed its departure, leaving ten minutes late.

I found myself surrounded by a bevy of wizened old men with weather-carved faces. One of them recited an English limerick in my ear; a limerick minus the last line which he didn't know. Halfway through this recitation a rock was hurled through the window, missing my head by inches, but I don't think it was aimed specifically at me. As the crush lessened I was able to move a little way down the corridor and this time my immediate companion became a male soldier half-surrounded by a circle of female soldiers, all adorned with carbines with fixed bayonets and wicked-looking grenades. It doesn't pay to get fresh with ladies in these circumstances, so I chatted up the man. To my delight he spoke some English. He told me about his schooling where he'd learnt my language and of the period of national service he was now undergoing which had taken him away from his engineering job.

'Everyone in Albania is a soldier,' he explained. 'In addition to arithmetic, science, and history our children learn grenade throwing and rifle shooting. We are surrounded by enemies and so everybody has to be involved in our defence.'

I tried gently to persuade him that Britain and all the other countries of Western Europe had no great antipathy towards his country and certainly had not the slightest intention of invading it, but he was not to be reassured. Already I had noticed the huge array of concrete blocks blossoming like giant mushrooms in every field and open space that were intended to check a tank advance by some supposed enemy. My new friend continued his recitation by airing a desire to visit England, though adding in some haste – as if he'd spoken treason – that there was nothing wrong with Albania. It had, he went on, progressed under the miracle of unadulterated Communism in spite of the treachery of Soviet Russia, Federal Yugoslavia and even the great Chinese People's Republic (all allied countries that had grown tired of Albanian demands and ditched it). I'd heard all this claptrap before a million times, so quickly changed the subject. We then ranged over our respective histories, his for the second time, aired our respective points of view (again) and all the while the female soldiers gathered round to listen to no more than the sound of our voices. I was in full oration upon the accomplishments of Winston Churchill, on which some doubts had been aired, when the train clattered into Durrës.

From a traveller I became a tourist again, coming to heel, behaving myself and being shepherded about at the whim of the state tourist office. Only once did I bring up the subject of individual rail travel with my guide.

'How could you or anyone stop me boarding one of your trains?' I asked apropos of nothing in particular. He looked at me pityingly.

'Albanian State Security is inviolate,' he assured me. 'We are ever vigilant. You could never even get into the station.'

He wondered why I smiled.

In 1983 I managed to visit Albania again, and though repressive measures in other European Communist-ruled countries had been softening over the intervening years, those of Albania had remained as strict as ever.

Again I had utilised the railway for my nefarious travels about the country, but this time things came unstuck. Taken into custody while my train idled at a wayside station, I was escorted by police car to Tiranë, there to be

arrayed before a senior official of the Ministry of the Interior and subjected to a severe reprimand.

Chastened, but not for long, I got my own back by taking photographs of everything that was deemed forbidden to photograph, which at that time was virtually everything.

Split was emphatically the end of the line so far as south-west Croatia was concerned. I just had time to take a glance at the great palace built by Diocletian, who was born in a nearby village, before boarding an overnight northbound train back the way I had come. A night journey suited me well as I had no particular desire to see more shell-blasted villages bordering the track while on Bosnian territory.

The Balkans have been no strangers to strife. Though they form part of our continent the fact does not immediately register, for the violent, irrational temperament of the Balkan countries is alien to our conception of an ordered Europe. For centuries men and nature have conspired to make this territory a hell on earth: Goths, Romans, Avars, Huns, Slavs, Magyars, Byzantines, Tartars, Turks, Venetians, Austrians, Germans and Russians have all fought for its inhospitable terrain. The history of the Balkans is a chronicle of atrocity interwoven with a fierce pride in the dark and bloody hills of a land sanctified forever by a burning love. These men of the Balkans have not had luck on their side. They have been brave but have all too often been beaten in battle. They have been industrious only to be broken by the terrible reversals of nature and human affairs. Prosperity invariably eludes them.

The region is a kind of microcosm of the universe. The modern states that have now emerged from the ancient empires – and in the case of Yugoslavia, an even more recent break-up of its territory assisted by civil war – hold within their grasp diverse cults, ethnic minorities and a passionately proclaimed uniqueness. Each nation has forged itself into an uneasy political entity proclaiming a

grandiose destiny that tumbles over the rock-strewn path of archaic national politics.

With the exception of Greece, each of the countries was a Communist state. True to form, even their Communism was of an intensely nationalistic brand and there was not one that would blend with the other. Yugoslavia flirted with capitalism, earning hatred from Albania and distrust from the rest of the communist world. Bulgaria was a loyal appendage of the Soviet Union. Romania, while seeking ties with the West, craftily continued its ideological ties with the East. Albania had become an irritant to Moscow, a short-lived ally of Red China and flaunted a hatred of most of the rest of the world. Even the exception, Greece, conformed to type for a while when she replaced her monarchy by a military dictatorship subsequently shaken off.

Back in Zagreb I turned north once more to enter Slovenia, another province of the former Yugoslavia elevated to country status, this one headed by the jumped-up capital Ljubljana. I was joined on the train by a couple of pleasant British lads with whom I was to join forces in the search for overnight accommodation and exploration of the city.

The line's approach to Ljubljana is by way of the *Ljubljana Vrala* or 'Ljubljana Gate', a valley, with its Sava River together with the railway, hemmed in by alpine foothills, making for not only a dramatically beautiful approach but a highly defensive one.

With the hostel full we were directed to a private house available to paying guests, which proved eminently satisfactory even though we all had to sleep on the floor, and our shared expense distribution requirements caused total confusion for the hostess who spoke only Serbo-Croat.

Our exploration of the city was a very worthwhile exercise. Ljubljana is centred, more or less, by its imposing Castle Hill, the castle in question not being particularly old or even impressive; in fact, the only hostile incident it had experienced was when it stopped a bomb in the recent Bosnian conflict prior to Slovenia

becoming independent. The view from the ramparts is fine indeed, with the red roofs of the Old Town half-encircling the hill. We ended our perambulations in one of the local beer houses that held a Bavarian air, the beer being equally good, but cheaper.

My divergence westwards from Budapest at an end, I returned to the Hungarian capital intent upon resuming the original southerly course deeper into the Balkans proper. And it was from that city's Nyugati station that I caught an express to the Hungarian spa town of Debrecen at the north-eastern end of the country.

On this superior train I came upon a problem that I had not met before but which I was to find on several further occasions on this journey. Seemingly I should have purchased a seat reservation prior to boarding the train because, without it, I was to be repeatedly ejected from a seat that held no indication of being reserved by indignant claimants waving bits of paper.

Debrecen I found to be an unremarkable, modest-sized town of flower-lined streets known for its annual flower festival. Its main attraction lies a mile or so out of town in Nagyerdo Park where a new spa resort had recently been opened. So recently, in fact, that my room, in which the Hungarian Tourist Office in London had invited me to spend a couple of nights, had not been completed. The complex contains swimming pools, sports amenities, children's playgrounds, multiple restaurants, snack bars and the like as well as modern thermal treatment facilities which, together with the hotel, cost guests far less than similar centres in Western Europe.

The weather had warmed up to a degree that had me immersed in one of the swimming pools over the middle of both days. But the unseasonable warmth triggered a massive storm from which, the second afternoon, I took shelter beneath the eaves of a drinks kiosk. The stall-holder handed me a beer, then another and another, joining me in their consumption to the point when both of us, I regret to say, reached a degree of intoxication. Even before

the downpour had ceased we had, clad in our underpants, thrown ourselves into the nearest swimming pool there to act the goat while still swigging beer. It all ended in trouble as I thought it might, with a senior member of staff bailing us out, he presuming me to be one of the stallholders. I had no reason to enlighten him.

Onward, refreshed by two whole days off the trains, out of Hungary and into Romania on the most *Personenzug* of all time that stopped at every wayside halt and often in between. At the border my visa, the only pre-arranged visa necessary for a British subject throughout every country covered by the interrail pass, was studied with exaggerated care and at the subsequent township – Valez lui Mihal – the wheezing old train gave up the ghost and pitched me out on to the station platform. Valez is hardly more than a village and a pretty humble one at that, yet it held two banks, neither of which could offer me any lei for my pounds and dollars.

'We have no money whatsoever,' explained an apologetic manager at the second bank – which said something about the continuing economic state of this unfortunate country.

The contrasts between beautiful, damaged Romania and its smart Westernised neighbour is best observed by a road crossing of the frontier. It is at its sharpest here. Hungary has buried the outer vestiges of Communism in one heady decade, but sadly Romania is taking longer. At the border are to be found forlorn lines of men on bicycles with bundles of goods that cannot be obtained in Romania queuing to return home. Hungary's well-repaired roads give way to pot-holed ones, their traffic mainly composed of bicycles and horse-drawn carts weaving erratically in an effort to dodge the worst of the craters and rutted verges.

A couple of hours later I was aboard another local train bound for Satu Mare, crossing flat terrain giving a hint of hills in the far distance, their outline vague in the unseasonable heat haze. Our wheels clickety-clicked and the coach rattled and swayed on the

unevenly-laid track which weaved around corners for no reason I could fathom. My fellow passengers were mostly gimlet-eyed village women accoutred with shopping baskets and string bags.

My previous incursion into Romania had been during the summer of 1993, four years previously. Then I had found a sombre and troubled country freed from the dead hand of Communism but not yet adjusted to the capitalism thrust upon it. And as my vehicle had been a bicycle and my accommodation a tiny bivouac, I had to share in the daily struggle for existence, queuing for rarely available bread in bare-shelved supermarkets of townships and villages. People stared at me as if I had come from another world. The influence of the vanquished Ceausescu remained strong; the baleful shadow of the secret police had not faded, though neither had it quelled the Romanian sense of hospitality to strangers. In the cities and larger towns the economic situation invariably appeared better, with at least some goods in the shops; more than could be said of the rural communities.

And so it was with Satu Mare. The town holds a trio of conspicuous but unremarkable basilicas – Orthodox, Roman Catholic and Calvinist – plus a castle-like structure of a significance that escaped me, a pleasant park or two, and the well-restored Shoemaker's Guild building transformed into a hotel. With some eight hours to spare before the departure of the next train to Bucharest, I had plenty of time to wander the town's central streets to gain a distinct impression of an expanded amount of goods in the shop windows since my previous visit. A kindly lady, to whom I asked for directions, insisted on giving me a brief tour in her small car and I ended my wanderings in a open-air brasserie awash with unsavoury characters, male and female, who couldn't keep their eyes or hands off me. My train was not scheduled to leave until after midnight, so I spent the final couple of hours waiting forlornly in a deserted station half expecting to be mugged. I could have caught an earlier EuroCity (EC) express but had selected

the so-called Rapide to give me more time in Satu Mare, which was a mistake.

The mistake arose from the fact that the second train was composed of sleeper coaches only and all fully occupied. So I sat myself down on the corridor floor at one end of a coach and prepared to endure an uncomfortable night on the tiles.

By the time the conductor found me we were well on our way so he couldn't chuck me out. But he wasn't going to have me dossing down in the corridor and at the first halt, Baia Mare, the good man arranged for a sitting coach to be attached to the train, led me to it and ensured that I was comfortably laid out flat on an empty bench seat.

I saw nothing of Baia Mare on this occasion and didn't particularly want to. Again it was a town in which I had dallied briefly earlier and from which I had been only too happy to leave. Originally a Roman mining settlement, there was little to show of its ancient past since the whole city had been inundated by a grotesque agglomeration of pollution-wreathed high-risery – courtesy of Mr Ceausecu – on the banks of the poisoned River Sasar, a tributary of the sizeable Tisza which, as I write these words, is recovering from the major disaster of having 100,000 tons of cyanide-contaminated water accidentally discharged into its flow from this very town.

Baia Mare, meaning 'Big Mine', supports a population of 150,000 and has been a centre for metallurgy since those Roman times; it was where the Magyar kings mined their gold, all of which has resulted in mounting pollution from the residue in the soil, the water and the air. Water from taps runs rust-red and lead pollution causes nausea and headaches, ensuring an average life expectancy that is 12 years shorter than elsewhere in Romania. No, I was quite happy to give Baia Mare a miss on this occasion.

For some hours I had the compartment all to myself until daybreak brought an influx of commuters and I was forced to relinquish my 'bed'. Further coaches had been added to the train

in the meantime, and it was a pretty full one that drew into
Bucharest Nord at breakfast time.

My first journey to Romania had likewise been by rail back in
the early 1970s, though on that occasion my route had been
different, having entered the country from Yugoslavia.

Once more my mind cast back through the decades:

*From the great empty plains the countryside had contracted into wooded
hills and valleys with villages, each with its onion-domed church half hidden
amongst the trees. The horizon had drawn in to settle close but dramatically
upon castle ruins atop the more unlikely summits. In this vein the new
countryside led us romantically to the walled city of Sibiu.*

*Originally known as Hermannsdorf, the locality was settled by German-
Saxon merchants in the twelfth century who, in spite of every kind of
vicissitude, managed not only to hang on but also to build themselves a
beautiful and prosperous town. It was destroyed by the Tartars in 1241
and again by the Turks in the fifteenth century, afflicted by earthquake, fire
and plague, and in the seventeenth and eighteenth centuries many of its
citizens, suspected of witchcraft, were butchered with astonishing frequency.
With so much violence no wonder Sibiu threw up fortified walls and watch-
towers and surrounded itself with moats. The town retains a medieval
Germanic appearance unchanged from its last disaster.*

*Brasov, Romania's second city to whence the train took me next, was
likewise settled by Teutonic knights from Saxony. It was called Orasul
Stalin when I was there, though everyone referred to it as Brasov. Situated
on the slopes of the Transylvanian Alps in a narrow valley shut in by
mountains on all sides except one, it is an unlikely place to find an industrial
complex. Yet the Steagul Roso – Red Banner – tractor and motor works
was one of the show places of Brasov if you liked that kind of thing. The
railway presumes you do.*

*It was dark as we crawled into the city and dark again as we crawled
out. The father of our small group in the compartment was Romanian by
nationality but German by birth, and proved it by speaking fluently in
both tongues. I had never realised how Germanic Transylvania was. The*

man was quite a railway enthusiast, so had something in common with me. He revealed the fact that the first railway in Romania, built in 1890, was a result of a concession granted to two Englishmen, John Barkley and John Staniforth, and it connected Bucharest with the Danubian port of Giurgiu, 72 kilometres distant. But building and operating railways by private enterprise did not last long, and in 1888 all railways in the country became state-owned and standardised to European gauge (except for a short length of mixed gauge, with three rails, to provide access for the Russian gauge of five feet).

With a cooperative group of people, even a full compartment can be a reasonably comfortable place. On this particular leg of the journey no overnight shakedown was necessary, but with the view outside denied us our attention became more localised. As was so often the case, nobody would hear of me not sharing in the communal meals, and since everyone had brought their own provisions I was, as usual, pressed on all sides to dip into the pooled resources.

Just as it had been on my earlier rail journeys across the Soviet Union, I detected a note of reticence during the conversations with my companions on the trains, a reticence born of a fear not only of the secret police – here in Romania the Securitate – but also their voluntary or involuntary agents. In line with all the other People's Republics, their hapless citizenry had learnt to look for the meaning behind every question of a political nature put to them. Informers had been created within the very fabric of the family structure so that one's own mother, father, wife, husband or child could, intentionally or unknowingly, release some scrap of information to the omnipresent Securitate and their network of agents. Thus I had come to realise that it was bad form to ask too many questions; polite query about matters we Westerners take for granted had long been taboo here.

However, this reticence again appeared to hold little sway when it came to discussion in the taken-for-granted safe refuge of a train compartment with only the two of us present. Consequently, given these circumstances, I was gradually able to build a picture of some of the more unpleasant aspects of the regime's hold on the populace, though these invariably reflected the same unpleasantness I knew about all too well; indeed, had experienced in

*other parts of the Communist empire. 'We cannot invite you to our homes,'
was a reoccurring bitter comment, and no surprise to me. 'Even talking to
a foreigner is frowned upon,' was another. The Securitate were everywhere,
ears straining for the slightest sign of dissent or dissatisfaction. If caught, the
perpetrator would be taken away for questioning, probably beaten and
heavily fined or even jailed. People sometimes simply disappeared altogether.
It was all horribly familiar.*

*Reading the 'wrong' book, writing to a friend in the despised West,
listening to a Western broadcast, airing an opinion that was not the party
line or grumbling about the chronic shortages of goods in the shops could
ensure the culprit would be followed by the Securitate and frequently be
forced to leave job or home or the right to live in a particular town. Relatives
and friends too would be harassed, followed and questioned to an
unbelievable degree. The Securitate in Romania, the KGB in the Soviet
Union, the STB in Czechoslovakia: it was the same dismal story.*

*Sinaia is known as the 'Pearl of the Carpathians', and has long been
one of the most popular and fashionable of Romanian resorts. All I saw of
it, again, was the station, but my companions filled me in with an abundance
of detail. One held a low opinion of King Carol II who, apparently, spent
his reign fornicating in the Royal Park with Magda Lubescu. The others
were more delicate, telling me tales of the three castles hidden amongst the
old trees in the parklands surrounding the Palace of Peles.*

*Peles Castle is like a fairytale come true. It was initially designed by a
Viennese, continued by another, with final additions by a Czech. The
interior was said to be packed with the oddest collectors' pieces, with not a
single item from a Romanian source.*

*The subject of oil in Romania invariably brings to mind the city of
Ploesti (much bombed by the RAF in the Second World War), which was
the centre of the country's considerable oil industry. The hours of darkness
were the ones to see the illuminated silver cobwebs of piping that made the
great refineries a fascinating spectacle. Ploesti means 'rainy' but, although
the town is the Manchester of Romania, the night remained dry. A serf by
the name of Ploaie is supposed to be the first inhabitant of the original*

village. No doubt he lived and died in wretchedness, not knowing he was sitting on a source of wealth beyond his wildest dreams.

We drew into Bucharest half an hour late. I was to spend a number of days in the Romanian capital which gave me time to discover that, though politics and war had scarred the fair face, the city wore its Communism on the back of its head with barely a red slogan to be seen. Its many bookshops contained works by British and West European writers; the few compulsory Karl Marx volumes were pushed out of the way to the back. The cinemas showed British and American films, the Soviet ones having long since been given the brush-off. The restaurants and nightclubs were of a high standard.

In spite of a rash of tower blocks in the Calea Victoriei, the main street was as long and handsome as Oxford Street and Regent Street put together. I beheld a city which was protracted and drawn out like the hours kept by its inhabitants. No shop opened between midday and five o'clock, because in the summer it can be as hot as in India.

I spent my last evening with my private accommodation hosts with whom I had been staying while in Bucharest. They took me to the 'Monte Carlo' restaurant in Cismigiu Park where we downed several bottles of extremely drinkable white wine. Some friends joined us later, amongst them a woman who spoke English and turned out to be the playwright Arnold Wesker's cousin. Like Cinderella, I had to steal away from the party at midnight to catch a pumpkin called the Bulgaria Express, taking with me an aspect of a city not yet despoiled by a future egotistic dictator by the name of Nicolae Ceausescu.

Bucharest. On the various times I've been pitched out on to its streets I can never find anything really nice to say about it. And I tried hard again on this latest whole-day leg-stretching exercise in the post-Ceausescu city before continuing my journey. In every direction I came across a litany of urban images that both confounded and depressed me: unkempt roads that meandered through the centre only to dead-end at some hideous and sometimes half-completed apartment block. The ugliest thing of all was the gigantic and ridiculous Ceausescu Palace, a monument

to madness that's so awful it's worth seeing. However, the shops were far from bare; in fact, they were positively brimming when compared with those I saw on my earlier visit.

Yet in spite of everything, the Romanian capital holds a kind of negative fascination. Beneath the melancholy can be discerned a city like no other. Though a hideous and shockingly painful reminder of the Ceausescu era, this somehow is its greatest strength. Bucharest may be unbearably overwhelming, but it is undeniably intriguing, a city that awes and tantalises even as it repulses.

When the concierge wasn't looking I treated myself to a wash and brush-up in one of the expensive state-run hotels and got a flea in my ear for my trouble. In spite of fatigue I was not the slightest tempted to spend a night in such a sterile and overpriced emporium, the huge vestibule devoid of clients and afflicted with the atmosphere of a morgue.

It was a relief to return to the dank and chaotic Gara de Nord where the 13.00 Bosphor Express abruptly held an attraction it hardly deserves. The station evoked, for me, a more recent (1993) memory:

Having cycled southwards across Romania and reached the Black Sea, I intended rewarding myself and my bicycle by a restful rail journey homeward. In the event the long-anticipated train ride was not only cut short but, except for the first few hours, was nothing less than horrific. Having arrived in triumph at Constanta following a near 2,000-mile pedalling marathon from the Baltic coast of Estonia, I was greeted by the news that Romanian Railways were scheduled to go on strike at midnight.

The three and a half hour ride to Bucharest held no problems beyond a slight fracas with a blonde female ticket-inspector who didn't know what to charge for the carriage of my bicycle. This ended amicably following what could be described as a Dutch auction.

The train reached Bucharest Nord sometime after 11.30 p.m. Wheeling and humping bike and baggage to the head of the platform, an indicator

board offered the information that a train would be leaving a few minutes
to midnight, the destination Timisoara about 170 kilometres short of the
Hungarian border. The station was a seething mass, the ticket-office besieged
by a sea of struggling humanity, so I abandoned efforts to acquire a ticket for
both self and bicycle. A huge crowd spread across the platform, alleged to be
the one from which the Timisoara train would depart, and by the time I
had ploughed a course through the throng, rumour had it that the train
would be arriving at the adjacent platform. Like a multitude of refugees
fleeing bombardment, everyone surged back to the head of the platform and
on to the next one. Three times this mass migration occurred, and for me it
was simply the luck of the gods that when the train finally backed on to its
allotted platform, I was in the right spot close against the steps up to the
door of a coach when the thing halted. By now adept at boarding coaches
with bike and baggage – difficult enough even without the scrum – I
managed, by superhuman effort, to heave everything into the corridor space
at the end of the coach and hold it against all-comers. There followed an
onslaught of crazed humanity, and both my bike and baggage disappeared
under a layer of bodies. Already exhausted, I hardly relished the prospect of
a nine-hour stand-up journey, but was nevertheless thankful for having
made it beyond Bucharest.

The deadline for the start of the strike had passed by the time our cruelly
overloaded train heaved itself out of the station. Further intending travellers
were left behind in droves simply on account of there being, literally, not a
toehold in any part of the coaches. I was painfully squeezed against the
handlebars of my bicycle, across which a couple of fellow passengers lay in
contorted postures. Everyone, equally relieved as I was to have succeeded in
boarding the train, made light of the situation and we became a close-knit
community in more ways than one. My neighbour possessed a bottle of
mind-searing tuica which he regularly tipped into my mouth since my own
hands were pinned to my sides. The fiery liquid deadened the aches in my
legs and I was hardly in a position to fall down in a drunken stupor within
such tight-fitting confinement.

That night was a long one. We reached Timisoara around mid-morning and it was a bedraggled mob of passengers that stumbled thankfully off the train. If nothing else it had been a free trip.

I boarded the Bosphor Express with some trepidation as, again, I held no reservation. Nor, seemingly, had anyone else, and in the garrulous company of half a dozen Romanians, Bulgarians and Turks we negotiated the territories of their respective countries to attain Istanbul. This involved a 22-hour journey extended by the late arrival at the terminus, a journey this time made painful by a raging thirst. I had noticed that everybody had equipped themselves with plastic bottles of water at Bucharest, but had neglected to do so myself. All through a stickily-humid night my tongue stuck to the dry roof of my mouth before the Turkish border produced an interminable delay for the purpose of the collection of £10-worth of entry visa, which at least offered the opportunity of liquid intake.

Except for the previous border station, that of Ruse, I saw nothing of Bulgaria on this journey. But I remembered the occasion of my second arrival on the Bulgar Express in the early 1970s:

For a relatively small country, railway construction in Bulgaria began on quite a large scale in 1866, with a main line 140 miles long from Ruschuk on the Danube to Varna on the Black Sea. A still greater milestone was, however, the completion of the international main line across the country from Dragoman near the Yugoslav frontier, through Sofija to Svilengrad, and providing the all-rail route to Istanbul and Asia.

From the point of view of observing the Bulgarian countryside my train timings were a disaster. Only as we drew sleepily into Sofija did the night relent enough to show me a capital I had seen before. But what my eyes had missed was compensated for by the spate of words that poured into my ears the long night through.

The Bulgarian lawyer had joined the train at Ruse. It was his town, he announced, the old Roman city of Sexanta Prista, or 'Sixty Vessels', now the fourth most important town in Bulgaria and I was not allowed to forget it. My new and volatile companion was a city councillor, a member of its liberation committee and chairman of the Bulgarian–Soviet Friendship League. In fact he was Ruse, for he was all I saw of it. Soon the compartment became his council chamber and his fluency in the English language lent wings to his oratory.

I ventured to suggest that the great Soviet Union might be milking his country dry and received a rap over the knuckles for my indiscretion. His vehement denials raised the eyebrows of the one other occupant of the debating chamber, who a little later found it expedient to withdraw

'Ever growing – never old' are the words inscribed on the heraldic crest (or device) of Sofija. It sums up the Bulgarian capital rather well. Little shows that it is very old, and the place is a patchwork of undistinguished building fads going back to the Ottoman occupation. As Serdica, after the Thracian tribe which lived there, it was considered as a possible capital of the Roman Empire, but greatness passed it by. Under a new name, Sredets ('Central'), it grew to importance in the Byzantine Empire, but many of the resulting new buildings were destroyed when the Ottomans besieged it. The Turk is therefore, architecturally, the most strongly represented of Sofija builders and many of his public edifices and mosques remain.

My previous visit to Sofija lasted a full three days. Now I was here for no more than three hours. Two of them I spent parading round the city's central square, a slavish copy of Moscow's Red Square with some Stalinist architecture to match. For the Lenin Mausoleum read Dimitrov Mausoleum, but there were no queues. For little reason other than to pass time, I looked in again on the Dimitrov corpse. It was difficult to slouch or stroll in such surroundings; goose-stepping seemed more appropriate.

Dear old Sirkeci station. I seem invariably to end up at this most modest of terminals at the end of Europe. And if Bucharest had been unseasonably warm, Istanbul shimmered in a heatwave. My first task was the acquisition of a modest hotel for a night between

sheets; undisturbed sleep had become a distinct rarity on this journey.

As I've intimated earlier, there is simply no city in the world like Istanbul. The place is tough, noisy, robust and ruthless and could be overwhelming but for the respite of the waters of the Golden Horn and the Bosphorus, though these too are alive with nautical activity. Whenever I come here my footsteps falter, my plan to stick to a certain route comes unstuck, as something strange and different confounds the itinerary. A thousand and one sights catch the eye and stir the curiosity, and for the best part of two days I imbibed a hundred of them to add to my recollections of this unique metropolis.

My hotel, close to Sirkeci station, was adequate and clean: clean enough anyway, and the following morning I made the ferry voyage to Haydarpasa to pay my respects to Asia. Then it was back to the trains.

The current friction between Turkey and Greece manifested itself at the Turkish-Greek border station of Athion and it is the likes of you and me that suffer the consequences. My train arrived at midday, a few minutes after the closure of the money-changing office. An hour later the EC Istanbul–Thessaloniki express arrived, but only those with drachma in their possession were permitted to board it, for there is a supplement levied from the border onwards. Neither love nor the hardest of currencies will be accepted at the ticket-office in payment for the supplement, so most of us had to wait multiple hours, kicking our heels on the sun-baked platform miles from anywhere, for the arrival of the lesser non-supplement train that went only as far as Alexandropolis anyway.

We arrived at this Evros coastal capital predictably in the middle of the night, and for me its chief source of delight was a surprisingly still-open exchange office in the town centre, resulting in my being no longer a pauper in Greece. But from what I saw in the dark of Alexandropolis (reputed to be so-named

after a 1920s king who was bitten to death by a monkey and not, as might be thought, Alexander the Great) was favourable, its wide promenade and expanse of sandy beach particularly enticing.

In fact, I would have preferred a sojourn there rather than Thessaloniki, to whence another consumptive and late-arriving train bore me. This preference stems from the fact that the promenade of the latter city overlooks, albeit magnificently, the Thermaic Gulf and the oil-polluted waters of the great harbour, completely unfit for bathing.

And the heat made it very batheable weather. The city is, officially, the capital of the country and its second port after Piraeus. Thessaloniki has no reason to envy Athens in terms of cultural life while, though it may not hold a relic of the fame of the Acropolis, its broad streets are littered with lesser but no less interesting Roman and Byzantine antiquities that are far more accessible. And the quality of shopping, I was assured, was a lot higher. Based at a small hotel of hardly Savoy standard, I spent a couple of days strolling the tree-lined streets, assimilating a city I'd only glimpsed before.

The line to Athens is worth the ride alone as the route curves through a sun-blasted terrain of rocky hills and valleys. I had no intention of remaining in the Greek capital for long; it is far from being a favourite city of mine, and since I reached it in time for breakfast and there was a night train out after supper, the hours between would suffice for a leg-stretch. Athens contains a myriad ancient bits and pieces besides the Acropolis if you're prepared to sweat it out looking for them; but I wasn't with 48-degrees of heat and another sleepless night behind me.

So I contented myself with watching the changing of the guard of *Evzones*, as the Presidential Guards are called – soldiers in fancy dress of white pleated skirts, white socks and shoes half-hidden by huge red pom-poms – and then wandering around Syntagma Square. I could see the Acropolis, wrapped in scaffolding and plastic sheeting, high on its hill in the distance but felt no

compulsion to re-acquaint myself with it. I smiled to myself as I remembered an incident while on an earlier visit to the Greek capital:

My route there had taken me to Athens by way of Larissa, capital of Thessaly, with its wide plains, distant mountains and lonely townships. Larissa means 'citadel', which may be appropriate to certain British gentlemen with receding hairlines who were instrumental in its stand against the German invaders of 1941.

One of the ravages of constant travelling is diarrhoea, and I was suffering a particularly violent bout as I wandered the Athens streets. I passed a hospital so retraced my steps and entered the building, intent on obtaining some sort of relief from my discomfort. By dint of facial grimaces and indication of my stomach I attempted to explain my condition to a startled girl receptionist. A youth in a white coat came to the rescue.

'I can help,' he announced triumphantly, having noted my performance, and dashed off to return with a potion of dark liquid. As I downed it I heard him say something about the stuff being a powerful laxative.

I stared, wild-eyed, into the empty glass. The youth saw my horrified expression and got the message. Away he went again, returning this time with a tumbler full of a white liquid.

'I give you double dose,' he told me, confident that 50 per cent of its power would cancel out the initial error.

I laughed uneasily. The youth laughed too, but not at his mistake. The girl at the reception desk had given him her own diagnosis of my ailment. How was I to know I'd blundered into a maternity hospital?

My onward 150-mile journey to Patras was by bus, laid on by the ferry company, though there was a perfectly good train service between Athens and Patras. Railways have long taken a back seat in Greek transport circles. A long and mountainous peninsula, with many equally mountainous islands, does not lend itself to easy railway construction or running. The country has a railway that is extremely sketchy, not much more than 1,600 miles of line in fact, much of it destroyed in the Second World War. To add

to the railway authorities' headache was the fact that there were four track gauges.

The town of Corinth, which was reached at midday, I found to be a ramshackle place virtually devoid of anything to show for its legendary and historic past, though not so the immediate neighbourhood. As the famed city of commerce, one can discern from its proximity to the canal, the sea and through its most famous export, the currant. But Corinth, the 'City of Pleasure', takes a very large hunk of imagination to bring to life. Yet was it not here that a thousand temple prostitutes, slave girls in the service of Aphrodite, made the secular sacred?

The road through the big 'island' of the Peloponnese hugged the sea with such fervour that on several occasions it became almost a wet embrace. It was like this all the way to Patras, winding through a cavalcade of charming villages and past graceful villas within luxuriant gardens. Darkness had fallen by the time we reached Patras.

'It's all Greek to me' has a very literal meaning where Greek railway timetables are concerned, and I was lucky to find my way to Patras on the night train for which I actually obtained a seat reservation. Pitched out at this sizeable ferry port before dawn, I dossed down on the platform for what was left of the night.

Greece's third city, Patras, merits little exploration, though with hours in hand before my scheduled night voyage to Italy there was no alternative except for brief immersion in a now Adriatic sea, this one the texture and temperature of tepid soup. A subsequent climb to the castle (closed) had me all of a sweat again.

The interrail pass is valid for the Patras–Brindisi ferry and, although I was unable to procure a berth, by lying out on the deck beneath a balmy sky I passed a most satisfactory night as the Balkans receded into the distance behind me.

There was little let-up from the heat at Brindisi. The town that marks the bottom end of the Roman Appian Way shimmered in the haze, but at least I could read and understand the train timetables and, up to a point, the lingo. I had the whole day to

spare since the through-express to Bologna didn't leave until nightfall, so I got my usual walkabout plus a bonus of a sumptuous meal to which I treated myself. The smooth efficiency of Italian trains made a joyous contrast to Balkan rail travel and my on-the-dot 04.00 arrival at Bologna was, temperature-wise, akin to finding oneself at the North Pole. And from Bologna on a local train, in company with a lady who insisted upon recounting her life-history, I was transported to a cool paradise called Trentino.

Many of us flock to Lake Garda but miss out on Trento, the small capital of the Trentino region spread about the Dolomite foothills. Putting up at the homely and comfortable Amerika Hotel, I was happy to remain static for three blessedly cool days. On the third, I took myself off on a private line known as the Trento–Male Railway. This runs through the lovely Rabbi Valley, part of the Stelvio National Park, tailor-made for trekkers, walkers, climbers and strollers wanting no more than to feast their eyes on stunning alpine panoramas and a plethora of wild flowers. And my hours of hill-walking here recharged my batteries for the rail-run homeward.

Back on the main line northwards I found myself, within one hour, out of Italy, into and out of Austria, and into Germany; in particular Bavaria, and in one of its celebrated ski-resorts, Garmisch-Partenkirchen, huddled at the base of a sensationally jagged mountain barrier. Having walked four miles to its out-of-town youth hostel I was turned away by virtue of a uniquely Bavarian by-law that forbade anyone over 27 from utilising its services. Instead a nearby B&B of pristine cleanliness took me in for a pittance; astounding value for a pretentious little town like Garmisch.

Back in Austria, Innsbruck, capital of the Tyrol, claimed me for half a day. Its Old Town is pedestrianised, the Hofkirche, Gothic town hall and other historic edifices grouped together conveniently in a town more often passed through on the way to

somewhere else, so I made up for the times I too had been but a transitee.

Eastwards now, via Linz, Austria's third city replete with a handsome cathedral and, more to the point for me, a youth hostel with no ageist hang-ups, and then on to the province of Carinthia (*Karten* in German). And here I landed up in a couple of pleasurable yet untouristy cities: Klagenfurt and Graz.

One good thing about Austrian railways is that they do not levy a surcharge for riding EC and IC (InterCity) super-expresses. Actually the supplement charge is extremely modest even in those countries that do: during 1995 just £2 or £2.50 for any distance covered.

From Linz I had turned about on a detour southwards again, a couple of EC trains bringing me swiftly and uneventfully to, first, Klagenfurt, the Carinthian capital on the shores of the beautiful 17-kilometre-long Worthersee. A fellow passenger not only turned out to be a highly enthusiastic devotee of his home town, but insisted upon escorting me to the centre there to ply me with ice-cream and cream cakes.

Though described somewhat tersely in my guidebook as a 'commercial centre', which doubtless it is, Klagenfurt's Old Town is an assembly of restored pastel-hued fairytale buildings from a variety of periods. But it was the atmosphere of this quite small and compact city that delighted me; I felt completely at home as I roamed the friendly streets. And the youth hostel situated between the town and the lake was the most palatial and amicable I had so far sampled.

Rail travel in Carinthia's alpine environment is a treat in itself; the high Alps of the Tauern are a sightseeing delight so, tired of cities, I caught a local train to little St Veit an der Glan, amongst wooded hills backed by alpine splendour. For me it was something of a holiday again as I took myself striding out into the hills, an endeavour I capped by a hefty meal at the chief hostelry where I spent the night in a non-hostel bed.

A couple of further trains transported me to Graz, the mountain views en route keeping me glued to the coach windows for much of the way. Again this city is dismissed as 'commercial', even 'industrial' in some guidebooks. However, I found it to be an enchanting place crammed with historic interest. The town lies astride the River Mur and encircles the impressive Schlossberg, a combined castle and palace atop an outcrop of rock that has proved more than useful as a defensive strongpoint over the centuries. The views from the summit across the red roofs of the Old Town, plus the strange *Uhrturn*, a huge four-faced clock tower equipped with a four-ton bell, make the steep climb worthwhile (there is a funicular for softies). A victorious Napoleon, warding off Turkish invaders, dismantled the ramparts but spared the clock in return for a substantial ransom.

The back streets of the city form a medieval maze of shops; a treasure-trove of possible (but unlikely) bargains reminding me of The Lanes of my own Brighton. And where the shops give out are picturesque arcaded courtyards, proud portals and secret stairs that have to be ferreted out. One such jewel found, another lies awaiting; my stroll through this old quarter made for a perambulation into the past, a fact that dawned upon me only when I noted that the hour and minute hand of the *Uhrturn* moved anticlockwise.

And time, for me, in the real world was running out so I set myself once more homeward, determined not to be deflected further off the route. A brace of EC trains obliged by carrying me to touristy, expensive Salzburg which demanded to be seen for its architectural flamboyance. This at least offered reason to catch a night express into Germany and so save a hotel bill.

I even won a few moments of sleep prior to gaining Hanover for a station breakfast. And so back to The Netherlands but not before the border township of Bad Bentheim had, damn it, interrupted my homeward bolt. So often had I had my passport examined at its station that I determined to see what the place it

was like. I was not disappointed. Lying in the shadow of a substantial castle, Bad Bentheim, as its title suggests, is a village spa, a fact of which few outside of Germany, and maybe Holland, are aware. A night in the comfortable town centre youth hostel and I was away again.

Rotterdam was my farewell and I might have ignored it but for a Dutch doctor in my compartment who insisted that I take a look at his city, and then virtually frog-marched me into its centre, pointing out the sights. Amsterdam may look back on its past with pride but Rotterdam, mortally wounded early in the Second World War, resolutely looks forward; it is a vibrant city of the future and I'm glad I stopped there for a day. I had intended catching the daytime Hook–Harwich ferry but the night service would serve just as well: and save another hotel bill.

Back at Harwich it was quite a shock to have to buy a rail ticket, the interrail pass not being valid in the country of origin. And to add to the shock, the train was more than half an hour late getting into London's Liverpool Street station.

Not everyone would consider such a concentrated rail marathon as I carried out within a three-week period, and I wouldn't blame them. But my objective was to test the pass on the railways of Europe and to prove my assertion that it is the biggest bargain in concessionary rail travel of all time. The more one uses it, the bigger the bargain. For my torturous perambulation over the rail networks of 16 countries it owed me nothing.

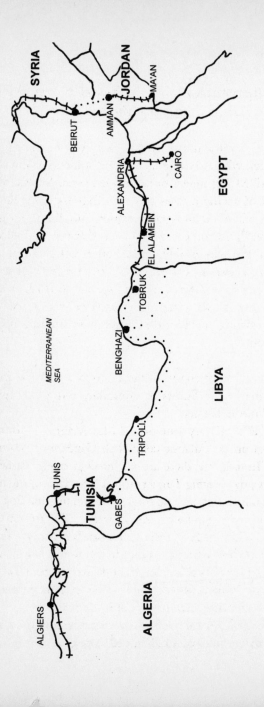

Mediterranean Circuit: Trans-North Africa and the Orient

Dreams of pushing uninterrupted railway lines and services to and through whole continents have a disquieting habit of never being fulfilled. Yet international express conceptualists were on the brink of seeing a Paris to Cairo Express enter the world timetables when war brought the notion tumbling to the ground.

The conceived route has long been that via the Balkans and the Levant but why should consideration not be given, I asked myself, to an alternate one that could run via the North African coast? To answer my own question I set out, in 1972, on a circuit of the Mediterranean – itself a challenge to be accepted – intent on using existing operational railways in an attempt to find out just why not.

Paris to Algeciras by means of the Intercity and Talgo Expresses brought me to the Straits of Gibraltar, and a decrepit ferry deposited me at Tangier.

There is a railway line across the Maghreb connecting Casablanca on the Atlantic coast with Gabès way down in the south of Tunisia, but there are no through trains. In fact, only two trains a day leaving Tangier stop at Sidi Kacem, the junction of the main line, but once on this eastbound line the first town is one that simply has to be investigated. William Lithgow, a Scotsman, wrote of Fez in the seventeenth century: 'There are some 12,000 allowed brothel houses in this towne, the Courtezans being neatly kept.' That was one man's observation. I had neither the time nor the inclination to confirm this statement, but a quick visit to this amazing town could not be denied.

To look upon Fez for the first time is a devastating experience. Clinging to the sides of a hill-ringed valley, all of it is visible as

one approaches from the new town and the spectacle is strangely disturbing. There is something unnatural about those densely packed houses, jostling and crowding one another within its outer walls.

If its exterior is disturbing, what lies inside is positively frightening. A quick visit is a hopeless quest; at least one day is needed to traverse the city, and another to find a way out. Moulay Idris knew what he was doing when he founded the city in AD 808; an invading enemy was likely to soon give up in the maze of streets.

Girding my loins I plunged recklessly into them to be confronted by anonymous walls of mosques and dwellings. These streets, that are more passageways than streets, defeat everything on wheels. There is no pattern. Occasionally I darted into a dark alley that breached the inhospitable walls to behold evil slums and magnificent palaces, often side by side in a contradiction of architecture and human behaviour. Near the centre of this confusion I came upon the city's oldest district where the souks break out in a rash of selling, arguing, hammering, carving, stitching, each thoroughfare specialising in a trade or product. To find my way back to the railway I was forced to pay for the services of a guide, which of course is a regular source of income for the lower strata of Fez citizenry.

That night was to be the first of many on the tiles. There were, again, only two trains eastwards out of Fez and both selected tortuous hours between midnight and the dawn to effect their departing.

The Moroccan railway, like its Algerian and Tunisian counterparts, is somewhat thin on the ground. Even after 30 years of independence from the French, Morocco had not added a single mile of line to the network left by them. In general the main line steers clear of mountain and desert and follows the coast; it is the only rail route between the two capitals of Rabat and Tunis via a third, Algiers; a distance of 1,300 miles. Yet in spite of this I found

it to be a despised railway, only fit for local travel by the *fellahin* (peasants), I was told. I was soon to learn why.

The train that drew in from Casablanca was well-loaded with spread-eagled humanity and to acquire a square inch of seat involved much manipulation of inert bodies, but Arabs sleep like the dead and will accept considerable buffeting before consciousness brings growls of wrath down on one's head.

We moved at a comfortable pace. But other factors ordained a very long night. The coach was cold and draughty, someone had removed my seat cushion for a pillow and the headrest protruded into the back of my neck. At intervals a dirty foot, emerging from a fragment of equally dirty sock, found its way on to my knees.

Streaks of yellow showed on the black palette of the sky when we stopped at Taza. Here the Atlas massif all but meets the Rif; only a narrow corridor permitting a thoroughfare to the East. This is the 'invasion corridor' through which first Arab, then Moorish conquerors marched to dominate the Maghreb. On a hill commanding the crucial gap sits Taza. Today it is a somnolent backwater; gateway in one direction to the steppe and desert of inner Morocco, and in the other the oft-troubled border with Algeria. The railway serves the new town of Taza Bas, pointedly ignoring the more inaccessible old city of Taza Haut that broods about its crowded houses, mosques and citadel.

Daylight showed a bleak countryside of near desert in an unseemly shade of pink. Wadis – deep chaps in the parched earth – cut across the steppe. Only cacti and tough clumps of desert grass could, inexplicably, hold on to life, though as if to disprove the point a rare stream or irrigation ditch drew a strip of cultivation around it. Bedouin tents and little groups of mud dwellings proved that humans too could live on next to nothing. Gliding in the clear air or foraging on the sandy soil, storks and cranes were other signs of life, but in those dismal surroundings they looked to me like vultures.

To complete this picture of doom there came into sight a great mound of rock rising high and sheer above the plain. Upon it squatted the Kasbah of Taourirt. An amazing conglomeration of buildings without plan or design, it was built in feudal days to house the Glaoui family and their retainers. The thing scowled at me as it does at all who pass this way.

Most of the complement of my compartment left at Taourirt, which gave me a couple of hours to iron out the creases in my neck and posterior. I made the best of it.

The wild, scrubby country continued to Oujda, a pleasant market town bordering Algeria. The border itself was open, though its guardians acted as if it wasn't. British nationals then did not require a visa, but that failed to discourage the immigration officials from trying to sell me one at an exorbitant price, and when I stood up for my rights it resulted in a savage search of my baggage.

Algerian trains were, if anything, less hygienic than Moroccan ones. Ruled by France from 1840 to 1960, Algeria was treated as a department of that country and given railways accordingly. Built to standard gauge, the trains ran with a speed and efficiency admired by many countries. However, with the departure of the French the conditions deteriorated. The coach of my Oran-bound 'express' contained one compartment minus a window, and in another somebody had removed the seats. What remained was old, worn-out and dirty. Along the way train wrecks proclaimed their rusty message of a revolution of years past.

Geographically, Algeria is a country of magnificence. Five times larger than Morocco, it contains majestic mountains and is fettered to a desert that sweeps southwards for 1,300 miles. Both its early history and geography are closely bound to that of Morocco and Tunisia, the whole fabric of the Maghreb being the fruit of a lengthy maturing, evolved through a thousand years of Arab-Moslem history which was itself rooted in some five-hundred years of existence as a Roman colony. Archaeologists speak of the

Maghreb as one of the Earth's oldest known inhabited areas. My attention to the passing terrain was diverted by an almighty row taking place between my neighbour, a rating of the Algerian Navy and a potential invader of the already full compartment. It appeared that, according to the intruder's reckoning, two children counted as less than one adult. Both were Berbers but obviously not of the same tribe since they shouted and swore at one another in different tongues, occasionally mixing in a little basic French. I'm certain they would have come to blows in the compartment had not the door been slammed between them, thus precipitating a fight in the corridor. This because the slam caught the finger of a third party, an onlooker who mistook the circumstances and so joined in the mêlée.

We were now back in alpine country amongst the Tlemcen Mountains, an extension of the foothills of the coastal Atlas, the Atlas Tellien. Small patches of cultivation forced from the red soil were interspersed with desert scrub and the ubiquitous cactus. Old men, young men, children and women with gold coins dangling from their heads watched goats in the cold and the rain. A flock of cranes swooped on a plough pulled by lumbering oxen.

Between Tlemcen and Sidi bel Abbés the railway enters the Atlas with a vengeance, attacking its brown crags with commendable gusto. The views were dramatic, the gradients considerable and the bends hairpin. It was all too much for one heavily-veiled lady in the compartment who began to exhibit sure signs of imminent vomiting. I pointed hastily to the window at which she promptly threw up. Unfortunately she didn't have time to open it.

At the Foreign Legion town of Sidi bel Abbés, looking Beau-Geste-like even in the rain, the mountains surrendered to both the railway's onslaught and a depressing plain. But a glimpse of the sea made amends as we rolled into Algeria's second city and port. I had half a day and an evening in which to sample the delights or otherwise of Oran. It is a busy commercial centre, old

and strongly fortified with massive walls, forts and kasbahs rearing upwards from an otherwise European-looking city.

'You must see the Ouled Nail girls,' advised a young Berber with whom I was sitting in a dockside café. I expressed interest, as any male would, and he went on to explain. Originating from a nomadic Arab tribe living in the foothills of the Atlas, the girls were brought up to be prostitutes and dancers, leaving their homes when barely in their teens to earn their wedding dowry. Ten or twelve years later, this task accomplished, they returned to their mountain villages to perform their final mission in life: the bringing of children into the world for the same profession. A mournful tale, but the dancing, he said, was exquisite and he gave me an address where I could watch it.

But I had another night train to catch so I had to miss out on the Ouled Nail girls. Instead I was caught up in charade that was being performed at Oran station where local travellers had a trick up their sleeves for ensuring seats in an invariably overcrowded train. Just before the whistle blew a rumour swept through the coaches that the train on the neighbouring track was the express for Algiers. In a flash, the corridor-standers were off, followed by bemused occupiers of seats, including me, in a whirlwind of baggage. But, of course, the train opposite is going nowhere and by the time this becomes apparent all the original seats have been taken by the rumour-mongers.

For me the disaster was mitigated by my fellow victims. A mixture of North African nationalities, they were a delightful bunch and I ended up with a bearded, if ever so slightly verminous, Bedouin on the corridor floor wrapped in the man's *djellabah* which was voluminous enough for both of us.

It is from the sea that Algiers presents its fairest face. Arriving by train one is taken on a tour of its port and industrial regions and ejected a long way from the centre. The station was a much lesser

building than that of Oran, and it was plain to me that Algiers, too, spurns its railway.

In need of a wash I followed the example of a cluster of soldiers who, stripped to the waist, were making use of a locomotive watering appliance. We scrubbed each other's backs, shared my battery electric razor and, refreshed, went our way. Mine was into the city.

I discovered Algiers to be a big brute of a place with some pleasing, elegant and even spectacular corners. Its face showed a sequence of white steps and terraces rising from the water's edge and backed by splendid buildings. Behind this rose the vivid green of the Sahel Hills. But I found Algiers to be two-faced. The Arabs may call it a diamond set in a frame of emeralds, but it was a pretty rough diamond. I had no time to venture far into the famed kasbah, but what I saw gave a foretaste: narrow streets, slippery with garbage, loud with aggressive vendors and high with offensive smells led into a rabbit warren of squalor.

The modern city was a complete contrast. Broad avenues built by the French, fine public buildings, luxury hotels and chic shops of not quite Boulevard Haussmann finesse. Somewhere in between lay the real Algiers.

My onward journey took me out of this urban pot-pourri to a far more enticing and nature-made entity: the violent eruption of the Atlas called the Massif du Djurdjura, a weird land of rocks weathered into preposterous shapes that led us towards Constantine.

With me in the new compartment was a young Algerian native of that city who was full of its marvels. We pooled our provisions and told each other of our respective home towns. My Sussex resort could raise a hill, but Constantine lay across a gorge. If the train was on time we should see the impressive Rhummel gorges and the delicate bridges that spanned them.

Of course, the train wasn't on time and it was nearly midnight when we reached the place. But a thoughtful moon obliged with

illumination more effective than sunlight and there, in stark relief, was the main gorge. With this giant cleft cutting the town in two, Constantine is a most impressive urban complex. It is very old and has withstood 80 sieges, which is not surprising when one notices that the town is guarded on three sides by ravines. My companion pointed out his university, but my eyes were for the Palace of the Beys that, for me, had come to life with his description of the harem protected by oft-replaced black women. These, and the older girls, were disposed of by being tied in bags and thrown into the gorge. Sometimes in a fit of do-it-yourself enthusiasm the Bey pushed them over, bagless, with his own hands.

Annaba received me in the middle of the night with a series of closed hotels. Annaba. A large sprawling city, but why hadn't I heard of it? Then I remembered. This was Bone, an agriculturally industrial city that was also a fine resort.

To stretch my legs I went for a walk. I was striding purposefully down the deserted main street when I was stopped by a posse of suspicious and heavily-armed police.

'Where was I going?' they wanted to know. 'Nowhere in particular,' had been my reply. Apparently nobody goes anywhere at 3.00 a.m. in Bone, so I was briskly returned by jeep to the station. But in the meantime, to keep out the strays, the gates had been locked, so for the rest of the night I had to doss down with the strays on the pavement outside.

The most dilapidated train of all rescued me from Annaba as dawn broke, and I was rattled through the majestic territory of Kabylia to Souk Ahras and the border with Tunisia at a commendably fast pace. There, my fellow-band of weary travellers and I were squeezed into the passport office of the station to await the convenience of an obnoxious policeman, who arrived in due course. He insisted on completing our exit forms himself to show, presumably, what a bright lad he was.

'Occupation?' he spat at me (having already misspelt my name).

'Pirate,' I replied facetiously, and watched as the word 'Pilot' went down on the form.

A big hunchbacked Berber took me into his confidence.

'They're all the same,' he whispered loudly. 'Jumped-up little thugs with uniforms and guns. We were better off under the French,' he went on. 'At least they were polite.'

The train crept into Tunisia and with red-hot eyes I looked upon a new country without great enthusiasm. One experience I'd missed in Algeria was that of an Algerian bed.

Even the Tunisians, with their knowledgeable handling of a considerable tourist industry, accepted no currency from their neighbouring state. Tourists were plainly not expected to arrive by rail; an oversight that was to the benefit of a band of ruffians who, with a great sense of the dramatic, changed my Algerian dinars into Tunisian dinars with considerable financial advantage to themselves.

The 118 miles of line between Ghardimaou and Tunis was narrow (metre) gauge, hence the practical reason for no direct connection between Algeria and Tunisia. Although a fraction of the size of its massive neighbour, Tunisia can boast almost as much track mileage. For a change my new train was clean and reasonably smart. Darkness overtook us for the second half of the journey, but before Beja I gained an impression of a gently rolling landscape with abruptly prosperous villages not afraid to come down from the hills.

The capital, when we reached it, was bright and civilised. And in Tunis I got my bed.

Continuing, the coastal run was by way of Hammamet, Sousse and Sfax, all geared to the whims and desires of the tourist. The train to Sfax was a joke. A jet-black locomotive producing prodigious amounts of smoke led us cheerfully along the shore, across the edge of the Bled and into the olive forest of Sfax. Our

coaches were spartan, badly sprung and communal. With me in mine were four men and a woman, and since everybody seemed to know everybody else it was like one big noisy family. Solemnly I was led from seat to seat to be introduced, hear a digest of the family fortunes and offer a version of my own. My name became Mister Porty; theirs, with individual variations, was Mohammed.

The man sitting opposite me possessed a transistor radio. Stations Tunis, Tripoli and possibly Baghdad poured out their wailing songs into that unlovely coach in a cacophony of competition with all the jabbering going on. Injected into this came another sound at irregular intervals. My neighbour, an unattractive little man in a badly-torn suit, had either 'got' religion or was an off-duty muezzin. Triggered by a particular musical note from the transistor, he would let fly a prolonged and blood-curdling howl of such volume as to drown the combined efforts of Tunis, Tripoli and Baghdad. Nobody took the slightest notice.

Between the howls there came an issue of cake. Arab cakes are sweet, syrupy and delicate. They do not travel well, particularly when lumped together in old newspapers and stuffed into overloaded baggage. What went the rounds was a gluey wreckage that still managed to retain its delicious flavour. The noisiest eater was, of course, our religious friend and his expression of gratitude must have deafened Allah.

The lone woman across from me said not a word during the whole five-hour journey. She was ignored by all. Just once she gave me a fleeting smile, a sort of near apology for the odd behaviour of her menfolk.

Sfax is a commercial city. I don't mean it has belching chimneys or rows of factories. It is, in fact, one of the most beautiful urban centres in Tunisia, but is an industrial city all the same. The fruits of its labour were visible long before we got there: olives by the million acre and belts of almonds, pomegranates and aromatic

plants and flowers, all of which Sfax puts to use. The air was heavy with the powerful aroma of exaggerated growth.

The town held little that was soft or seductive. Its great walls, spiky with merlons and pierced at intervals with embrasures for cannon, were workmanlike in themselves and provided frame and shade for the great variety of handicrafts going on at their base. Inside the walls the streets were heavy with sculptured doors and ornamental embellishment on gate and mosque. Sfax, it must be said, is a handsome city and its blatant prosperity a reward for centuries of unbroken toil.

From Sfax there were only two trains a day to Gabès. That I was nearing the end of the line was patently obvious. The railway authority of Tunisia virtually gave it up at Sfax, and what continued to Gabès was simply an expensive toy. Some bright spirit had built a track decades ago and industrious Sfax was not going to be the one to terminate a labour of love, so, since two trains a day (I notice there are currently three) kept the rails clear of sand, the service continues.

The Sahara invades Tunisia from the West, coming in like a tide via the great salt lakes or *chotts* that almost cut the country in two. It clogs the valleys near Gafsa, brushes the foothills of the high steppes, and around Gabès rivulets of sand dribble to the sea. Huge herds of camels dot a landscape that doesn't know if it's a desert or a steppe, but civilisation continued to be represented, if only by Arab children spending their days looking after camels and making obscene gestures at our toy train. The two coaches were nearly empty and the loneliness of the desert reached out to touch me.

I don't know where I got the idea that Gabès was a town. It looked a sizeable place on the map and gives a bay a name. And it *could* have been bigger if one rolled all its bits and pieces together. As it was, there was simply a collection of untidy villages, a cinema standing incongruously in the middle of nowhere, and a rash of petrol stations. Probably for the traveller from the South, Gabès,

with its tufts of date palms, offers the first faint promise of a greener land. Rank thickets of apricots, pomegranates, tobacco, henna and bananas cuddle the inland springs, defending this last oasis from the drying action of the sun. Once Gabès was the northern limit of Tripolitania and, as Roman Tacapae, the terminus and wholesale market of the Saharan slave trade. Fragments of history form part of the living of today, the market-place sporting a grandiose portico of Roman columns entirely out of place and proportion. But the heart of Gabès is dust, boredom and the end of the line.

One of the finest institutions in North Africa and the Middle East is the *servis*. Cheaper than a taxi, more personal than a bus, the *servis* runs between two points touting for customers at its point of departure or along the way. The favourite vehicle of the *servis* driver is the Mercedes and its maximum complement is usually seven. The subsequent 1,500 miles of my journey I was to travel, largely, by this mode of vehicle.

I picked up my first *servis* in a back street in Gabès. Perhaps it would be more accurate to say that it picked up me. A string of placenames was flung at me by the local *servis* agent: Turns, Sfax, Gafsa, Nefta, Ben Gardane. I recognised Ben Gardane as the township close to the Libyan border and held up my hand.

Squeezed between two bearded Arabs, I was whirled out of Gabès in a cloud of dust. At the checkpoint at Ben Gardane we picked up a policeman. There being no seat space available, he sat on my knee to solemnly tell me that, even with a visa, the Libyans would not let me over the border.

'But the English is coming with *me*,' announced one of my companions. 'He will accompany us to Tripoli on my lorry.' This was news to me, though I didn't see how it affected the visa situation.

In a region of *ghorfas* – cave-cell indented crag summits – and empty horizons the Libyan border station makes almost as much

impact as does the El Jem amphitheatre out on the Tunisian plain. Suddenly a palace of chromium-plate and marble stood before me, rising like a genie from the dust. However, its promising appearance was deceptive. Inside was a chaos of confusion – which might have been the reason why I got by. We had dropped off the pessimistic policeman and my potential new chauffeur accompanied me to the window where our passports had to be shown. The new authority was not exactly rude or unpleasant, their minions simply insisting upon going through the rigmarole of officialdom with heavy-handed precision. Everyone wanted to know my father's name.

Outside it had begun to rain. Also outside was the lorry. It was a boneshaker of great antiquity with a Morris Cowley bonnet. The buck was piled high with crates of live chickens. A man in the cab grinned a welcome. The question arose as to where I was going to sit, as if I didn't know.

Tripoli was all of 125 miles away. The rain was of the solid North African variety. Though the surface of the road was smooth tarmac and noticeably superior to what had gone before, the lorry contrived to move with a most peculiar gait that had me rolling about on top of the heaving crates even while clinging to a handhold as far from the edge as possible. It was one hell of a ride.

Somewhere along the way, out in the wet darkness, was Sabratha. Sabratha was an ancient city of Africa founded in the sixth century BC by Tyrian settlers and flourished under the Phoenicians. Though but a satellite of Carthage, its excavated remains are the more magnificent. But with water dripping down my neck my interest was, to say the least, tepid.

We lurched into Tripoli at about midnight. I was dropped outside what was alleged to be a new hotel, so new that it hadn't yet opened. I wandered miserably down the road puzzling over a scintillating array of neon signs that spoke only Arabic. I forced

open the door of what looked like a factory to enquire the whereabouts of a completed hotel.

'This *is* a hotel,' came the reply.

I was to see much of Tripoli over the next two days. Ancient Oea to the archaeologist, Tarablus-al-Gharb to the Arabs, Tripoli is the only city in what the Phoenicians called the 'Land of the Three Cities' to have survived and prospered. The other two, Sabratha and Leptis Magna, have died, and in their dying they settled permanence upon a town that has become capital of Libya.

More Western than Arab, the city has grown up around a lush oasis situated on a promontory extending into the sea. The residential area had spread along a broad palm-shaded boulevard facing a ship-infested port, while the inevitable old quarter, with its narrow streets of trades and approached by way of the castle and the Arch of Marcus Aurelius, was the cleanest and most un-North African I had seen. In the centre of new Tripoli lay the king's palace; no longer a palace and so, since a revolutionary colonel could hardly have the nerve to live there, was something of a white elephant.

Tripoli to Benghazi is about 650 miles. Yet these *servis* drivers made the journey nearly every day or night of their lives. Admittedly the roads were good and traffic light, but it was still quite a performance bearing in mind that a lot of the way lay across open desert with special hazards of its own.

There is no railway in Libya, but this is not to say that it has always been a trainless nation. Once there were four independent sections of line, totalling some 230 miles. Fragments can still be found but for long Libyans have put their faith in roads, many built for them by Mussolini's Fascist Italians.

And for me it was the road again, and a heavy dose of it at that. By the time my *servis* driver had got himself two more clients – a minimum long-distance load – it was dark. We stopped at Horns, close to the remains of Leptis Magna, and consumed a hearty meal in a simple stone restaurant that might have been part of the

celebrated ruins. The driver was a close friend of the owner and his family, so we ate in style in their cosy kitchen-living-room seated around an ancient stove, while outside rain beat upon the tin roof.

The rain gave way to wind, a hot searing torrent of air called the *ghibli* which stirs up the vast sandy wastes. In compensation, the moon rolled out from behind departing clouds to illuminate the desert in all its awful desolation. We bowled through palm-fringed Misurata to enter the Syrtic Desert, an arid crescent lacking in fresh water but immeasurably rich in crude oil. Beyond Sirte our progress was made slow and painful by the appearance on the tarmac of hard-packed wedges of sand blown across by the howling wind. Each had to be circumvented or driven over in bottom gear, while all the time a mist of sand crept into the car and stung our eyes.

At intervals we came upon lone transport cafés, little concrete structures hugging petrol stations, welcoming and brightly lit in the oppressive solitude. Here we drank beakers of mint tea in the company of other travellers of the night while flying sand lashed the walls as, earlier, the rain had lashed the roofs, to turn strangers into friends.

Entering from the desert is not the most flattering approach to the second city of Libya. This is reserved for the sea and the air, the latter ending with a drive along an impressive dual carriageway sweeping into the centre from Benina Airport. We more humble travellers entered by the back door through an odorous suburb mean of streets muddied by the recent rain.

Most towns are built on or by a hill, astride a river or at the head of a valley. Benghazi's only claim to a geographical raison d'être is that it is by the sea. Dead-flat desert and salt marshes stretch away on three sides. The place suffered cruelly during the fighting of the Second World War, changing hands five times in all before the British and Allied forces finally drove out the combined Italian and German armies in November 1942. The

scars had healed, leaving it a surprisingly attractive town overlooking its harbour across a wide sweep of promenade.

I left Benghazi oblivious of the fact that I would be returning there within a very few days. My vehicle was again a *servis*, my destination Tobruk. There were six of us tucked inside an old Packard and the driver said he could do the 310 miles in five hours including stops. I didn't believe him, but he did.

When I mention to any Eighth Army veteran that I spent a couple of days voluntarily in Tobruk, he invariably asks what the hell I want to do that for. But the place is not that bad. I arrived in a sandstorm, though the short streets and small shops were strangely peaceful, as if the 1942 siege had been lifted but yesterday. A taxi driver, asking no fee, insisted upon driving me to the military cemetery outside the town. Maybe my blond sand-caked hair deceived him, for it was to the sombre German cemetery I was taken. To make amends the good man took me to the beautifully kept British cemetery containing 8,000 graves, and would have thrown in the French one too, given half a chance.

The furthest east anyone wanted to go was Bardia. The town's *servis* agent eventually managed to persuade four lost souls to go there, and squeezed another half a Libyan pound out of me for the extra 12 miles to the Egyptian border, where seemingly nobody at all went.

The main road bypasses Bardia, but we had to go into the town to drop off the four clients. A slap-happy dusty place, it put me in mind of the film setting for *High Noon*. At Urn Sa'ad, in a slight dip of land that likes to think of itself as a pass – the once-famous Halfaya Pass – a Libyan policeman checked my passport and waved me on. The border station between Libya and Egypt was not quite so grandiose as that between Libya and Tunisia; its inmates, however, were more relaxed with seemingly little to do. Plainly transitees between the two countries were a rarity. A Libyan emigration officer searched my bag, counted my money and cancelled my visa. A little further on at a large ramshackle shed

an Egyptian official searched my bag, counted my money and then discovered that I was British.

'The land border here is closed to foreigners,' I was told with great firmness, and his statement went a long way to confirming a notion that I'd tried to put to the back of my mind for some time as, currently, Egypt was at war with Israel and certain restrictions were placed on entry to the country.

'The Libyan authorities should not have let you pass. You'll have to go back.'

But Libyan authority wasn't having me back. They had devalidated my visa and processed me out of their territory. Without another visa from their embassy in Cairo or London or somewhere equally inaccessible, I couldn't return. I was a non-person. Nobody wanted me.

The Egyptians were adamant that I couldn't go forward either.

'There's a war on,' they explained.

'Yes, but that's on the next border.'

'It doesn't matter. All border zones are forbidden to non-Arabs.'

'What's to be done then? I'm here now, so you might as well let me through.'

But it was not to be. Only recently I'd read a newspaper report of a stateless man being shuttled between Britain and France for weeks because neither country would accept him. Did the same fate lie in store for me? In the event my initial sojourn on Egyptian soil lasted the best part of a day, the time it took to coerce Libyan authority into taking me back. And it could well have been longer had I not been making such enthusiastic inroads into Egyptian police rations and their stocks of cold lager while they held me under loose guard in and around the border post. Except for the disappointment of having to break my circuit, I quite enjoyed my enforced detention; everybody was exceedingly kind, one officer in particular who, I think, fancied me.

With some difficulty – for there was a marked lack of *servis* vehicles going west from the border – I got back to Benghazi

from whence a jet whisked me to Cairo. This section of the journey was something of a bore, for I had been looking forward to further train riding, if not from the railhead at Soloum then at least Mersa Matruh. But I was not going to accept things as they stood. Once in the Egyptian capital I would backtrack by rail to cover the territory denied me by my abrupt about-turn.

Cairo is huge, impressive, historic, traffic-jammed and inflicted with a howling poverty. I lost myself in the Mouski on my first night. At first this was amusing. Everywhere in the evil little streets men were earnest in the pursuit of money. There was little friendliness, but no hostility. A man without legs tried to entice me into his shop by pulling at me from a tabletop. A dumb child, for the price of a duty-free cigarette, led me in the direction of what he thought would be Ataba Square, but succeeded only in losing himself too. A policeman shrugged at my attempt to elicit information and a soldier confided to me, with much expressive drawing in the air, where the most voluptuous girls were to be hired. I walked many miles that night.

My second morning I returned to the trains.

A strange method of acquiring tickets greeted me at Cairo Main Station that had me scampering from one kiosk to another collecting an assortment of pieces of paper deemed necessary for rail travel to Alexandria. Porters and touts were quick to smell out a foreigner, and I was directed from pillar to post by a retinue of little men all clamouring for reward. One had an original line in rackets.

'Foreigners need a special permit to travel,' he told me. 'I'll get one for you,' and away he ran. But I followed him to a crowded railway transport office where I watched him pause, draw a piece of paper from a sheaf in his jacket pocket and return. I looked the man in the eye and smiled grimly. He had the grace to smile back sheepishly and I gave him three cigarettes for his initiative.

My train, I found, was air-conditioned and occupied mostly by businessmen. Not my sort of train at all. The 129-mile journey, normally of two and a half hours, took three. It was also dull. Dull, that is, except for the panoply of the green, cultivated Nile Delta with its palms and exaggerated lushness through which the silver-coached so-called express, headed by its heavily-armoured diesel unit, sped importantly. As well as air-conditioning there were sun visors and smoky-blue windows and uniformed waiters who dispensed refreshments at the flick of two fingers. I yearned for my broken carriages and verminous Bedouins.

The Nile came into sight between Tanta and Damanhûr when the train rolled across a large bridge spanning the wide main stream. Thereafter a system of canals criss-crossed the flat countryside and high-masted *feluccas* glided disconcertingly across the fields. Alexandria I found to be something of a sham. The seafront was modern, impressive and European. Graceful stone buildings and slender mosques pleased the eye. The old city was long ago destroyed and buried by desert sands that lap at the doorstep. In its place had appeared the standard Egyptian phenomenon: mean streets and unsavoury smells.

My request for a ticket was greeted with patient resignation. The man behind the grill indicated a notice in Arabic and English above my head.

'Special permission has to be granted by the Government to go to or beyond Mersa Matruh,' dictated the man in case I couldn't read.

I asked how far I *could* go. There was a brief consultation in the ticket-office. It was clear that not many Britons used the Western Desert line. A consortium of officials decided I could go as far as El Dabaa. I wasn't sure where El Dabaa was, but decided it would do.

My train was pure Arab. No businessmen's special this, and no pretences of being an express either. Instead it was a happy little train of village elders and merchants who could afford the

run into Alex at regular intervals. After an initial show of distrust I was accepted into the brotherhood and invited to tea.

Out in the desert there was a sudden cleansing. The stone walls of Amriya and Hamman were bleached white by the sun, while nomad tents studded the sand to lend a romantic air. One small station name held more impact than the others, an impact quite lost upon my chattering companions. But why should they bother themselves about a place called El Alamein? To them it was just another hamlet in which to eke out their days. To me, as a soldier, but not in the famed 1942 battle, there arose a feeling of trespass.

I did not alight at El Alamein because its dunes and depressions would have meant nothing to me. Instead I continued to El Dabaa, another hamlet that could have been El Alamein, Amtiya or Hamman. I tramped its sand-blown, uneven street and drew curious stares, for not even old soldiers come to El Dabaa. Thereafter the road and railway passes through territory of a dying fame. Names like Fouka, Mersa Matruh and Sidi Barrani are its roll of honour.

But for me El Dabaa was the end of the ride. About 180 miles of desert separated me from Soloum and the point of my fractured land journey. Perhaps I could have wangled my way through. In fact I'm sure I could, for rules and regulations in the desert get worn by sand. Instead I called it a day and returned the way I had come to Alexandria and Cairo. I must have had indigestion for all at once I was eager for a new country.

The new country was the Hashemite Kingdom of Jordan. It wasn't on my planned itinerary but it was the route I had to take. This came about through my failed endeavour to pass through the territory of Israel, a forlorn attempt that got me only as far as the Suez Canal which I managed to reach by local train from Cairo by dodging various checkpoints. Finally, my onward progress was firmly bulked at the hands of a slightly ruffled colonel of military

transportation who wanted to know how the hell I'd got that far in the first place. 'Didn't you know there was a war on?' he barked.

Thus I was forced into the air once more, this time to Jordan. After teeming Egypt, little Jordan was a comparative oasis of peace. Actually, the kingdom is not so little, but its cosiness gives that impression. At Amman Airport policemen dressed as British bobbies took me in hand and fixed me up with hotel accommodation.

Jordan contained the sandy beaches of Aqaba, the rose-red city of Petra, the Dead Sea shared with Israel and a toehold in divided Jerusalem, but the big attraction for me was the Hedjaz Jordan Railway. I was now too far south of any embryo Cairo–Paris line, but the new country into which I had been deflected promised some interesting trains. And the promise was not a false one.

It came about through my hotel, a modest hostelry near the centre of Amman. And it was while I was laying bare my life history as demanded by the registration form that I mentioned to the manager the fact that I was acquainted with the current Jordanian queen; a wild exaggeration since actually it was my father who had once met Colonel Gardner of Ipswich, near my former home town, who was Queen Muna's father. Before I realised what was happening, the man had phoned the palace and received, on my behalf, an invitation to breakfast the next day. My wardrobe, or what there was of it reposing unwashed and crumpled in my small bag, was far from fit for a royal breakfast so I borrowed the manager's trousers.

Following a well-earned night's sleep, I presented myself at the palace adorned in my only reasonably clean shirt and a pair of oversize trousers that periodically threatened to drop to my ankles. The breakfast was substantially British, the meeting with King Hussein and Queen Muna fleeting, the conversation with Colonel and Mrs Gardner prolonged. Having divulged the reason for my visit to Jordan I came away with the offer of no less than the freedom of the Hedjaz Jordan Railway.

In consequence I found myself ensconced in the cab of a gigantic black oil-burning Japanese-made locomotive at Amman station heading a 20-wagon train bound for the terminus of the southbound line at Ma'an, close to the Arabian border. Having taken me for a senior British Railway's driver I was invited to take over the controls, but wriggled out of this situation without losing face by explaining that I was trained only to operate diesel and electric traction. So, in the spirited company of a Jordanian driver, his fireman, a guard and a character brandishing an old Lee Enfield rife – designated as our anti-aircraft protection against marauding Israeli aircraft and guerrilla infiltrators – I took my appointed place on the footplate for one of the rail highlights of my then 60-year career. We performed various loading and unloading tasks en route, though much of the journey was taken up with tea and chat with the garrulous trackside staff along the line.

At each halt these railway employees were invited by the driver to make the acquaintance of the crack BR driver from the United Kingdom and close friend of their royal family. This invariably produced more tea and a great deal of handshaking with smiles and bows all round. I'm ashamed to say that I revelled in my new-found status.

Between these lineside receptions I was given control of the train in spite of the fact that I hadn't the faintest idea of what I was doing, though the locomotive appeared to have no great objections to my lever-pulling and handle-turning. At the tiny village of Qatrana we stopped to greet another reception committee, and on a section of double track await the passing of a northbound train. A few miles away stood the celebrated ruins of Petra, the most sensational of archaeological sites, but my allegiance that day as we trundled into Ma'an was to the railway. Petra would have to wait.

A night in a railway hostel of shambolic condition and I was back in Amman, my conscience prescribing that I cease playing

trains and resume my circuit. The northern section of the Hedjaz Jordan Railway into Syria was closed by one of the frequent disputes, inflated by war, arising between the two nations, so it had to be a *servis* again that conveyed me to the border. But this one, at Dera'a, was closed too. However, I was learning the ropes so that when one official denied me passage I simply hung around until another came on duty who approved of my face and let me through.

My *servis* driver on the Syrian side was a jovial Palestinian who claimed to be the father of 16 children but was outshone by a passenger boasting of 18. The road accompanied the railway with trains conspicuous by their absence.

Damascus, they say, is the oldest continuously inhabited city in the world, as it is said of half a dozen others in the Middle East, but it matters not at all. The city is alive with biblical reminders and old Damascus is a step backwards into a school divinity class. The most celebrated building is probably the Omayyad Mosque, but it was the way to it that fascinated me. In the bazaar of the old city you have mankind and womankind, as you may never hope to see it again. Within the hubbub of the souks were white-turbaned Druses from the mountains, Bedouin women jangling with necklaces and coin earrings, and the true desert Arab in his *kaffiyah* headgear with the colour of his tribe woven into the cords. Over the narrow passageways of the souks were roofs of corrugated iron sheets offering stark contrast to the abrupt appearance of the great mosque itself, a classical vision of Greco-Roman architecture formed from the Temple of Jupiter that once stood upon the site.

I suppose it was inevitable that I should end up at Damascus railway station. I went there at the instigation of a friendly airline clerk at PanAm's booking office who claimed close acquaintanceship with the deputy station-master. And it was only

through this tenuous connection that I could hope to catch a train of some sort to Beirut.

A narrow-gauge railway linked the Syrian and Lebanese capitals. It was a goods-only line and I'd seen its Lebanese end three years previously. Occasional goods trains plied the single track through the mountains and it was upon one of these that I pinned my hopes. Alas, here I could brandish no royal or presidential names to further my case, but even so, the deputy station-master was impressed with my enthusiasm, and possibly my cheek, so promised to do something about it.

I duly reported to his office next day as requested, but no train to Beirut of any sort put in an appearance. Neither did the deputy station-master. I gave it up as a bad job and made tracks for the *servis* station.

The road to Beirut was a surprisingly fine undertaking, splendidly engineered and supported by magnificent scenery. All of which encouraged the speed cravings of both Syrian and Lebanese drivers. On that Friday afternoon the road was a battleground of drivers released from offices and the pile-ups were legion; I saw two smoking wrecks within the first ten minutes of the drive. A huge cement plant thrust its ugliness into the beauty of mountain and forest, while a rash of tin-roofed restaurants lined the hairpin road out of Damascus.

On the crest of the Lebanese mountains the panorama of the Bekaa Valley held me breathless. The horizon was full of the long rampart of the Anti-Lebanon with snowcapped Mount Herman to the South, and at my feet a corrugated trough of waving grass. Orchards, villages and rich cereal fields extended to the limits of vision.

The frontier barriers between the two countries were some five miles apart. The great Arab unity proclaimed by Syrian propaganda posters seemed to have come unstuck here as machine and anti-tank gunners aimed their weapons convincingly into each

other's territory. Since my earlier visit to these parts, the whole region had erupted into either open or near-open war.

Traffic jams were as bad in Beirut as they are in London or Paris with, additionally, taxi and *servis* drivers exhibiting a wild addiction to courting death (there are few old or middle-aged taxi drivers in Beirut), and it was a startling sensation to be driven at speed by a young Levantine in his shirt-sleeves, one hand on the wheel, while with the other he gestured – usually rudely – out of the open window at other drivers.

Having a cousin residing in the city, I stayed with him for a few days hearing his stories of the civil war afflicting the country. I was warned against undertaking much exploring in the torn streets, so contented myself with no more than local wanderings. On this trip wars seemed to be following me around.

From the Lebanese capital I attempted to do what I had done in Egypt and backtrack along the rail route denied me earlier. This involved a *servis* drive to beyond Tyre where I dodged two checkpoints and nearly found myself in Israel. But a miss is as good as a mile and I ended up, as you would expect, being ever so slightly arrested and returned to whence I came with a flea in my ear. If nothing else I had, for nearly 60 miles, followed closely the one-time coastal line constructed by British engineers between Beirut and Cairo, its broken sections still visible half-buried in the sand.

It was hardly surprising that nobody had heard of St Michael's station. It turned out to be little more than a wayside halt, yet it was the Grand Central of Beirut. But, this notwithstanding, it was a pleasure to be back aboard a train, even if the little red two-coach diesel was of minimum inspiration. We left the city by the tradesman's entrance, slinking out through a jungle of dilapidated tenements divided by mean refugee-choked streets and, on the seashore, filthy black beaches.

The working railway, or what there is of it, north of Beirut obviously took a back seat in Lebanese economic circles, but was

a fine vehicle and safer than the roads for viewing the sensational coastline. In unison with the *Corniche* road it took hairpin bends, ploughed through tunnels in the rock headlands and only strayed inland to avoid the seaside towns.

Banana palms growing on the shores of the tideless sea heralded ancient Byblos. A paradise for the excavator with its prehistoric, Phoenician, Roman and medieval sites in muddled array, it was the sea and the land that stole the show, particularly the rocky gorge down which the Dog River scampers. Near Tripoli – another Tripoli, this one the second city of Lebanon – we trundled past the terraced saltpans that turned the countryside into a chessboard with little iron windmills as its pawns.

Back in Syria we came to classical Emesa which is now Homs. Far older than its Libyan namesake, the modern blocks of flats compared no more favourably with its unimaginative minarets, 'square black towers of basalt' as someone called them. The market-place was full of Bedouins on a shopping spree from the desert.

If Homs was disappointing, the next city along the line made up for it. Hama sat astride the Orontes in a valley of blood-red soil sprouting great bursts of blossom. But what makes Hama unique is, of course, its water wheels. The creaking of the *norias*, as they are called, is something one becomes aware of the moment of entry into the town. The biggest is 120 feet across and it creaks and groans in a never-ending tortuous clamour as it lifts water into ancient aqueducts. Smaller ones dotted the Orontes valley around the town, each one groaning miserably. I asked a native of the town how he could stand the eternal racket. 'What racket?' he replied.

Across the great plains we stumbled through the granary of Syria – and stable, too, for here were reared some of the finest Arab horses. Then in the midst of boredom came the unique sight of the northern beehive villages. At first they were diluted with mud houses of standard pattern but eventually complete

communities of windowless beehive dwellings materialised, each housing one family.

The train ended its run at Aleppo. Here I was back once more on the Baghdad to Istanbul line. On the northbound Taurus Express the familiar stop at Adana felt like home ground. And home was calling loudly; I'd had enough wandering for the time being. Turkey, Greece, Bulgaria, Yugoslavia, Italy and France were the homeward stepping stones covered with no less hassle and no more incident than the previous occasion I had come this way. In France I could have closed the Mediterranean circuit more assiduously by following the rail route along the Riviera to Spain, but this would have been but a gesture. So I made straight for Paris where I had commenced the whole journey.

I had, I suppose, answered my own initial question. Maybe those Paris to Cairo Express conceptualists had better stick to the conceived and prescribed route laid down in their dream.

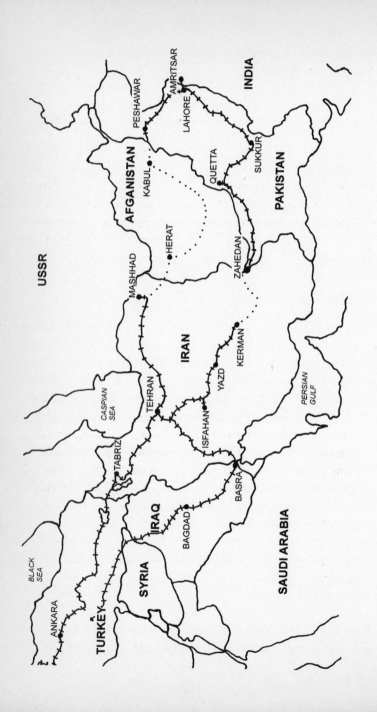

Trans-Asia

It is not, perhaps, universally realised that you can pick up a train at Calais and jog quietly and amusingly nearly all the way to the Taj Mahal and beyond by rail. Unfortunately the spotlight must be aimed firmly on the little word 'nearly'. The dream of a through train from Dover to Delhi has receded though, in point of fact, the mechanics of such a service have become simpler by virtue of certain track extensions currently being undertaken by Iran. There are, actually, two routes to India where the railway can offer a vehicle for a considerable proportion of the way. The more northerly of these is via Afghanistan, a trainless nation that sits stubbornly athwart the lines of Iran and Pakistan. To the south the gaps are narrowing. Some 30 miles of sand-embedded date palms and a considerable river are not insurmountable geographical barriers to a link-up between Iraq and Iran, while further east Iranian State Railways are already closing the gap between Yazd and the terminus of the Quetta line at Zahedan.

In 1973 I girded my loins with the requisites for a rough ride and set out to test both routes. My plan was to travel out via the traditional 'India route' to Teheran, continuing on the railwayless section across Afghanistan, then return on the more southerly route including the Baghdad 'detour'. At that time Afghanistan was not engulfed in war, but between Iran and Iraq there existed a hate that was about to ignite into one. Also then there had been no rail extension southwards towards Pakistan beyond the southern Iran town of Kerman. Given these conditions, my journey promised some eventful travelling, and I was not to be disappointed.

I saw little of Lake Van on my long slow ride across Turkey because the strictly non-express train was late and it was dark when it

arrived at Tatvan pier to catch the ferry across this considerable body of sometimes storm-afflicted water. Tabriz was my entry point to Iran. The city is, of course, famous for Persian carpets, many on sale in the bazaars of this capital of Azerbaijan province. I remained there a couple of days, which was the length of time it took me to obtain a compulsory seat reservation and await the then twice weekly Istanbul–Teheran express; the only rail service that ran between Tabriz and the capital.

In spite of the exalted nature of the new train, my compartment contained an assortment of Iraqis, an Australian, a roll of carpets and two live turkeys. The turkeys were persuaded to perch aloft on the luggage rack to make room for me. The goat came later.

For mile after mile the line ran parallel to the snowy rampart of the Elburz Mountains over a desolation of stone and sand, a land of no flowers and no birds. One town on route was Qazvin, once the Persian capital, as were Isfahan, Shiraz, Suleimanieh, Ardabil, Nishapur and Mashad (sometimes spelt 'Meshed'), Qazvin having its fling in the sixteenth century under the great Shah Abbas. Its blue domes and shrines offered a touch of capitalship to an otherwise nondescript town. The Australian in my compartment was a garrulous Queenslander on his way home after an itinerant year in Asia. When not talking to me he was noisily engaged in conflict with the Iraqi owner of the carpet roll that kept digging into his ribs.

The current Iranian capital, Teheran, made something of a relief. This basically modern city was the creation of Reza Shah. 'An opera house, a stock exchange and no camels,' he ordained, basing his idea on Ankara which was about the only other capital he had seen. But the opera house, faultily conceived, could not be completed and the stock exchange remained on the drawing board. The camels, however, vanished. Gone, too, were the old ramparts built chiefly with money sent from Europe for the Persian Relief Fund. The railway station into which I emerged,

liberally sprinkled with turkey droppings, was a grand affair though it served few trains.

I remained several days in the Iranian capital, raising little enthusiasm for it. Traffic-snarled and containing a lot of hideous art nouveau, as well as the occasional truly beautiful building, I was happy to leave. There were then only three trains a day to Mashad on which to do so, and I got lumbered with the slowest. Before 1939 Iran had no railway, but the Second World War brought in British and American railway builders who laid a line from the Persian Gulf through Teheran to the Russian frontier and the Caspian Sea which was to carry enormous freight loads supplying the Soviet Union with munitions. Things sprouted from there and the line across the edge of the Great Salt Desert towards Afghanistan was one such to blossom. Teheran could be described as the clearing house of the India route, since here one can go south towards Yazd and beyond to the Quetta line or, the way I was now going, towards Afghanistan.

While my overnight train skirted lonely Mount Damavand and the Great Salt Desert I joined my latest male companions on the corridor floor. This left our two veiled ladies with the privacy of the compartment. My European clothes made a poor substitute for the *chapan*, a garment so practical for train corridor travel, and once more I envied those who could find sleep in the most uncomfortable of situations.

At dawn the alarm clock of the morning call to prayer shivered down the train. Taken unawares I was overrun by scores of Allah-fearing stalwarts who, when we stopped at a wayside station, left the carriage to prostrate themselves upon the platform. Then, with devotions brought to an abrupt end by a blast from the impatient locomotive, I was pressed to accept various breakfast offerings by my companions. There was another halt at Nishapur and, a few miles ahead of this garden and park-ornamented town, a stir of interest indicated the modern abomination that is the tomb of Omar Khayyaám, revered by Persians young and old.

Mashad introduced itself with another cathedral of a station, this one marking the terminus of the Trans-Caspian Railway. Nearly but not quite did it eclipse the marvel of the golden dome and the palaces of this most holy city. The Tomb of the Imam Reza is the equivalent of Mecca for the Shi'ites, and to go with such distinction were buildings of sublime magnificence.

With the end of the line well over 500 miles away I elected to remain in the city a couple of days. The place owes its foundation to the burial there of Harun-er-Rashid of *Arabian Nights* fame, who died nearby. In the same tomb lie the bones of Reza, the eighth Imam who died after eating a bunch of poisoned grapes a year or two later. The holy buildings are firmly out of bounds to infidels and the likes of you and me which all adds to the mystique which had me, incautiously, dodging the guards to get a peek inside. I managed to sneak into the inner courtyard wearing a *djellabah* before being thrown out. I suppose I could well have had my throat cut. Mashad is that sort of place.

For the overlander the route eastwards is by road or nothing. There was a regular bus service to Taibar, the Iran-Afghan border town, and the road ran straight across a broad plain with blue and white mountains barring the horizon. By the roadside, as we left Mashad, were yellow irises, scarlet tulips and a dead camel.

Because of a poor connection and non-cooperation between the bus companies, it was necessary to spend a night in Taibar. And if it's the same one today I do not recommend the 'hotel'. As for the Afghan-bound bus, it had to be seen to be believed. Tall and ungainly, half as long as it should be, made almost entirely of orange crates, the whole thing luridly painted with unveiled cherubic-looking women, camels and aeroplanes, I was surprised it could move. But not only did it move, it moved fast. In it I arrived in Afghanistan.

Herat, Kandahar, Kabul, Jalalabad. These were the topsy-turvy cities that were to make my stepping stones across that rugged, sun-baked country to the next railhead. Time jerked to a standstill

three centuries ago. There's cholera at Kandahar, went the rumour, but nobody bothered. For sure there was cholera at Kandahar. And no doubt at Herat, Kabul and Jelalabad too. History stalked their primitive streets but the edifices were all falling down. Beggars flaunted their deformities, holding out withered hands in supplication and murmuring 'Welcome to Afghanistan'.

Four tall chimneys marked Heart: four minarets against a horizon of brown desert. Most of the town's old buildings were levelled on the advice of a British military adviser in 1866 to make a field of fire against a Russian attack that never came. Four minarets remained, crooked fingers scarred and pitted, that will one day fall to join the brown earth. Perhaps they already have.

Kandahar was a community of bazaars where, allegedly, the best skullcaps, waistcoats and silk shirts were made. Here I was accommodated in a hotel room shared by an Indian snake-charmer who had lost his bag of cobras. The toilet was outside on the flat roof of the building, and if it *had* to be used there was a three-to-one chance of one's effluent falling into the restaurant below. I slept badly, worrying about where the cobras might be.

I had my pocket picked in Kabul, the Afghan capital. It took me a whole day to attempt to obtain from the police a certificate confirming the loss which involved me taking an officer of the law around the skein of bazaars to pinpoint the exact spot where the crime had taken place. They then ducked out of it by telling me they had no official rubber stamps so, eventually, I had to obtain the certificate from the British Embassy.

All Asia could be seen thronging the streets and bazaars of Kabul. Tall Pathans, black-bearded and turbaned, flat-faced Mongols, long Tajik profiles, Indo-Iranians, Uzbeks from the upper Oxus, and the bright eyes and uncombed heads of the pagan hillmen of Nuristan. Only the women presented a uniform picture, though their fragile silk *chadari* offered mysterious and colourful anonymity. Adventurous modernity pushed out from

the booths and dried brown mud as the untidy sprawling city struggled for form amongst the hills.

During my stay in the Afghan capital I made an excursion by local bus to Istalif, reputed to be a colourful village atop the Khair Kana Pass in the snow-dappled Paghman Mountains. On the return journey I learnt a lesson: never wear shorts in Afghanistan. Sitting on the roof of the bus minding my own business – my favourite position in the stifling heat away from the crowded interior – my bare legs attracted the unwelcome attention of a set of ruffians who were accompanying me. One by one they sidled up to me and, grinning inanely, began fondling my knees and thighs. Slowly I backed away from the growing threat of a fate they say is worse than death, until I came to rest hard against the guardrail at the front of the roof. I yelled for the conductor who promptly appeared up the iron ladder at the rear and I beckoned wildly to him. Over he came in one bound and without so much as a 'welcome to Afghanistan' joined the mêlée, his hands halfway up my calves. A passing lorry had me on my feet in preparation for a James Bond-type leap from one moving vehicle to another, but I was forcibly restrained by my amorous assailants. Fortunately we drew into the Kabul suburbs before my self-respect was entirely despoiled.

The Kabul Gorge to the south-east, through which my continuing journey took me, was an incredible contortion of nature along a zigzag road over which my latest, and as always overloaded, bus hurled at breakneck speed. At its further end I wondered what had hit me and discovered it was the heat. The temperatures had been sky-high earlier, but this was searing.

The last Afghan town before Pakistan was Jalalabad. I had read descriptions of this town as being the nearest one can get to paradise and, indeed, the cypress trees and lake at the approaches tended to encourage optimism. But my optimism was short-lived; the town sweats in its own humidity, disease and filth. My overnight accommodation was the Majestic Hotel which turned

out to be the local dosshouse. The beds were no more than frames lined up close together, and it was just my luck to find myself in the middle of half a dozen bearded and booted tribesmen sporting tattered robes and exuding powerful smells. With them in bed went their daggers, assorted rifles and AK47s. Towards the end of the night I not only wanted to scratch myself but also visit the toilet, but was told in no uncertain manner to lie still. Trapped in the middle of this snoring mob I perceived, in the early hours, a bulbous, hairy-legged spider slowly descending on its web from the ceiling towards my face. Unable to use my arms which were pinned to my sides, I blew hard at the thing trying to cause it to swing and fall on anybody's face except my own. The five pence tariff for the bed was sheer robbery.

Yet another bus took me to the Pakistan border and a jeep taxi to Lindikotal at the head of the Khyber Pass. Lindikotal is a den of thieves if there ever was one, with a population armed to the teeth, but for me the township had one priceless attraction: a railway station. And luck was with me for once, since the no-charge weekly train to Peshawar (which the Pakistan government runs as a demonstration to show that *they* run the region, not the tribesmen) was due to leave that very morning.

There was, however, not an inch of space to spare on the three-coach train that waited at the platform, so I took up residence on the left-hand front buffer of the Sheffield Vulcan Foundry-made 1923 steam locomotive, sharing it with a jovial Pakistani since the right-hand buffer was similarly occupied. And my 40-mile ride that followed was a high spot of many years of train travel as we wound down the famous pass.

Empty forts made a walnut topping to every hill and a jutting rock proclaimed the names of regiments – British, Pathan and India – including my own carved in stone where years and blood lay eaten by the sun. The Khyber is the steepest non-rack-and-pinion stretch of track in the world, and even with two engines (there was a 1936 German oil-burner at the rear) progress was

heavy going. The route took the form of a letter Z, the train changing direction at each apex, the locomotives taking it in turn to lead. On the steepest sections, safety track had been installed so that runaway trains could be diverted up into the hills. In the short tunnels I was wellnigh suffocated by the smoke, as were others who made a necklace of humanity around the coaches.

I took a *tonga* (two-wheeled taxi) into Peshawar town from a station that, like those elsewhere in the Indian subcontinent, still hold fast to the old traditions of the British Raj with their strictly segregated classes of waiting-rooms and restaurants. If the mall remains vitally English in conception, the town centre was equally as vitally Indian with its maze of mean streets of trades.

Another overnight sojourn in a cheap hotel had me spending it on the roof with a horrific dose of the 'runs', but a couple of vultures that came with the dawn and perched on the surrounding wall as if waiting for me to die provided the best medicine and it was surprising how quickly I recovered. In spite of my condition I managed a bus trip next day to Kolhat, a village that is given over entirely to the manufacture by hand of guns of every description, to offer me another slant to this rebellious region.

From Peshawar, shimmering in its heat and flies, there were reasonable Pakistan Railway services to Rawalpindi and Lahore. This last-named city of Northern Pakistan was, at that time, another railway terminus resulting from the hate with India that, alas, has not much abated today. Thus the tracks to Amritsar, across border in India, lay broken and ensnared with barbed wire. The border road was open only on two days of the week, so I suppose I was lucky again to have no more than two days to wait.

But two days is not nearly enough to see something of this city of faintly decaying beauty, so I increased my days there to four. Mogul history with a dash of Kipling is one way of describing Lahore's past, but my strongest impressions were of the turmoil in its streets where the people fought, lived, slept and died; it was all so visible here.

I crossed the border into India and Amritsar, stronghold of the Sikhs, by taxi. After the flat, dull terrain of the Punjab this city of the Golden Temple was exciting. The temple was set like a jewel in its polluted 'Pool of Immortality', surrounded by some of the meanest streets and most dreadful human squalor imaginable. What Mecca is to the Moslem, or Benares is to the Hindu, the Golden Temple of Amritsar is to the Sikh.

From here I caught the Delhi Mail to spend a sickening 14 hours standing with three dozen others in a compressed gel of sweaty, unclean humanity in a compartment meant for eight. Next morning, at New Delhi station, I watched a corpse being deposited in a refuse-barrow from my coach and I can't, in all honesty, say I felt much better myself.

Delhi is the only one of India's larger cities – and it is not the largest – to offer more than a millennium of history in its stones. When Bombay and Madras were but trading posts and Calcutta a village of mud flats, Delhi had already been capital of an empire for 500 years. An assortment of Hindu and Moslem dynasties, the Moguls, and finally the British, established their seat of government with the British realising their dream capital of New Delhi just in time to turn it over to the new independent nation it had spawned. To this day the city wears its Britishness with style and pride, the stately buildings and cool spacious avenues contrasting oddly with the labyrinth of small crowded streets studded with mosques, temples, monuments and bazaars. Contrast. It is a word that crops up again and again in any narrative about India. Alas, it is not just a contrast of architectural styles but, more starkly, that between the people who have and those who have not. While in the Indian capital I varied my accommodation accordingly between a cockroach-prone pad in Connaught Place and the luxurious apartment of a prosperous acquaintance in a well-to-do suburb. In their different ways both were to prepare me for the long and incident-full haul home.

The route I had set myself was to follow that of the once-designated Trans-Asian Railway at least as far as Qom in Western Iran. Thereafter my railway wanderings would take me south to the Persian Gulf, then north-west into southern Iraq and Syria and back into Turkey along a frail and sometimes broken line.

I left New Delhi station on another mail 'express' along the same route covered earlier as far as Lahore. The train was, again, packed. Even before it had pulled up at the station the coaches were assaulted by a crowd of would-be passengers using their baggage as battering rams to struggle through the windows against intense resistance from those who had already got into compartments. The mood was ugly. Me? I was simply washed aboard by a sea of people. I counted 40, this time in my compartment; even the luggage racks were two deep. After a few miles the crush lessened. Later I was to win a 'seat' by sharing a step at the open door of the coach with an amiable Afghan, our feet dangling out of the train.

From Lahore my next train was to be the Quetta Mail. To acquire a seat I selected the toughest looking of the red-jacketed porters on the platform, offered him a rupee to get me a seat and another to follow if successful. The train arrived late from Rawalpindi and before it even stopped the man had taken a header through an open window into a second-class coach to hold on to my window seat against all-comers. He earned his two rupees.

My new companions were a mixed bunch. All were Pakistanis, but of assorted ethnic groups. One was busy carrying out his devotions up on the luggage rack, a tricky business on a swaying train. The others squatted cross-legged on the wooden seats, watching me and smiling every time they caught my gaze. If I took out my notebook to scribble an observation all would crowd round to look.

The line ran straight as a die for a hundred miles over flat, uninspiring territory, our electric locomotive coping effortlessly. We were travelling the old Indus Valley State line that formed

part of an undertaking, started in 1853, to link Karachi with Calcutta as a step in the larger concept of a fast transport complex to improve transit between Britain and Calcutta.

On through Multan and Sukkur, and a dull roar in the night coupled with stabs of light showed we were passing over the Lansdown Bridge, opened in 1889, and then the largest cantilever bridge in the world. Below us was the wide Indus River. Soon after dawn I was to gaze upon a brown plain of desolation supporting no more than an occasional mud village and the beseeching arms of stunted trees. The Quetta Mail's defection northwards from the Karachi line had allowed it to escape the worst of the Sind Desert's excesses; a flat expanse of sand and scrub winnowed by hot winds and scoured by limitless horizons. And dust there was in plenty; it piled up against the doors and window ledges of our train while tiny avalanches slithered to the floor at every halt.

With the change in scenery came a change in the composition of my fellow travellers. The Punjabis had become swarthy-faced Balochs flaunting fierce bushy eyebrows and beards. They stared at me with a prolonged and disconcerting intensity, and when they spoke their questions were sharp and to the point. Why had I come to Baluchistan, they asked, as if my invasion of their ancient and terrible land was a grotesque anachronism. Up until then I hadn't realised that we *were* in Baluchistan.

Sibi town sat on another junction of the line. Its scattering of houses, cowering beneath a merciless heat, served a railway that was as grotesque an anachronism in this land as myself. At intervals along the track were white-painted markers carefully framed in painted stones that showed a devotion to duty inherited from a past generation of railway staff.

Pakistan Railways have been overtaken by history. Its eastern section, once the pride of the then East Pakistan, has been lost to Bangladesh. Long before Partition in 1947, the then Pakistan Western Railway had been the Kandahar State Railway. The story

of its construction has no parallel in all the history of the railways of the subcontinent. It is a tale of appalling muddle in the beginning, of extreme privations in the face of frightful heat and bitter cold, and of success achieved through sheer determination to force a route through some of the most forbidding territory on Earth. Much of the line was built in record time in spite of destruction by flood, landslide and earthquake, and the very fact that the line is kept open today in the face of the additional handicap of Balochi hostility is evidence of a quality of endeavour unsurpassed anywhere.

Onwards we rolled, through the historic Bolan Pass where General Roberts bade farewell to his troops after his epic march from Kabul to Kandahar, and on to the Dozan Gorge. This was the third line to have been constructed here since the original was laid along the stony bed and, when not in tunnels, it crossed the ravine nine times within four miles. Once through the storm of rock we emerged into the calm of avenues of Chinar trees that grace the former capital of Baluchistan, Quetta.

It is quite a small town with little of the concentrated bustle of other Pakistan cities. The buildings that were once the Residency and the Commissioner's Secretariat remained, still exuding an air of English upper-class life. At the further end of town stood the memorial to the British victims of the 1935 earthquake. Fifteen thousand died, but only Christians are commemorated.

My overnight accommodation in Quetta was one of a series of cabins surrounding a muddy square. I shared the single room with a cheerful American hippie couple; in fact, we all shared the same and only bed, but because of the amorous activities of my bedmates it was hardly a tranquil night.

The next leg of the journey was that to Zahedan in south-eastern Iran. The purchase of my second-class ticket included advice on how to dodge the ticket-inspector and travel first class. The train was a mobile oven and was headed by a museum piece, an ancient

steam engine circa 1930. It stopped for the slightest excuse, and on one occasion long enough for the playing of a football match: locals versus a team of captive opponents. Being a single-track line the delays were necessary, it appeared, to allow another train to pass though; there being so few of them on this route, I was convinced that the signal system was geared to the football schedules.

This lonely line was once known as the Nushki Extension and was built during the First World War as a strategic expediency. It runs hundreds of miles past Nushki, 50 miles into Iranian territory, and commences with the bifurcation from the Quetta line at Spezand, homeground of the first football match of the series, to run parallel with the Afghan frontier.

Between Dalbandin and Nok Kundi, a distance of 104 miles, the landscape was wholly without habitation, virtually devoid of vegetation and can only be described as a hell upon earth. The track crossed stretches of ground covered with sharp black stones broken only by patches of coarse sand. For eight months of the year the heat is intense and the '120-day wind' lashes the sand so that it lacerates the skin like a sand-blast. The whole desert is coated with sulphur dust, and water, when it is obtainable, is a concentrated mixture of common and Epsom salts. When there is any rain the year's fall may occur within an hour. The riverbeds, bone dry for 99 out of 100 days, then hurl a mixture of water and stones it has picked up at the exposed railway. To overcome this disconcerting obstacle the engineers constructed Irish bridges or 'dips', and the steam-engine drivers using them were expected to rely on their discretion as to whether or not they could get through without the water putting the fire out.

Another surprise on this blood-curdling route is the *do reg*, or marching sandhills, which driven by the wind are constantly on the move. Time and time again new track is laid to avoid this obstacle and the duplicated rails left in position so that there is a chance of a line clear of sand at a particular time.

These then were the potential vicissitudes of my trans-Baluchistan Desert journey. Another was to come. Caught by the ticket-inspector while dozing in a first-class compartment, I was banished back to second class. With every seat occupied I took refuge, during an unexplained halt, in the cab of the steam locomotive where I was welcomed like a long-lost brother. However, the transfer was akin to jumping out of a frying pan into a fire, the heat of the roaring boiler easily matched that of the sun. By sticking my head out of the cab I caught the pitiful remnants of a breeze while, periodically, tumblers of oily, sweet tea went the rounds of the crew to lubricate parched throats. I felt it expedient to earn my keep so, as well as taking over the duties of look-out, I fussed around undertaking odd jobs, including stoking the furnace, whenever necessary.

My fellow crew were a couple of friendly Baluchis who shared with me their meat-stuffed *chapattis* while I kept them supplied with duty-free cigarettes, thus forging a close bond. The scenery, shimmering in the savage heat, was of austere desert backed by a long low range of lifeless mountains. I stripped down to my underpants and suffered an endless day in a lather of sweat, oil and dirt. Evening brought a delicious coolness; the horizon joined forces with the dying sun in a great suffusion of vermilion and gold. Then darkness.

It was early next morning, while on lookout duty, that I spotted the bent rail. I'm sure if I hadn't seen it nobody else would have. We slammed on the brakes and, together with most of the complement of the train, walked over to examine the damage. The blistering heat had caused excessive expansion and it was obvious that the rail would have to be replaced. With spare rail alongside the track and a potential workforce to hand, the problem of rectification was minimal.

Having done my stint I wandered off into the desert intent on investigating a tiny mud-walled village I had noticed in the distance. I was to pay for my nosiness. About a hundred yards

short I was intercepted by a gun-toting warrior of bearded magnificence who stuck his musket into my ribs and demanded money. And he wasn't joking. I hunted about for loose change and flung a handful of rupees on to the ground with the idea of belting him when he bent down to pick them up. Perhaps fortunately for both of us a commotion in the village sent him into retreat, while I prudently returned to the train.

We limped into Mirjaveh, the Iranian border village, many hours behind schedule; hardly, it seemed, a rare event. The faint outline of a live volcano, the sometimes smoking Koh-i-Taftan, stood out in an otherwise empty landscape, and in the grey shrouds of another dawn we finally drew into Zahedan.

For a town on the edge of eternity Zahedan was not really a bad little place. An oasis in the midst of purgatory, its simple amenities were the more remarkable and welcome. But the one amenity it lacked so far as I was concerned was a vehicle to get out of it. The Army came to the rescue. Presenting myself at the nearby barracks and introducing myself as a British soldier (and I had my regimental association membership card to prove it) I gradually worked through the ranks until I found myself before a full colonel who, much to my surprise, told me he would be delighted to help with my transport problem. And this was effected by one of his minions taking me in a military vehicle to a road junction just outside the town and stopping the first lorry going in the direction of Kerman, 200 miles away and the next railhead.

The lorry was high-sided, the buck full of sheep and with three Baluchis jammed in the cab. I shall never forget that drive. The road led into satanic hills that we crossed in a series of zigzags, at never less than 70 miles per hour, in a cloud of choking dust. On the straight the speed and density of the dust increased, and whenever the driver braked all sixty-odd manure-caked beasts catapulted into me. All the while individual beasts stood or relieved themselves on my feet, which wasn't funny since I was wearing

open sandals. The lorry halted briefly at a couple of villages and scores of amused peasants clambered aboard to stare and prod at the funny 'Ingleesh'. But twice I was offered tea and yoghurt from these folk, who seemed kindly in spite of their aggressive curiosity.

I was thrown out at Bam, a town 125 miles short of Kerman. At an all-night transport café I teamed up with a Good Soldier Schweik-like character, cross-eyed and unbuttoned, who kept urinating in the most public of places. Together we caught a bus bound for Kerman in the early morning. The bus was luxurious compared with the lorry but the driver quite plainly was another of those who fancied me to the point of acute embarrassment (mine), and at Kerman I was inveigled into being his guest for the day. I accepted because his vehicle was going further westwards to Yazd that night, which was the direction in which I wanted to go. Once I had made clear the limits of our friendship I enjoyed his hospitality, which included a substantial lunch and the ecstasy of a Persian bath.

Settled in the reserve-driver's seat next to Momeny – we were on Christian name terms by now – much to the jealous rage of most of the other passengers, I looked forward to reaching the railhead at Yazd. Repeatedly I fell asleep only to be awoken by the affectionate Momeny.

Both Kerman and Yadz were reputed to be famous for their shawls, which allegedly rival in quality those of Kashmir. But while Kerman seemed to me a very mediocre, if sizeable, town of bazaars, Yazd raised a skyline reputed to be the most picturesque in all Iran containing, as it does, the highest minarets in the country. However, again arriving in the middle of the night, neither quality shawls nor picturesque skylines were very high on my agenda. And what I missed of Yadz in the darkness I looked upon, bleary-eyed, in the cold light of dawn.

My train towards Qom dropped me off at a junction where, with a little bribery, I was allowed on to a goods-only train to Isfahan, sitting in an open wagon with a couple of railway workers

who spoke to me in a rapid tongue of which I understood not a word. I dallied a whole 48 hours in this fabulous city. The Maidan and Royal Mosque is the crowning architectural achievement of Shah Abbas, and the Great Square is seven times the size of that of St Mark's in Venice. The curve and swell of the turquoise dome of the mosque is beautiful, if anything in the world is beautiful. The court of the *madreseh* is lined with students' cells and makes a fine sight though, to me, Islamic mosques and sacred college construction has a depressing similarity about it. But is was all so worth seeing. A small but clean and comfortable hotel offered me a much-needed bed for two nights, and the third day it was another bus, rather than a train, that I caught with the idea of reaching Khorramshah, close to the southern border with Iraq.

But through a misunderstanding coupled with mispronunciation I found myself on the way to Kermanshah, in the opposite direction. The two places being some 240 miles apart, my ride to the latter city was something of an exhausting mistake which at least showed me a little more of the country. The way between Hamadan and Kermanshah was spectacular. A well-paved road ran straight over the range of mountains which included the 12,000-foot Mount Alvand, offering superb views across a fertile plain cradled by yet more mountains, these displaying skirts of green and sharp peaks of alpine perfection.

Kermanshah turned out to be a city populated by Kurds, a pleasing enough town giving no hint of the rich archaeological treasures from prehistoric to Babylonian and Parthian times to be found in its rocky terrain. I have nothing against Kurds as a race, but those of the younger generation I found in Kermanshah were a thoroughly objectionable lot. Strolling in a back street I was met by not only verbal abuse but also by a barrage of stones. I took refuge behind the wall of a derelict house plentifully endowed with similar ammunition, and made to give as good as I got. Fortunately a misfire from the opposition went through the window of an occupied house and the tinkling of broken glass

brought the affray to an inconclusive end. We all fled in different directions.

A mail van backtracked me as far as Qom. With a tea stop at Arak, I slept intermittently in the back of the van and we reached Iran's second holiest city as its citizens were stirring themselves for another day.

Qom looked its age, and as Fatima, sister of the Imam Reza, is buried here it was consequently full of pilgrims and infidels, the latter being no more popular than in Mashad. The Shrine of Fatima, with its golden dome and four blue minarets, excitingly oriental, is one of the visions of Persia. Again the mere presence of Christians was frowned upon by devout Muslims, but commercialism seemed to be a more potent force as, again and again, I was entreated to buy a selection of pious junk. I was solemnly warned not to enter the court of the shrine, so I dutifully desisted from a repeat of my Mashad incursion. Muslim hypocrisy was making me not a little bored anyway.

At the station I purchased a ticket for Khorramshah, making the ticket-office spell it out to me, so ensuring that I would be going to the right place. Sometime around tomorrow's dawn I would be upon the threshold of Iraq – if I got my pronunciation right.

It came to me that I was seeing too many dawns for the good of my health, and yet another was to present itself at Ahvaz. The train was excruciatingly slow, stopping at stations and between stations along the route. We were hauled by a sorry specimen of steam locomotive, and the compartment floor of my coach was again my bed for the night. Approaching Khorramshah I could smell the sea and oil of the Persian Gulf.

Passenger trains on the Trans-Iranian line had their southern terminus at this garden city where the scent of mimosa and luxurious flowering growth was almost able to counteract the stench of the neighbouring oil tanks of Abadan. Technically an

island, Abadan, seat of the great oil-pipeline terminus and refinery, was a few miles ahead.

Khorramshah came into prominence at the beginning of the nineteenth century when, as a village, it was demolished by the Turks on the grounds that its commercialism was a detriment to nearby Basra. The British and Russian governments stepped in to keep the peace by allocating territory separated by the river to both sides, with a view to a fair distribution of potential wealth. But they reckoned without the Karun River, a tributary of the Shatt-al-Arab, which promptly upped and changed course, inserting a watery spanner into the works. Basra, once in Iran, is now of course firmly Iraqi, but the hate continues to boil. War had not broken out when I was there; only the border was closed, which was inconvenient enough for me. I tried half a dozen taxi drivers before I could persuade one, with the help of an exorbitant bribe, to take me to the frontier post. His vehicle was another Packard, and on the way out of town he picked up three labourers and a soldier. They all got out short of a place called Shalamcheh, and since none of them paid I perceived I was subsidising the trip.

Shalamcheh turned out to be a hamlet of five houses, all taken over by the military. I detected an air of the front line with barbed-wire coils ineffectively laid, clusters of khaki trucks and a lot of rubbish. At the last house in the row the taxi dropped me. Inside the house the customs and immigration officer was in bed. From his pillow he eyed me without enthusiasm, rose with reluctance, and carefully strapped on his revolver belt over his flame-coloured pyjamas. Dressed for duty as it were, he enquired as to whether I was carrying hashish, firearms or precious metals and when I said 'No' to all three, he stamped my passport and let me go with the parting shot, 'You'll be back you know. They won't let you in there,' as he jerked his head towards Iraq. Then he went back to bed.

With an Iranian dog snapping at my heels I set off on the four-mile hike across open desert that was no-man's-land lying between Iran and Iraq.

At the Iraqi border post I was steadfastly ignored. Finding another officer in bed, I tapped my passport idly against the headrest and raised a grunt of irritation. I searched his table for the correct entry stamp with the idea of doing the job myself, but my back-to-front Arabic was not up to it.

A commotion outside materialised into a trio of Serbs intent upon crossing into Iran for a business conference. The officer rose reluctantly to a sitting position and surveyed his tormentors balefully. Quite certainly he wanted to refuse the Serbs's request to leave Iraqi territory but was aware they were folk of substance. Yet his book of rules stipulated that no more than two persons per day could proceed through his post in either direction. Yet here was a determined unit of three making his life a misery. The officer glared at me and I perceived a repugnance of things British clashing with expediency; and expediency triumphed. He would swap one incoming Brit for three outgoing Serbs. The ratio, with its implications, plainly stuck in his gullet but it provided a solution. He banged stamps into everyone's passports and the room emptied.

Revenge was sweet. The officer, joined by his minions, upturned my bag and rummaged through the contents. From them was extracted my portable electric shaver, to him a fiendish electrical device of capitalistic cunning. Suspicion turned to childish delight as I gave a demonstration of its magic and, in order of seniority, the personnel of the post went to work on their five o'clock shadows.

The senior officer then demanded a return of the shaver for a trim of his moustache. And that's when the battery gave up the ghost, since Iraqi stubble is the stuff of porcupine quills. It took a firm grip on a tuft of bristles and clung on like a limpet. The

scream of agony and terror echoed round the room as, with difficulty, I prized off the offending apparatus and fled.

'Welcome to Iraq' read the notice outside. Possessed of no Iraqi currency, I had to tempt the one and only driver of a non-military car with pound notes before he would take me the 13 miles to Basra, and then he only did so because he was an incurable romantic who liked the look of the Queen on the banknotes. Within sight of the city I met two further hurdles: one was the wide Shatt-al-Arab River with Basra the wrong side of it, and the other was the fact that my arrival coincided with a Friday when, as in all Moslem lands, the banks and change offices are closed. The ferryman, no fan of a British queen, refused to accept sterling and directed me to a posh hotel eight miles up the river. A boatman was persuaded to take me there and accompany me to the hotel to collect his fare but, upon arrival, the cashier refused to accept my Barclays Bank travel cheques. 'Lackeys of Israel,' he maintained darkly. So I changed the last of my pounds which amounted to enough to pay for my river voyage and no more. But at least the boatman dropped me on the other side of the waterway.

Wondering how to continue to Baghdad, I walked the two miles to the station through a town I found to be more Arab than most towns I'd seen in Iran, and where its citizens seemed well-disposed towards visitors – even British ones. The place was a hotchpotch of other people's development: Carmathian, Mongol, Turkish and European with a thin veneer of Moslem construction. And in Basra station, quite by chance, I met the station-master who invited me to tea. He was an educated man and showed great interest in my recent rail journeying. Then, learning of my financial predicament, the good man promptly donated a first-class ticket valid for the air-conditioned de luxe overnight express to the Iraqi capital.

Basra to Baghdad is 380 miles and we covered the distance in nine hours, which is good for a Middle Eastern train. The route

follows the Euphrates River for some of the way and passed within two miles of Ur, of the Chaldees fame. We also flashed by a short platform designated 'Babylon Halt' which even local trains pass with a derisive whistle. And in the morning we drew into West Station, the Grand Central of Baghdad.

I have already charted the course of the railway between Baghdad and Istanbul and back to Europe in Chapter 2, so let the further impediments arising from such a journey speak for themselves. A Paris to Delhi Express may not appear in the world timetables yet, but in the meantime its fragmented local predecessors make for an incident-packed ride as you may discern.

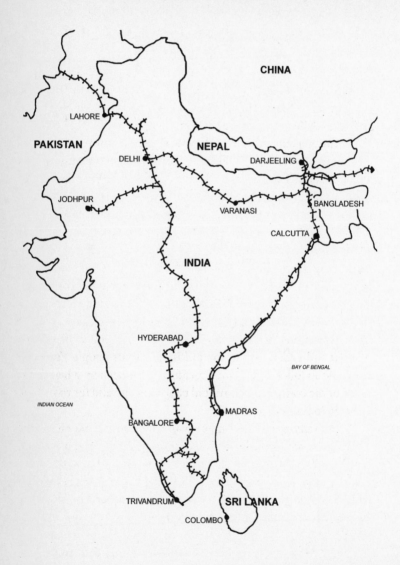

- 8 -

Round and About India by Rail

The man by the hotel pool in Bangalore was incredulous.

'You mean you're travelling all over India by railway! How do you get on? What's it like? How do you survive?' he burst out, shaking his head in wonderment.

Admittedly the man was American so was more attuned to airlines than other forms of public transport, but some Europeans I met likewise displayed disbelief. Yet those same Europeans, and even some Americans, catch trains back in their respective countries, so what's so different about Indian trains? When I was riding Indian Railways in 1973 there existed a third-class mode of transportation which, as I've made clear earlier, *can* be something of a trial, but since then third class has been assimilated into second class with a corresponding improvement in conditions except, perhaps, on some local services. However, even today Indian trains are not, in general, as fast, sleek or elegant as those of richer nations, but they can offer a foreign traveller the reward of sight and experience of the *real* India and its people. And this for a cost so low it'll take your breath away, especially when use is made of the concessionary Indrail pass which is valid for the whole gigantic Indian rail system.

Indian railway statistics make daunting reading, which maybe dissuades some from the notion of train travel when it is realised that 11 million passengers board trains every day – and these are just the ones who buy a ticket. The total route mileage is some 61,836 kilometres covering 7,000 stations; another awe-inspiring figure, while those visitors who venture into a major railway station, and many a minor one for that matter, are dismayed by the sight of its seething human content. How, you might ask, with that mass of humanity, could anyone get *near* a train? Of course, many of those ant-like denizens are permanent or semi-

permanent inhabitants of the station; not all are bent upon *boarding* a train. But there was one real deterrent: the acquirement of a ticket.

At least that was the case during the 1970s and 1980s but, though change is slow in India, the proliferation of computers has, to a considerable extent, lessened this deterrent.

My first, and finally successful, attempt at the acquisition of a railway ticket went something along these lines:

1. Am told by a beaming railway official that my quest for a ticket provokes 'no problem', a favourite Indian expression but spoken with such sincerity that I believed him.

2. Make my way to the end of the queue at the ticket/ reservations booth.

3. Fight to hold my place in said queue, since Indians are inveterate queue-jumpers.

4. At the grill, having stated my required destination, I am handed a form (I could have obtained this from the enquiry office if I'd known) together with a torrent of instructions in Indian rapid-fire English which has to be repeated before I can get the drift of what he is saying.

5. The form, which I carry away with me so losing my place at the front of the queue, demanded all manner of personal details; virtually a potted history of my life, in addition to where I wanted to go and by which grade of seat/berth I wished to utilise. It also required me to stipulate the *number* of the train.

6. That necessitated a trip to the station departures board to ascertain this requirement.

7. The form competed, I return to the ticket/reservations booth to join afresh the queue, again struggling to hold my place.

8. Reaching the grill once more I hand in the form with an air of accomplishment, whereupon the clerk checks my entries and laboriously copies them, in scratchy longhand, into a dog-eared ledger.

9. Am told that my requested train is fully-booked but am nevertheless issued with a ticket, even though I'd been told that one had to have a reservation on a long-distance train.

10. Worn out, I turn towards the station exit and am accosted, two hours later, by the same beaming official I'd met earlier. 'I told you there'd be no problem,' he trumpeted.

But there were short-cuts available to all this once you'd got the hang of things, while the Indrail pass (obtainable for all classes of travel and for different periods of validity from the Indian Railways' representative in your own country or at major Indian railway stations) was, and is, the open-sesame to the system as well as giving the bearer priority. The classes of travel available are air-conditioned, first and second.

In the late 1980s these ticket acquisition antics were again awaiting me at New Delhi station as I launched myself into the process that, if I remained sane, would allow me to set out on my further rail wanderings that would take me, in somewhat more comfort than before, over much of the Indian rail network. What follows therefore is the narrative of a composite journey made over a period of years which would circumnavigate as well as traverse this huge and diverse country.

I left New Delhi station at midday on the Kerala Express, its route carving a great arc through central India and which would, within two nights and three days, deposit me at Trivandrum, Kerala's provincial capital down south at the sharp end of the country. It is one of the longest – in excess of 3,350 kilometres – passenger through-services run by Indian Railways. My Indrail pass stipulated first-class accommodation that allows daytime use of the air-conditioned coaches, though I found these to be too cool for comfort.

The Kerala Express was, as expected, an express in name only, dawdling and stopping everywhere. My compartment converted, at night, into four bunks though bedding was not supplied.

However, such were the outside temperatures that none was needed and I made do with my sleeping-bag liner (Indian travellers lie on their *lungis*, a kind of enlarged dishcloth they wind around their waists). The compartment windows, as on all Indian trains, were barred but openable, the walls paint-lacking but reasonably clean, while a battery of ceiling fans maintained a noisy but cooling flow of air. There are no dining cars as such on most Indian trains, meals being ordered ahead and picked up by coach attendants at certain stations. It was presumed that I wanted meat, but my initial curried chicken was stringy and tough; thereafter in the country I became a vegetarian. Such dishes cost me no more than 35 pence and hot, sweet tea in flasks was brought in on demand. Cutlery was not supplied (it is on the de luxe expresses) so, until I could procure a knife and fork I had curried rice and gravy dribbling down my chest. On this initial leg of the journey my fellow travellers were a series of individuals with whom it was all too easy to effect the most amicable of relationships.

Station halts were prolonged, the station occupants, throughout the night, the noisiest ever. At Agra there were fleeting glimpses of the Taj Mahal; 400 kilometres on was Gwalior, a name synonymous with its fort; then Jhansi at the 500-kilometre mark where our evening meal came aboard; and Bhopal, still recovering from the Union Carbide plant disaster when scores of workers were killed.

Dawn found us rumbling across a wide placid river on a newly repaired bridge. My neighbour, a Mr Arya (MSc(Ag)Hort) – or so his card indicated – imparted grim details about the flood that had washed away the original structure just a couple of weeks earlier and a train with it; the death toll in this instance being 140.

Nagpur, Warangal – where Mr Ayra made his fond farewells – and Gudur were our main scheduled stops next day and a second dawn had us at Coimbatore where Mr A.'s replacement, a garrulous sales executive of the Premier Cable Company, joined me. At Ernakulam, the junction for Cochin Harbour in the

province of Kerala announced itself with its distinctive forests, lakes and coconut plantations, abruptly picturesque after the parched flatlands of central India. Rice paddies were being 'ploughed' by water buffaloes, men and beasts thigh deep in liquid mud. Alone in my compartment I was visited by the train commander for social chit-chats. Then around midday we drew into Trivandrum, just 20 minutes late. This I perceived as something of a miracle when it is recognised how many hazards Indian Railways has to put up with, additional to its appalling bureaucracy.

My first static night was spent in a British-inspired institution, now uniquely Indian: the railway retiring room where I was given a bed in an eight-bed dormitory with showers, toilets, clean linen and a lockable baggage locker, all for the equivalent of 75 pence. The night, however, was not much less noisy than those of the stations through which we had passed, with the shrieking of diesels, the eternal roar of passing trains and now the hawking and spitting of my bedfellows plus, in this particular case, a disconcerting dirge from a religious tableau set in the station square outside the window. I could have had a room to myself, but none was available. My breakfast next morning was 35 pence-worth of vegetable curry.

There was time for a few hours' exploration of the town which, for an Indian city, I discovered to be a sedate sort of place. It was once known by the tongue-twisting name of Thiruvananthapuramand, the abode of the sacred serpent Ananta upon whose coils Vishnu lies in the main temple. I strolled through its narrow winding streets of whitewashed houses with red-tiled roofs in cool, green gardens, glad of the exercise after so much sitting. Then I returned to the station for the final leg of the journey to Kanniyakumari where the tracks run out. And lo and behold, there on the departure noticeboard and displayed on the side of a coach was my name – albeit misspelt – and reserved seat number. Though I had made these initial bookings in faraway

London, my reservations had managed to filter through the bureaucratic maze.

Kanniyakumari (Cape Comerin) was no more than a short hop and here, if the Almighty had given us three legs, one could stand in a trio of oceans that meet here in thunderous embrace. Between Trivandrum and the Cape lay the exotic Kovalam tourist beaches, but on this trip I spurned them for a risky dip in the turbulent waters at this southernmost tip of India. The small Indian resort at the end of the line was a distinct come-down from the flamboyance of its rail terminus, and my cautious bathing activities were watched in amazement by bevies of Indian citizenry since no foreign tourists venture here. Which is not surprising, for the place was not much more than a sun-blasted slum. My night was spent in a hovel and the only liquid refreshment available was local 'potable' water which I drank without ill-effects while watching a sunset of fabulous intensity.

A day and a night was quite enough for Kanniyakumari. I don't know quite what I expected of it, but I had not quite finished with southern extremities. The island of Sri Lanka was the subsequent landfall and it titillated my roving instincts. There was a snag, however: Sri Lanka's civil war was raging in the north of the island so I could expect restrictions, if not cancellation, of ferry services.

To reach the Indian embarkation port for the island I had to return, the way I had come, as far as Coimbatore. So I stopped off en route at Ernakulam, a component of Cochin and a junction furnished with a trio of railway stations, with the idea of taking a look at this historic city. Outside the station I was befriended by a bright young man who took me into town on the back of his motor scooter. He also found me an inexpensive but reasonable hotel and offered to give me a scooter tour of the sights.

Cochin, of Portuguese ancestry, is spread about both the mainland and a number of islands that made it, for me, a most confusing place. At its southern end I was shown old merchant

houses still exhibiting remnants of past imperialistic glories amongst bazaars reeking of pungent spices. I even managed a swim of sorts in murky oil-polluted water close – too close – to the huge docks on Willingdon Island. Back at my hotel confusion reigned. Somebody, certainly not me, had left my washbasin tap running and water was pouring down the stairs. By this time, too, I had discovered the real motives for the attention I was receiving from my scooter-riding friend when he abruptly took to stroking portions of my anatomy and suggesting sharing my bed with him. Here we go again, I thought, as I politely declined his overtures. So I sweated out the night alone and unmolested in a sauna of a room in which the fan had broken down.

The morning brought an excited knocking on the door that could only have been my gay acquaintance, so I pretended to be asleep and eventually the pounding desisted. An hour later I crept down the still-damp stairs, paid my bill, and left to explore more of the city on my own, a project that included a peek in at St Francis Church of imposing Dutch façade and wooden interior where Vasco Da Gama was buried before being transferred elsewhere.

My train to Coimbatore was due at noon, the hottest time of the day. While waiting at the station I was entertained by the sight of a child peeing at the platform edge and a prosperous-looking sari-clad mother sweeping the liquid on to the track with her bare feet removed from elegant sandals for the purpose. There's never a dull moment on Indian railway stations.

I was repeatedly to find myself on Coimbatore station. On this occasion it was to pick up the overnight Rameswaram Express, Rameswaram being the ferry port serving Sri Lanka, with a berth previously booked in Cochin. The following dawn showed the train creeping over the old, broken-down bridge to Pandram in the shadow of the skeleton of the then partly-constructed dual-purpose structure alongside that would give improved road and rail access to neighbouring but isolated Rameswaram.

The terminal station was another of those modest-sized but faintly majestic affairs that flamboyantly introduced me to a small town, far from majestic in itself, but which is a pilgrimage centre. Its temple, where Hindus came to pay tribute to Rama – the hero of the epic *Ramayana* – is the centre of attraction that elevates Rameswaram into a shrine of the calibre of Banaras.

As half expected, the ferry that plied the Palk Strait to Talaimannar on the Sri Lankan shore was not operating. Walking disconsolately along the beach I was approached by two sets of fishermen offering to take me across the strait at dawn next day when the fishing boats went out. Nobody would notice, it was inferred, if one of them dropped me ashore on the island. Though a highly illegal method of reaching Sri Lanka, I nevertheless negotiated with one set of fishermen a fee of 400 rupees – then about £20 – to cover the round trip, this to be paid when I was picked up 24 hours later.

It all ended in trouble, of course. The scheme was thwarted, I think, by the boatmen whose offer I had not accepted and who reported my intentions to the authorities. This brought along a corporal of the military police shouldering a rifle who firmly read me the riot act. As I received my dressing-down for a scheme that I hadn't actually proposed I wondered if envy and treachery were normal Tamil traits. With my tail between my legs I partook of a swim, toured the massive temple and reverted to the trains. (A few years later I legally reached Sri Lanka to traverse the island by a steam-hauled train known as the *Viceroy Special*, more about which appears in Chapter 11.)

En route back to Coimbatore, my night express halted at Madurai around midnight where I was involved in an altercation concerning ownership of my bunk. The result was that I was pitched out on to the platform by an irate conductor. I took my grievance to the station-master who agreed that, indeed, I was in the right. He offered me a berth on the early morning train to Madras but I had no wish to go to Madras, thank you. So I spent

the rest of the night in the bell-trilling station-master's office swigging sweet tea with the intention of catching the next Coimbatore-bound train 24 hours later.

At least my enforced delay enabled me to cast my eyes over perhaps the most famous man-made landmark in Southern India: the Temple of Minakshi, the Fish-eyed Goddess, another Hindu shrine. Madurai is a town of great antiquity made the more special by the huge and astounding temple, a town in itself. Within its confines are a prodigious number of carvings; some say as many as 33 million, though I found this hard to believe. Certainly there were more than I could count.

Back at Coimbatore once more, and somewhat bleary-eyed, I set out for the garden city of Bangalore where I caught up with lost sleep at the plush Windsor Manor Hotel before catching a series of trains that, on a serpentine course, eventually dropped me at Bombay (now Mumbai). On the way I stopped off at Goa to renew my acquaintance with this one-time Portuguese enclave, Matheran to sample its small-gauge mountain railway, on to the Nilgiri hills and 'Ooty' (Ootacumund) holding ghosts of the Raj, and reached by another narrow-gauge line, the Blue Mountain Railway, to end up at the Malabar coastal town of Poona (Pune) known to generations of British soldiers. Bombay terminated my whistle-stop rail tour.

By courtesy of Oberoi I spent a luxurious night in their hotel being pampered by uniformed flunkies including a personal butler who frightened the life out of me. I took refuge in the city's teeming streets, being carried along by the throng. Finally I came to roost in Bombay's St Pancras-like Central Station.

Here my measure of high living continued by virtue of a reservation on the crack Rajdhani Express which covers the near 1,400 kilometres to Delhi in 17 hours instead of the 28-odd by less prestigious trains. My Indrail pass entitled me to the ride as it did to the inclusive afternoon tea, dinner and breakfast as well as pillow, sheets and blankets in a sleeper compartment. This train,

they say, is *never* late. Nor is it permitted to arrive early at its destination. And to prove it we left Bombay on the dot and drew into New Delhi station exactly at the scheduled arrival time of 09.15 next morning.

There are two Rajdhani Expresses, the second one covering the 1,505 kilometres to easternmost extremities. I could have reached Assam, my final destination, on a through-coach from Bangalore, the longest through-journey on the Indian rail network, but my northbound wanderings from that city had precluded it.

Calcutta is a much maligned metropolis. With a population of around 12 million it is, after Shanghai, the largest in Asia and comes fifth in size in the world. One associates it with a horror story, an urban nightmare peopled by deformed beggars and skeletal children begging for scraps of food in stinking disease-ridden gutters skirting tumultuous streets. Our history books vigorously chronicle the occurrences of the infamous Black Hole of Calcutta; an incident that grips the imagination of at least those of my generation with a clarity that, again, imbues the city with an even darker hue.

These were my conceptions upon arrival at the ant-heap of Howrah station. And crossing the huge Meccano set of the girder bridge spanning the Hooghly River into the city proper, my first impressions confirmed my worst fears. Buildings rose higgledy-piggledy from the dust, wobbly verandas leant out from upper storeys, incredibly dirty windows were half obscured by corrugated iron or enormous cinema hoardings; power and telephone cables looped and dangled from leaning posts. It all looked decayed and old but strangely British, which of course it was, as the more enduring reminders of the British Raj – the Victoria Memorial, St Paul's Cathedral, Dalhoussie Square, not to mention a plethora of still operating exclusive clubs – give ample evidence.

Yet, like everyone else who comes to this city, I was soon captivated by it. The place is astonishing, bewildering, repugnant and exhilarating. It is scarred by hideous poverty. But it is also a prosperous metropolis; the only one in India, so they say, where one can, if it has to be, live on a rupee a day. And millions do. An urban horror story perhaps, but it is a living legend, too.

I remained in the city for some days, roaming its teeming streets and visiting outlying districts. Calcutta was in the grip of the annual Durga Festival, an event celebrated throughout India but with not half the fervour as here. In back street workshops I watched people putting final touches to the vividly coloured, often fearsome-looking effigies painstakingly being made which would later be cast into the Hooghly River. And on the big day itself the fireworks, torchlight processions, religious displays and general mêlée made my brief visit a particularly exciting event, and got me off the trains for a while.

To reach India's easternmost states from Calcutta it is necessary to go north and then east to avoid the territory of Bangladesh (which I was to visit the following year). However, first my onward route was south-west on a deflection that would take me into the province of Orissa. My train was the Coromandel Express, its final destination being Madras (Chennai) but, at least initially, I was only going as far as Bhubaneshwar, Orissa's chief city.

And in Orissa lies the greatest concentration of temples to be found anywhere, Bhubaneshwar itself being dominated by the huge Lingaraj Temple of vintage 1050. Others, in varying states of preservation, are sprinkled about the town; some protected, others mouldering away beneath the searing sun in backyard or paddy-field. Despite the fame of the Sun Temple at Konark and the Jagannath Temple in Puri, the province remains one of the least visited in India. And this in spite of the fact that its coast holds excellent beaches, ideal for swimming and surfing amongst the rollers of the Bay of Bengal, if you're not too fussy about unmentionable things found on Indian beaches.

Once part of the ancient kingdom of Kalinga, the region grew prosperous through trading before being crushed by the Mauryan king Asoka around 260 BC. This worthy underwent a total reformation after experiencing the horrors that accompanied the conquest, and became a fervent Buddhist to preach the philosophy of peace and goodwill to all men; an episode that is recorded for posterity in the Udayagiri caves near Bhubaneswar and in the superb and erotic stone carvings that adorn the countless temples concentrated within the triangle formed by Bhubaneswar, Konark and Puri.

The stupendous Sun Temple at Konark simply *has* to be seen. Conceived as a mythical chariot of the Sun God, Surya, borne on 24 carved wheels and displaying plenty of erotica as if to prove that sexual display is not just a modern phenomenon, it rises phoenix-like out of the landscape.

During my short sojourn in Orissa I stayed in a number of so-called guesthouses, some of dubious nature, but on my last night I treated myself to the gimmicky Toshali Sands Resort on the coast which described itself as paradise. Accommodation was vested in individual chalets and luxury tentage, and compared with some of the overnight pads I was experiencing on my travels, paradise was not all that of an exaggeration.

For no more reason other than for the hell of it, I continued my journey south-west from Bhubaneswar on a subsequent Coromandel Express reaching Madras the following evening, thus covering the rail route I had missed when leaving Bangalore. This would complete a circuit of the whole country by the time I had accomplished my current journeying. And, as may be seen, I'm a sucker for completing circuits. I saw little of Madras beyond its station and was back, with a bunk sleeper, on the next express out to return to Calcutta.

And once there it should have been very few hours before I would be rolling northwards into West Bengal. However, back amongst the pandemonium of Howrah station I was to find that

the northwards-bound Kamrup Express had been 'rescheduled' for an 02.00 departure resulting in a nine-hour wait, much of it after dark. But I have kicked my heels in less entertaining places than Howrah, and with every conceivable activity going on from cooking through shoe shining to dentistry being undertaken alongside a hubbub and confusion that defies description, my extended loiter offered barely a dull moment.

West Bengal spread flat but enticing to end at the base of the Himalayas. It is a jar-shaped state, bounded by Bangladesh to the east and with the one-time British hill station of Darjeeling on the neck. For the rail traveller from Calcutta to Assam in the North-East, the journey entails two days of rattling over endless bridges all the way to the Nepalese border, then on through the narrow corridor between the former East Bengal, Nepal and Bhutan, and down the Brahmaputra valley. For me, however, this arduous journey was to be broken at New Jalpaiguri, the junction and unassuming gateway to the Himalayas.

The train arrived there two hours later than even the 'rescheduling' had dictated and, worse still, the line of the famous 'Toy Train', which would have taken me the 88 kilometres to Darjeeling in nine idyllic hours from neighbouring Siliguri, had been blocked by a landslide which entailed its miniature trains running only from the halfway station of Kurseong.

The result was that I had to make my way up into the cloud-flecked hills that shielded the dim outline of the great Himalayan chain by taxi. The vehicle was driven by a maniac with suicidal tendencies on a road of corkscrewing inclinations. I could have reached Darjeeling by road in less than half the time it takes the train, but that's not the point. Darjeeling and its 'Toy Train' are inseparable. So at Kurseong I transferred back to the tracks: miniature tracks, these carrying a minuscule train, its wooden coaches hauled by a diminutive steam locomotive of around 1880 vintage. And what a ride it is with mind-blowing views as, moving hardly more than walking pace, we wound a tortuous way,

sometimes doubling back on ourselves on multiple loops, gaining ever-higher altitude, on a vehicle that once carried weary colonial administrators up into the cool tranquillity of this former favourite hill station of the British Empire.

Darjeeling derives its name from the Tibetan *Dorj Ling* ('Place of the Thunderbolts') and, at an altitude of some 6,000 feet, it presents a face common to such resorts comprising a mall, a very British-looking church, the usual hill station array of bungalows, and stern public buildings of the type one sees in, say, Leeds. It also has the unbelievable Windamere (sic) Hotel, an institution stuck in a time warp of circa 1920.

I remained in the town for a number of days enjoying the distinctly cool temperatures and exploring the different terraces upon which it is built, their levels indicating the strata of society its residents had attained. I found most pleasure in the bazaars and crowded lanes of the bottom rung of the class ladder where its denizens went about their noisy, aromatic and vulgar business.

Darjeeling is probably the best known of the hill stations, mainly on account of its celebrated narrow-gauge railway, though other hill stations likewise possess similar rail links. The upper level put me in mind of a small and exclusive seaside resort – minus the sea. But as far as I know, the likes of Frinton do not embrace a Tibetan refugee camp such as the one here, its occupants encouraging visitors, and I made regular pilgrimages there to hear stories of escape from a repressed homeland in exchange for goodies I bought in the town. I also received an invitation for dinner from the redoubtable and venerable Mrs Tenduf-La of the Windamere Hotel – a considerable honour this – who showed me autograph books sprinkled with guest's names, a kind of roll of fame, that whisper of recent history and vanished epochs. Before I dared show my face there I felt it expedient to undergo a half-day of clothes washing and sprucing up prior to presenting myself to an establishment that impudently defies the vulgar modern world.

But one doesn't go to Darjeeling simply on account of its urban charms. Further north is a sequence of some of the highest Himalayan peaks; the mighty Everest is visible 120 miles away if you are prepared to rise at dawn to watch the sunrise from atop Tiger Hill to progressively illuminate the distant summits in pale yellow, green, purple and, finally, glowing gold. Closer, at only 45 miles, is Kanchenjunga, its grandeur enhanced by the fact that it rises sheer from the Teesta River valley shrouded in mist.

Being myself shrouded in light summer clothing, I soon yearned for the warmth of the plains and so was not displeased to be winding down through the tea plantation-flanked foothills back to Siliguri and a berth on the Kanchenjunga Express. It was to transport me in 24 hours to Guwahati, the chief town of the north-eastern hill states that include Assam. There was considerable political unrest in the region and, to enter Assam, I had had to obtain a special permit from the Indian High Commission in London.

The route of my latest train was an interesting one, taking me out of West Bengal and along the narrow 20-kilometre-wide strip of Indian territory called the Siliguri Neck, pinched between Bhutan and Bangladesh. In addition to the unrest, Assam was bordered by some potentially hostile nations including China and Burma (Myanmar), this latter one likewise in the grip of semi-civil war. A land of touchy frontiers is Assam.

In the morning, looking out of the window of my berth, I beheld the enormous Brahmaputra River that rises in Tibet, plunges through the Himalayas and debauches into the Bay of Bengal. The train followed its brown sullen waters into Guwahati, arriving hours late.

I had an appointment in the city with the then Assam director of the Indian Tourist Board, a Mr Kamal Lochen Das (later moved to Amsterdam), who awaited my late arrival with some anxiety. I found my way to his office across a great brute of a town of wide

highway intersections over which madly-driven traffic hurled; drivers completely ignoring the traffic lights and the police sent to enforce them.

I found Mr Das to be one of the most engaging of human beings. His office formed part of his home, and the whole family were summoned to meet me. Tea and chat followed before I was taken to the city's top hotel, the Brahmaputra Ashok, a cold stone palace-like building of sparse furnishings and a seeming deficiency of clients. Here we dined before returning to the Das household for a nightcap, or to be accurate, a series of nightcaps, partaken on the flat roof of the house under a balmy star-studded sky.

Over the ensuing days I was given a whistle-stop tour of the Guwahati hinterland; all too short a time to obtain even an inkling of what Assam has to offer its visitors. The state is the second largest of the North-Eastern Hill States which comprise, in addition to Assam, those of Meghalaya, Arunachel Pradesh, Nagaland, Manipur, Mizoram and Tripura. Assam itself is a land of rice paddies, bamboo plantations, tea estates and hidden temples divided by the gargantuan Brahmaputra. The terrain is utterly beautiful; its varied tribal people kind and generous and extremely appreciative of the rare visitor like myself, even when I rudely poked my nose into thatched cottage dwellings tucked away in the coconut forests.

With Mr Das I crossed the two and a half kilometre-wide river on the British-constructed Saraghat Bridge to see the archaeological site of Madan Kamdev, a secret place of ancient exotically and erotically carved stones; the silk-weaving community of Sualkuchi; the temples around Guwahati including that on Peacock Island in the middle of the Brahmaputra reached by a current-fighting boat, and the sacred Nilachal Hill believed to be an ancient Khasi sacrificial site which we climbed to marvel at a blood-red evening sky reflected in the huge spread of the river below.

Gujjar nomad wedding party. Karakoram Mountains, Pakistan.

In the cab of the locomotive *Fort of Jodhpur* heading the *Palace on Wheels* train.

The Desert Queen heading the *Palace on Wheels*. Rajasthan, India.

Rameswaram railway station. Southern India.

Foraging for coal. Udaipur, Rajasthan Province, India.

Prayer flags at Kardeng Gompa. Lahoul, India.

An engine shed of the East African Railway (now Kenya Railways). Kisumu, Kenya.

Lions on the road. Masai Mara National Reserve. Kenya.

The Ecuadorian Railway – an old British Leyland bus on rails. San Lorenzo line, Ecuador

Steam traction on the Fort William–Mallaig line. Arisaig Station, Scotland.

The Canadian in the Canadian Rockies.

Alaskan highway road-sign forest. Watson Lake, Yukon, Canada.

Rail approach to station. Cape Town, South Africa.

Viceroy Special waits at Colombo station. Sri Lanka.

A deficiency of sleep caught up with me during my last evening with Mr Das. Invited to a banquet provided by an assembly of newspaper editors and local radio programme presenters at the Nandan Hotel in Guwahati, I was plied with questions and beer to the point where my head kept falling on to my plate.

Had there been time I would have taken a peek at the famed Kaziranga Wildlife Park, the last remaining haunt of the Indian one-horned rhino, and Manas, a wildlife sanctuary in the Himalayan foothills. Instead I made my way by an erratically-driven bus to Shillong in neighbouring Meghalaya, which translates into 'Abode of the Clouds'. It was an appropriate name, too, particularly for Shillong which was once another British-patronised hill station and is a cooler, calmer urban centre than grinding Guwahati.

At the back of my mind had reposed the idea of attempting to reach the town of Kohima in Nagaland or Imphal in Manipur, both in heavily restricted border areas with Burma. My regiment – then the Dorset, now Devonshire and Dorset – fought around these two areas during the Second World War and I had determined to visit the war cemeteries there. In support of this endeavour I possessed letters from the top brass of both my regimental association and the current regiment. The very fact that no authority had demanded to see my Assam permit encouraged me to flout the rules again and enter a restricted zone.

As is the case with a lot of my plans, this one also came unstuck. Its attempted execution involved a continuation by one of a trio of named expresses – the Brahmaputra Mail, the Assam Mail and the Kamrup Express – from Guwahati towards Dibrugarh, emphatically the end of the line. I'm unsure which one of these I actually boarded, but it dropped me at Dinajpur, the halfway mark, at an inconvenient three o'clock in the morning. Dinajpur, or what little I saw of the place, struck me as something of a den of thieves, albeit the pleasantest of thieves, and my presence there

drew much attention particularly when, at the bus station, I commenced making enquiries about road services to Kohima.

'Didn't you know they weren't running?' I was asked. 'They are shooting up the buses.'

'No, I didn't know,' I had replied, uncertain as to who 'they' were. Alas, as I should have realised that bus stations, like railway stations, harbour minions of authority and the attention I was receiving, helpful though it was meant to be, focused the eyes of both the military and the police. The Army captain who questioned me about my intentions was really quite nice, sympathetic even when he heard about my mission. The police officer was less so. He told me, in no uncertain terms, that I would be breaking the law by entering Nagaland, the border of which was just down the road, and sent me packing.

Thereafter I debated whether or not to continue further eastwards to Dibrugarh and so chalk up another attainment of an Indian extremity, or return to Delhi. Instead of tossing a coin I allowed Lady Luck to dictate the decision; I'd catch whatever train came in first. In the event the Guwahati-bound Kamrup Express came down heads and, even without a reservation, I obtained a seat. And from Guwahati the North-East Express gave me a 40-hour ride right through to Delhi.

By this time my tolerance of rail travel was being pushed to the limit, and an added burden arose during this long final leg of the current journey. An excess of sitting must have trapped a nerve in my thigh, causing increasing pain that reached agonising proportions. I have arrived in Delhi in a variety of ways, but never have I had to emerge there from a train on hands and knees.

I have mentioned and commented upon several Indian narrow-gauge railway lines in these pages; those of the Blue Mountain Railway, Matheran, and Darjeeling in particular. Another worth a few words is that of Simla.

It was in 1981 that my wife Anna, on her first trip to India, and I came to the Himalayan foothills to join a trekking group. From the Simla Mail we transferred at Kalka to the innocuous white-painted Viceroy's rail-car for the five-hour haul up through the green hills to Simla. As we stepped into our carriage, and had rugs solicitously wrapped around our legs, we might have been the viceroy and vicereine ourselves, though five o'clock in the morning is not an hour for viceregal airs and graces.

For much of the way the line runs close to the road, their paths crossing at frequent intervals. To enable trains to climb the 5,000 feet to Simla, two miles of viaducts and 107 tunnels had to be constructed over a track length of 60 miles, such is the terrain. Two hours out, and we halted at the little station of Barog, where the rail-car waits while its passengers partake of a leisurely breakfast before setting off again into the tumbling cloud. Occasionally this cloud and mist were rent by shafts of light to reveal a valley floor thousands of feet below, ignored by the busy rail-car with more than views in mind as it hooted indignantly at buffalo and goats straying on to the track.

Solan Brewery Halt has been both a brewery and a railway station. But the station came afterwards, the brewery having been erected in the nineteenth century by a British company that found good spring water here in the hills of Himachal Pradesh. In 1904 when the railway was built, the line cut right through the brewery, and passengers thereafter were treated to the rich aroma of malt and hops at the station approaches.

With its meadows of asphodel, of hyacinth and celandine, of carmine rhododendron trees surrounded by solemn forests of *deodar* and towering pine, Simla retains the ghost of bygone splendours in the same manner as 'Ooty' and Darjeeling. Golf and cricket are still played and the town's architecture is an uncharacteristic mix of late-Victorian colonial, mock-Tudor and modern spa resort. Higgledy-piggledy, it lurches up and over the steep slopes, one ramshackle building piled upon another. The

Ridge is the centre where the sallow Christ Church and mock-Tudor library provide the tourist-acceptable face of Simla. The precipitous back alleys and narrow passages between the houses are, however, pure India. The Viceregal Lodge itself is a splendid over-the-top baronial affair and from Scandal Point, where a European lady is reputed to have been abducted by a maharaja, the town can be seen wreathed in the smoke of thousands of cooking fires pungent in the chill morning air.

Anna and I based ourselves for a couple of days at the elegant Woodville Guesthouse, a raja's former residence, while we explored this smiling caricature of an English county town. Then we were off into the hills where no railway dared venture.

It might be noticed that my Indian rail wanderings have taken a turn towards the luxurious end of the amenity spectrum. And as a climax of superabundance to them I now relate a peregrination through Rajasthan made in 1982, on the ornate *Palace on Wheels*.

Rajasthan is the obvious choice of states through which to run a maharaja's train. It is a land of rock and desert, lakes and gardens as well as enchanting fairytale forts and palaces. From the human angle the region is still living in its historic past, despite the changes of the last few years. Home of the Rajputs of ancient lineage, it is a legendary land of chivalry and knightly prowess. Its very name means 'Abode of Kings'. Palace and fort, garden and lake speak of love and loyalty, of proud prestige and deeds of derring-do. Resisting every invader since the time of Harsha in the seventh century, the feudal lords and princes of Rajasthan valiantly defended their independence and, in this, they were helped by the British, for whom its colourful peoples maintain a high regard.

Awaiting my pleasure, the prestigious tour train *Palace on Wheels* hid its light under a bushel as it stood amongst hardly less exotic trains at Delhi Cantonment station. The long line of dun-coloured coaches gave little impression of a palace, wheeled or otherwise. The windows, set low, were the usual barred variety and there

was no corridor. The train's chief power unit was the steam engine and this, externally, was where its grandeur lay. On my journey there were two such locomotives, magnificent monsters both, each bearing a golden coat of arms and the proud names *Desert Queen* and *Fort of Jodhpur*.

The outside of the coaches may have been unimpressive, but inside was another story. Upon being ushered into my own private coach – in its time it had borne both the Maharaja of Bikaner and Mrs Indira Gandhi – I gazed in awe upon the spacious sleeping compartment replete with wardrobe and double bed, plus refinements such as table lamps, fans and a telephone. The lounge contained a sofa and armchairs of quality brocade and the walls were lined with heavy polished mahogany. A well-fitted toilet and bathroom as well as two further bedrooms completed the suite of rooms, beyond which lay the servants' quarters, the domain of two most gracious Rajasthanis attired in crimson and gold tunics and turbans to match; their sole object over the ensuing week being to wait upon me hand and foot. Further along the train, the restaurant car was a reflection of what I can remember of the one-time *Brighton Belle*: pink lampshades at each window, the tables agleam with monogrammed china and cutlery, while the lounge car was plentifully endowed with soft cushions around long, low divans and oblong coffee tables of polished carved oak, the whole menage tastefully encased by the luxuriant folds of curtains glittering with gold thread. An end section housed a bar and a library, each well stocked with its particular requisites.

Indian Railways it was that carried out this major refurbishment of rolling stock rescued, item by item, from railway sheds and disused sidings at remote railway stations all over India. Saved from the grave, but rusted from the monsoons and bleached by the sun, they were assembled and painstakingly restored to their former glory, or rebuilt from a basic framework.

The first meal of the trip in the restaurant car was representative of them all. There was a choice of meat or fish between the usual

ancillary items, but the paramount attraction of that particular meal was vested in the assembly of its consumers: the gathering of the clan. Across the soup, the veal cutlets, the halibut and the crème caramel, we eyed one another in critical appraisal, pondered upon the type of person who would choose a train for a holiday and launched into a fever of introduction. Thus, with the coffee and mints, I was to discern that our numbers included lawyers and doctors, stockbrokers and company directors, a naval captain and a nuclear scientist. That such an upper stratum of society should be so strongly represented was surprising only in that it showed who is the most adventurous class; so long as the adventure is diluted with comfort and there is the money to embark upon it. The coffee and liqueurs concluded, we bade one another good-night and scurried to our respective bedchambers to await the maharajan movement.

And indeed, the maharajan movement took us all over Rajasthan. At Jaipur, the 'pink city', we were greeted by a cavalcade of elephants, not pink but vivid nevertheless in glittering headdress; a band of folk-musicians warbling boisterously, and the first of seven marigold-garland welcomes from smiling girls of exotic allure.

There was a perfect tonal harmony about the salmon-pink dawn breaking over the faded red-ochre sandstone of the city that owes its name and symmetry to Maharaja Jai Singh II. Encircled on all sides, except the south, by rugged hills surmounted by forts, Jaipur is enclosed by battlemented walls. Within them is medieval bedlam. The Hawa Mahal, 'Palace of the Winds', is the landmark of the city, though its elaborate, fanciful, pink façade stands amidst the high street chaos of clogged roads and rude dwellings.

At Amber came the scheduled elephant ride on which we progressed regally up the hill, musically escorted, to a deserted Mogul edifice before a lesson on sundials at the Jantar Mantar Observatory, tea on a maharajan terrace, and dinner amongst the floodlit remains of the ruined fort of Nahargarh.

Came Udaipur, another sprawling city, this one given a romantic air by the steel-blue waters of a lake. Moated Udaipur, ethereal, unreal, holds island palaces galore that sparkle with pinnacles of coloured glass, of amber and pale jade, created by Maharaja Udai Singh in the sixteenth century. His palace-fort, massively bastioned and gated, erupts from the crest of a ridge and is the largest such pile in Rajasthan. In the less sombre palace that takes up the whole of an island in the artificial lake, we lunched very adequately on asparagus and venison.

'Island in the Sun' describes the next port of call, and for most of us it was the most fascinating city of all. In a scarred, romantic land amidst shifting sands, barren ridges and jutting rocks of sandstone, limestone and flint under a brazen sun lies Jaisalmer, a forgotten feudal outpost where temples, palaces and bazaars created a magical city of the Orient. At every turn there were glimpses of an older, fiercer way of life, a life made hard and vital by its remote and austere setting. Proud, turbaned figures; impressive faces atop slow, swaying camels; graceful *panharis* walking from village wells, brass water pots balanced on their heads; the clamour and clangour and colour of bazaars; kohl-rimmed eyes, bangles and ankle bells; a hundred ancient secrets kept behind fortress gates amongst the streets and alleys of the teeming city.

Jaisalmer's history dates back to the twelfth century when it became an important trading post between East and West. The discovery of the sea route to India by the Portuguese three centuries later nullified its commercial *raison d'être*, but successive flamboyant maharajas maintained its splendour with temples and palaces encrusted with stone carvings. Only in the last couple of decades has this exotic city become accessible with the construction of both road and railway.

On camels now, we sauntered in single file across stony expanses and over smooth dunes towards the Pakistani border, each of us perched precariously on the blanket-covered wooden

saddles as the animals rocked back and forth. Our return hack looped over parched earth framed by a featureless horizon, our mounts maintaining their air of haughty indifference, contemptuous of their desert joyriders.

Northwards, still on the railway, lies Bikaner. 'Out of the silken darkness of a desert dawn emerged the dream of Bikaner.' For 30 years after leaving his father's capital of Jodhpur, Rao Bhika and his followers lived from skirmish to skirmish on the edge of life in a hostile land. Gujars, Pratiharas, Chauhans, Afghans, Bhattis and Rajputs fought with one another for supremacy and here, in a wilderness of sand, Bhika won a kingdom for himself and ruled as 'Lord of the Desert of Bikaner'.

And so to the last city, Jodhpur, once the capital of the state of Marwar, built upon the brow of a low sandstone hill, again in the heart of the desert. A rocky eminence immediately behind dominates it from the sand that stretches away on all sides, and at its summit soars a massive fortress, its towers and bastions standing out like tough sinews gleaming with a copper tinge where the rock was hewn to form the walls and ramparts. From these the view commands the horizon; indeed, on a clear day the tower of Khumbhalgarth may be seen, 80 miles to the south.

These then were the cities of the tour, plus Bharatpur with its bird sanctuary, an ornithologist's paradise, and as a grand finale, the jewel of the Taj Mahal at Agra. But for me, the height of evocation came with my repeated transfers from the luxurious splendour of the mobile abode of the Maharaja of Bikaner to the sooty confines of the cab of the locomotives. Here, my eyes full of smut and a tummy full of sweet, oily tea, I rediscovered a joy of travel that was in danger of eclipse beneath a welter of high living. Within a shuddering cab packed with dials and levers, I was back in a corner of real India and in the company of Indians, sharing the whiff of steam, the searing blast of heat from a raging furnace, the ear-splitting scream of the whistle and the sheer exhilaration of riding a mechanical monster vibrating with

unleashed power. On the last morning aboard the *Desert Queen* I was given a revisionary lesson by an appreciative crew on the rudiments of an old-fashioned semaphore signalling procedure and, in farewell, received a big bear hug from the driver and his fireman who had tolerated – even aided and abetted – my numerous incursions into their domain.

Back at New Delhi station there were no garlands; we were maharajas no more.

Trans-East Africa

For a long time I had natured a desire to ride the one-time East African Railway. Not only for the universally-acclaimed purpose of being able to observe big game from a moving train, but also by reason of the very evocativeness of its history. My chance came in April 1976, but the timing was both lucky and unfortunate. The year was the last before the complete break-up of the confederation of railways of Kenya, Tanzania and Uganda so I was fortunate to be able to ride a considerable portion of the network while it still *was* the East African Railway. My misfortune stemmed from the fact that the despotic ruler of Uganda, Idi Amin, was not only at the zenith of his power but, that very month, was on the brink of sending his Army into Kenya. Yet another near-war was to dog my journeying; this one turning my dream ride into something of a nightmare.

When construction of the railway began in 1898 it became known in Britain as the 'Lunatic Line' by virtue of the fact that it was seemingly going from 'nowhere through nowhere to nowhere'. In spite of the fact that its creation was a very considerable feat of engineering, few could raise great enthusiasm for the project even though one of the declared purposes of the railway through unknown East Africa to the remote landlocked country of Uganda was to put down the Arab slave trade. But the builders and promoters maintained their faith and the line took shape, snaking its way through the uplands, meeting but overcoming obstacles such as hundreds of miles of sponge-like quagmire, hostile tribes, waterless desert, man-eating lions, tsetse flies and malaria. The route brought the workforce over the mile-deep volcanic Rift Valley escarpment, down which trains were lowered on an inclined plane assisted by ropes. It continued across

the Highlands and over the fierce Mau Summit and on to the shores of Lake Victoria.

At first the line was known as the Kenya & Uganda Railway, and British indifference to its conception and construction is illustrated by the fact that its metre gauge was a direct result of being supplied with cheap, second-hand rolling stock and equipment from India. The Tanzanian section was originally metre gauge anyway from the time of its construction by the Germans when the country was known as Tanganyika. The two railways merged in 1948. Under British influence the union was effective, but political and economic differences since independence have gradually wrenched the three systems apart.

Looked upon in the early days as no more than an imperialistic manoeuvre aimed at enabling Britain to control the upper Nile and thus maintain her hold on Egypt and the Suez Canal, the outcome was surprising. As well as being virtually instrumental in putting down the slave trade the railway opened up Uganda, created the country of Kenya and developed what has become East Africa's major metropolis, Nairobi. Nowhere else in the world, and at no time in history, has a journey been so dramatically shortened from a six-month walk fraught with danger to a four-day ride in comparative comfort and safety. Freight movement gained spectacularly; no longer restricted to what a black human head could carry.

In spite of the truncation of the complex, the Night Mail still covers the 308 miles between Nairobi and Mombasa, but the famous and luxurious Uganda Mail has fallen victim to man's folly. I was lucky, very lucky, to have ridden from Mombasa in what turned out to be the last through-express that ran between the two countries.

Against the endless Athai Plain fading into dusk I contemplated East Africa's premier city as I set off on the Night Mail from

Nairobi to Mombasa. For anyone then coming to black Africa for the first time, the Kenyan capital served as the perfect decompression chamber. The steel and glass shopping centre, parking meters, red post-boxes, Wimpy's, Woolworth's, fish and chip shops and traffic that circled roundabouts clockwise in the British manner made homely touches. Today it is a metropolis of skyscrapers rising from avenues adorned with statues and lined with bougainvillaea that fails to hide suburbs of disease and poverty. Even in my father's lifetime Nairobi had grown from a malarious swamp to a city of well over a million. In 1902 this former railway construction camp called 'The Cold Well' – or 'Nai'robi' – held but one small shop and a tin shanty that served as a hotel.

My dinner in the dining car was no more than adequate and afterwards, when back in my compartment, a steward brought me my bedding. He had been with the East African Railway for ten years and expressed relief that he would soon be working for just Kenya Railways.

'Might get paid more promptly,' he observed.

I gave him ten shillings which was the cost of *reserving* bedding rather than for the loan of it. He bade me good-night, promising to wake me early next morning to see the African wildlife on the plains. I turned out the light and lay looking out of the window at the train's flickering reflection.

I awoke at Voi, the junction for Dar es Salaam and Tanzania. Somewhere back down the line was Tsavo where the famous man-eating lions had so effectively depleted the railway construction workers and their master, Superintendent Ryall, who was dragged from his sleeping car and devoured. There have since been enthralling stories of lions and other wild animals resenting the passage of trains and hurling themselves against the coaches, while a heavy Garrett locomotive was reputed to have been derailed by a charging rhino. But over the last decades the four-footed

inhabitants of the plains have come to terms with the railway and there are no more such exciting stories to record.

Kilindi announced the approach to the outskirts of Mombasa and we were in the city proper as soon as our train had clanked across the bridge to pull into the eastern terminus of the line. A row of cubicles attracted my attention: '1st Class Ladies & Gentlemen's Toilet' pronounced one, '2nd Class Ladies & Gents' read another, and '3rd Class Male & Female' was the notice on the last door. Shades of India.

And assuredly Mombasa is not only a slice of India but all Asia as well. It is a town reflecting, in both character and architecture, mixed cultures that have joined in true unison. Arabs and Asians, Africans and Europeans live together more or less contentedly in a blatantly humid oriental sprawl that could be ten thousand miles from Africa. I spent the day feeling uncomfortably sticky and walking the narrow streets of the Old Town in the shadow of tall houses of elaborately carved ornamental balconies and slender mosques. Itinerant Arabs sold coffee from traditional long-beaked copper pots, while oriental music drifted from the shops of goldsmiths, moneylenders, tailors and tinsmiths. On a massive hill, Fort Jesus and its silent guns covered the harbour, looking out beyond English Point to the line of shipwrecks that had become as permanent as islands.

I returned to the station in the evening in good time to catch the Uganda Mail. Given the wrong sleeper number, I came face to face with two formidable English matrons who held very definite ideas as to how first-class travellers should be attired and made it plain to me that I failed to measure up to their exacting standards.

'Sir,' they observed in stern reproach, 'You appear to be in the wrong class.'

An English Electric diesel unit hauled us through rich dark palm groves into the gathering dusk and a land of endless thorn

trees. These waterless wastes and the red dust of the Taru Desert ensured East Africa's isolation from the world until the end of the nineteenth century. For me it was a first sight of the African bush, and with the dawn my first living perception of the size of Africa. Tall grass, as far as the eye could reach, swayed like a vast field of ripening corn in a perpetual summer wind.

In the grey light the plains of the Masai presented me with its fruit: water buck, gazelle, wildebeest, zebra and giraffe steadfastly ignored the train, continuing with their grazing as if we were no more than some insignificant caterpillar.

It was not my intention to continue straight on to Kampala from Nairobi but to catch a later Kisumu-bound train. This would entail travelling the same line as far as Nakuru and then branching north-west towards Lake Victoria. The railway, which had created Kenya simply as a by-product of its construction, was, in the late 1920s, to open up new and empty territory for development. The high wastelands through which it passed on the way to Lake Victoria had been settled and found lucrative. Farms had spread all over the green highlands to the west of the great Rift Valley, near Eldoret and around the Uasin Gishu country. A new main line started to crawl towards them, branching off from the Kisumu line at Nakuru, itself a growing town, and climbing to a height of over 9,000 feet, the highest point ever reached by a British Commonwealth railway. Since that time the Kisumu line has become subordinate to the Kampala route by virtue of the fact that the Ugandan capital was later linked by rail instead of by the original ferry service from the Kisumu railhead. But for me the old Uganda Railway route was one I felt I had to see and cover.

Hardly had we left behind the suburbs of Nairobi when the track started climbing. It rose through green pastures towards the summit of the eastern wall of the Rift Valley. The first sight of this phenomenon is indelibly marked on my memory. Abruptly the forest thins and there, 2,000 feet below, at the base of a sheer

escarpment, is the Rift, quite certainly the most gigantic valley in the world. Thirty miles away the opposite wall rose, dark purple against the sky, a procession of clouds drifting across the peaks. The colossal fault in the Earth's surface is as though some immense thermonuclear plough had dug a furrow striking right across Africa from Lake Baikal in Siberia to the Red Sea. The geographical disturbance must have convulsed half the world in some prehistoric age to become an inland ocean from which the waters have receded, leaving a succession of lakes to this day. Dozens of volcanoes have erupted in the Rift, the greatest being Kilimanjaro, and their threat still hangs in the air like the curl of smoke I could see rising from a herdsman's fire.

The town of Nakuru lies on the floor of the valley and at the foot of the Menengai Mountain, the top of which is reputed to have subsided into some subterranean vacuum. To the south of the town is Lake Nakuru, a large expanse of shallow, saline water, the shores of which are the sacred nesting ground of ten thousand flamingos. An acrid smell of soda rose from the lake to increase the allure of this mysterious region, while great flurries of pink-white feathers made a fairytale snowstorm that was reflected in the water.

Nakuru, not an unpleasant urban centre by any means, makes no use of its lake which is a mile or two away. But what it lacks in lakeside scenic backdrop it makes up for in friendliness. Simply through asking directions I was invited home to tea by two African ladies. The tea expanded into a double scotch and, subsequently, the biggest mixed grill I have ever consumed. I was also pressed to have a bath, perhaps because I looked as if I needed one. The good ladies were all for me staying the night, but I had a train to catch.

I suppose my interest lay as much with the railway as it did with Africa, for continuing towards Kisumu and Lake Victoria I found myself pondering the fact that it was not the steep climb to

Fort Ternan but the easy terrain to the lake that had troubled the line's builders. Americans in 1903 built the tunnels and dozens of bridges within a section of 50 miles, but found problems with the soft littoral which caused an uncanny number of derailments. And the locals *would* keep nicking material like telegraph wire for their womenfolk's decoration and tools for adaptation into weapons. But Kisumu entered history with the Uganda Railway which terminated at the then Port Florence.

Kisumu aspires to bigger things than Nakuru and makes better use of its lake; as it should, since Victoria is the second biggest lake in the world. Like Mombasa, Kisumu is a mixture of Africa and Asia and, additionally, is something of a garden city. In the main square a conglomeration of exponents of Christian religions were militantly competing for custom and recognition amongst a Sunday crowd of onlookers. Even the Salvation Army, beaming black faces under stiff bonnets and peaked caps, was represented, although the band was composed entirely of percussion. The weather turned from warm to sweltering and, together with a gang of African boys, I managed a quick dip in the lake in spite of dire warnings of crocodiles and other deterrents. Back at the station I obtained permission to visit and photograph the engine sheds full of greasy old steam locos, but not before a fracas with an obstinate member of the railway police. This ended in a draw when he agreed that I could have the run of the sheds so long as he was included in every picture I took.

Back in Nakuru a new emotion assailed me. Ever since I had decided to cover what I could of the East African Railway network, the situation at its western end had been a nagging worry. World newspapers had been screaming about the tension on the border for weeks as the then Ugandan dictator, Idi Amin's crack troops stood poised to invade Kenya. For weeks Uganda had been pouring invective at Kenya, Britain, Israel and anybody else who had failed to support his monstrous edicts. Just ten days previously the

Israelis had scored their triumph against Amin with the successful raid on Entebbe Airport, so the hate across the border was fresh and vitriolic. That Amin and his regime were bad the world was learning fast; just how bad it had still to discover. But in the meantime the border was allegedly open, albeit with long delays.

I had some hours to kill at Nakuru, so spent them exploring this quite large and prosperous town. Its railway station was the smartest in East Africa, I was told, and certainly its locomotive sheds held offerings that deflected my morbid thoughts from the gathering crisis up the line. I had arrived at this paragon of stations at 3.30 a.m., having spent a night on the tiles. However, my Uganda Mail, when it drew in soon after 3.00 p.m., was resplendent with sleepers, one of which was mine. The very fact that the train had not been cancelled or seemingly curtailed and showed every sign of an intention of going through to Kampala cheered me up no end.

Nakuru vanished and, out of the window, I caught more glimpses of the Rift Valley, only now it was becoming more fertile as the red soil deepened and lush foliage folded round the line.

Eldoret, they will tell you, is where the bank was built around its safe. Again, it was the railway that made the town, though it was through an accident that the big safe fell from a wagon; found to be too heavy to move, a building was constructed over it and things grew from there. Unfazed by its unscheduled beginnings, Eldoret flourishes as a busy market town, the last sizeable community before Uganda.

I had several companions in the compartment who drew me into animated conversation and pressed me to edible delicacies from an assortment of newspaper packages. One of the men was a Ugandan law student from Nairobi University who was returning to Kampala to see his parents. He thought he could stay a couple of days and make it back to Kenya before the border finally closed. This, likewise, cheered me up some more since

my plans were to remain in the Ugandan capital just for one day. The train schedules offered a nine-hour stay, which I felt was adequate for a brief glimpse of the city. The coach in which we were travelling was composed of compartments making up into four beds at night.

It was nothing less than pure bloody-mindedness that kept the train standing at the border station of Malaba for all of five hours that night. Neither the law student nor myself were able to sleep with the rumours and counter-rumours that were circulating as money-changers and Kenyan border police stamped up and down the corridor. Cold daybreak saw us stomping impatiently alongside the stranded train, so that when the Ugandan authorities finally gave us the green light to let the train go we almost missed it, and in retrospect I rather wished we had. Rolling across a wide brook I glimpsed a notice reading 'You are entering the Republic of Uganda' which evoked in me a similar sense of foreboding to that of crossing the one-time East-West German border into the totalitarian Communist East.

Ten minutes later we drew into Tororo, on the Ugandan side of the border, and the train filled up again. An immigration official examined my passport, acidly pointing out that I had no need of the visa I had prudently obtained from the Ugandan High Commission in London.

'This is a free and democratic country,' he added. 'We welcome British visitors wholeheartedly.' He stamped the passport and afforded me two days on Ugandan soil, though I only wanted one.

The train did its best to make up for lost time but, with numerous scheduled halts en route, it was a forlorn hope that I would get more than a fraction of my nine hours in Kampala. Every station was a hive of activity, the colourful crowds having little to do with the train's arrival, but grouping there simply because the station represented the local community centre; the

place where the action was, and where they would be most likely to sell their goods. Even though I possessed no Ugandan currency, I nevertheless became the recipient of a bunch of thirty bananas on account of the fact, it was explained, that I looked hungry.

As we crossed the Nile over the great bridge at Jinja – Uganda's Sheffield – I sensed an air of crisis at its station. The crowds were less exuberant here and uniformed police more in evidence; indeed even while the train stood at the platform I watched two of them arresting a man.

This region of Uganda is a green and pleasant land, well watered and fertile. Exotic blossoms and bloated leaves pressed against the track and my student friend treated me to a running commentary on their botanical details.

It was raining when we reached Kampala and the grey clouds did nothing to enhance a city of nearly empty dual carriageways, tall buildings in need of renovation and beautiful colonial homes run to seed. I estimated that my planned nine-hour sojourn had been cut to four, which worried me not at all. My friend escorted me up the stairs to the station concourse.

An officious-looking man in civilian clothes stood behind a desk close to the ticket barrier surveying the happy jostling crowd with distaste. His gaze fell on me.

'You. Here!' he bawled.

'You talking to me?' I asked with equal hostility.

The man demanded my passport and that of the student. To me he barked, 'Why have you and your friend come here?' as he thumbed through the pages. I sensed the start of something more ominous than mere immigration control, and noticed too the unease of my companion.

'I've come to spend a few hours in Kampala,' I explained, adding hurriedly that I had met the student on the train and that we were not together. The student gabbled his own reasons for his visit.

'Wait here.' The man moved away, taking our passports. We watched him arrogantly pushing through the crowd, knocking a woman almost to the ground as he went.

He returned a while later to take us to a bare office where a colleague sat, smiling sardonically, at a table. We were not invited to sit down. The second man started to question me.

'Why have you come to Uganda? What is the purpose of your visit?'

I answered his questions as best I could, expressing my interest in the East African Railway network though aware that my reason sounded inadequate, even provocative to an African unappreciative of his railway. The student was steadfastly ignored though, out of the corner of my eye, I caught his unease growing into stark terror. He was sweating profusely, plainly aware of what these evil men had in mind.

'What is your connection with this man?' came the question I was half expecting.

I repeated the fact that we were no more than travelling companions and that once out of the station we would be going our different ways. Neither of our questioners seemed to believe this, and a few moments later the two of us were taken outside and pushed into the back of an antiquated black saloon car. As we were driven through the town the rain fell in buckets and I almost managed to convince myself that, in the circumstances, this was the best way of seeing Kampala.

Seldom have I witnessed a more depressing city. The shops were no more than eye-sockets in a face of empty streets where policemen hung around the intersections. Halfway up a hill the car engine began to cough and the driver to moan loudly about the shortage of fuel coupons even for official vehicles. I now understood the reason for a deficiency of traffic. When the engine finally expired we all had to abandon its dry interior and push the

thing all the way to the Kampala Police Headquarters. In minutes we were wet through.

Inside the blank-faced building a stench of stale sweat, rancid tobacco and an unidentifiable sweet odour permeated the bare-walled corridors. Handcuffed prisoners, wild-eyed and perspiring, passed by in the charge of young policemen. The student's face had gone deathly pale and I guessed he knew more about Ugandan security police methods than I did.

In an office almost as bare as the corridors we found ourselves before another inquisitor, this one likewise in plain clothes. The furnishings were a cheap desk, a couple of hard-backed chairs, a filing cabinet, a telephone and, on the wall, a lop-sided photograph (unframed) of Idi Amin. Previous interrogation scenarios of which I had been witness went through my mind. Such sparse furnishings fitted the Gestapo, the Czech STB and the Soviet KGB, though nobody in Nazi and post-war Communist days would dream of displaying a lop-sided Fuhrer or an unframed Stalin.

Ugandan interrogation style differed too. Not particularly unpleasantly did the new man sitting opposite me repeat the same questions, though adding a new emphasis. It wasn't so much why had I come to his country, but why for so brief a period? To this I gave him the double reason; this being that my passport had been endorsed by the Ugandan authorities at the border for only two days, though one would suffice since my chief interest lay with the railway. He also wanted to know why I was in a carriage with a Ugandan exile returning to his country (when everyone else was leaving), and why we had exchanged addresses (the 'incriminating' scraps of paper had been found when my wallet and pockets had been searched). This had been the student's request and a very harmless one but, abruptly, I was aware how small incidences could be blown up into a balloon of guilt and suspicion. Then came the next hurdle.

'How is it your passport indicates you are a company director and this card pronounces you a journalist?' (At that time British passports had to show the bearer's profession).

To explain that I was once a company director and had retained the title in my passport in preference to the sometimes provocative 'journalist' would only complicate matters, even though here was an example of just such provocation. So I offered the white lie that I was still a company director and that I was a journalist, though only a travel journalist, in my spare time.

To two fresh interrogators in another room I repeated these explanations, which sounded even less plausible each time I uttered them, but I stuck to it. And you know, there comes a moment when you actually begin to believe that you *are* a spy or whatever it is they are trying to suggest you might be. It creeps up on you when they catch you out on some harmless answer to a question. I felt the symptoms and resolved to keep my answers *simple* and to stick to them the second and third time round.

For instance: What school did I attend? I was asked. I gave the one I attended the longest. There was no need to bring up the other two.

My regimental association membership card came up for scrutiny. What rank did I hold? they wanted to know.

'Corporal,' I replied, giving the lowest rank I had held, though I had actually risen to that of captain. Pride alone stopped me from saying 'private'.

'Which army?' came the next enquiry. I had to admit it was British.

My camera produced much attention. I was asked what photographs I had taken on Ugandan soil and truthfully reported that I had taken none. They made sure I was telling the truth by exposing the film.

Every now and again I would point out the fact that if they were going to charge me with anything, I had the right to see a

representative of my government, though this seemed to be of no consequence to my interrogators. And there comes, too, a point in all interrogations when there is a lull in proceedings during which one can mount a counter-attack of the 'Why the hell am I here? What crime am I supposed to have committed?' sort of thing which, if nothing else, raises morale if not the roof.

No longer was my student friend with me and I was never to set eyes on him again as I was taken from room to room to be harangued by a sequence of questioners all demanding to know what I was up to. Occasionally I was asked if I was hungry, to which I replied, truthfully, that I was.

'What would you like?' they enquired.

Optimistic to the bitter end I suggested steak and chips.

'Do you want some tea?'

'That too, please.'

Neither the steak nor the tea put in an appearance, of course, but I felt grateful for the enquiry. It added a slice of normality to the proceedings.

Sometimes the questioning was undertaken in an abusive manner with accusations flung at me in angry outbursts. I was a spy sent by Kenya to make contact with somebody. I was intent upon prying into the workings of the railway. I was sent to undermine the Ugandan regime, the student being my contact. Mostly, however, the questioning was mildly administered of the 'Come on, you can tell us everything and we'll let you go' sort of manner, which was the more ominous.

Everything I said had to be typed in triplicate by a series of clerks who were no more than one-finger typists. Everybody with whom I came into contact wore the depressing air of a black Gestapo, this emphasised by the fact that I had finally recognised the source of the sweet smell my nose had picked up as we had entered the building. It was of rotting flesh: a recollection dredged up from my wartime experience.

The questioning, together with repeated searching of my duffel bag, continued for two whole days and nights with little respite. Occasionally I was left alone, presumably so that I could ponder upon my alleged sins, and I took the opportunity for a catnap. But just as I nodded off, in someone would come with the same line of questioning and it would all start again. A single glass of water was all I could manage to extract to keep body and soul intact.

And then, suddenly, I was told I could go. A moment of disbelief kept me rooted to the spot and then I was off, bundling my belongings, strewn over the table, into my bag. My sense of urgency to get to the railway station must have communicated itself to my guards because they broke into a run to get to the car. Abruptly they were no longer my guards but the means of catching a train, if there was one, to Kenya, or as near as I could get to Kenya.

At the station I found I had to wait for several hours for a train to Tororo, some five miles from the border, and my return ticket was still valid for it. Not that this mattered, for when the train did arrive it was overrun by a huge crowd that overflowed on to the outside of the coaches. I joined a trio of anxious youths on the steps of a second-class coach. Rain still splashed down but I was too relieved to care.

For 15 minutes nothing happened and then, without any warning, the overloaded train slunk away through the suburbs of Kampala. I never felt so pleased to see the back of a city as I did this one.

But my good fortune was short-lived, for as we approached the gradient to Seta, the English Electric diesel ground to a halt. A wave of panic washed through the coaches. Up front a crowd gathered round the green locomotive with its distinctive yellow stripe. Everybody yelled advice and instructions to the driver and, such was the desperation to proceed, some passengers began trying

to *push* it. The atmosphere was tense, with more and more men joining the pushing contingent while their womenfolk stood in silence by the track, under the downpour, with their babies and small children. At the third attempt the wheels gripped the track and we were away again, everybody hurling themselves back into the coaches. In the mêlée I won a seat in a coach.

Back at Tororo they grabbed me again. I couldn't believe it. As everybody left the train with, presumably, the intention of joining an expected connection that would take them into Kenya, a posse of uniformed police intercepted me, gave a cursory glance at my passport, and bundled me into an office in the station. And there I was grilled again, this time by uniformed interrogators. I complained loudly that I had been officially released by their compatriots in Kampala, but this seemed to cut no ice with them. Instead I was curtly told not to answer back. Then came the bombshell. *I would be returned to Kampala on the next eastbound train.* My sense of relief plummeted to that of grave concern.

However, there was no train to Kampala scheduled until the following morning. In the meantime I was consigned to a draughty waiting-room, the door securely locked and a sentry placed outside it. At least my new oppressors fed me as I was becoming weak with hunger. I had also fathomed a superficial reason for my re-apprehension since my permitted stay in Uganda had expired which, technically, made me an illegal alien. But I felt this to be no more than a ploy in the general scheme of things. It was all becoming a bad dream.

The room into which I had been put was, to all intents and purposes, a prison cell. It held no more than a wooden bench on which previous inmates had carved their names, and one window, high in the wall, which was too small to use as an escape exit. As darkness fell the elderly guard with an old Lee Enfield rifle joined me in the room. Beyond an occasional grunt he never spoke a word. We sat in stoic silence through the first half of the night,

with me trying to get some sleep on the narrow bench. The darkness of the room was confounded by a low-wattage bulb suspended from the high ceiling.

Escape was now firmly in my mind; the idea of a return to that hellhole of Kampala Police Headquarters was unbearable. The border was not more than five or six miles distant and, though the Ugandan Army was supposedly massed along it, I presumed it would be facing the other way. And, after all, nobody was stopping the massed migration out of the country. Furthermore I was unable to believe that the Amin regime had caught up with the finesse practised by the European Communist regimes so far as their methods of discouraging illegal emigration across the former Iron Curtain was concerned.

I pondered upon these matters as the night wore on, even managing a brief doze too, until my guard, snoring stentoriously, had fallen into a deeper sleep. And, glory be, he had left the key in the inside lock of the door. All I had to do was to pick up my duffel bag and let myself out, which I promptly did. It was all too easy; I even felt a pang of conscience about allowing the man to take the rap for losing a prisoner.

Nobody was about the station platform as the first streaks of dawn showed in the sky. And the rain had ceased. I made straight for the almost complete darkness of the trees and, keeping the railway to my right and in sight so as not to lose direction, strode out for the border. I fastened my eyes on a distant hill, now visible against the lightening sky, which I judged to be in Kenya. Foliage dripped incessantly as if it were raining again.

I bumped into the Army a moment before I became aware that I had company: a bunch of soldiers trying to get their radio to work. Too late to take avoiding action, I exhibited interest in what they were doing and, telling them that I was once a soldier myself, offered my help since I knew the type of Second World War apparatus they were using.

The group seemed more concerned with the state of their equipment than with my presence amongst them, but I still felt obliged to explain that I had missed the last train to Nairobi and was therefore walking to the border. After all, an Englishman walking into someone else's war zone at dawn I felt needed some explanation.

Though the soldiers had no need of my assistance, which was just as well, they could not have been friendlier, one of them presenting me with a bottle of lager. Rashly I enquired whether one of their vehicles and a driver could be presumed upon to give me a lift to the border. The corporal said he'd have to ask his officer, and I wondered whether I was pushing my luck too far.

But not so. A lieutenant came over, showing not the slightest surprise at my being where I was. He apologised for not being able to take me to the physical border, though a driver would drop me close by. This suited me fine.

And so it came about that, in the warm, petrol-reeking cab of a 15-hundredweight Bedford truck I made the border area without even having to walk there. The driver pointed me in the direction of the border post and, with a wave, returned the way he had come.

With the vehicle out of sight I left the road and struck out across pleasant rolling country in front of the conical hill for which Tororo is known, and also the landmark I had wrongly gauged to be in Kenya. And there was the railway again. Parallel with it I turned eastwards and came to the brook that forms the physical demarcation line between the two countries. I got my feet wet by failing to jump the obstacle.

In Malaba I boarded a bus to Eldoret, and there I caught up with the trains again. Relaxing in my compartment on the journey back to Nairobi I thought wistfully upon the remainder of the old East African Railway tracks that I had not covered; the line beyond

Kampala, and eastwards across another then closed frontier into Tanzania. Tanzania I was to visit a year or two later, but, for the time being, I had lost my appetite for closed borders.

Trans-Andes

In 1977 I turned my attention to riding the railways of South America, in particular those of Peru and Ecuador, plus brief dalliances on lines in Bolivia and Colombia.

The most evocative railways on that continent are, without doubt, those of the trans-Andean lines. Two connect Chile and Argentina, three give landlocked Bolivia access to the Pacific, one links Lima with the mountain valleys and mineral region of central Peru, and the most northerly connects Guayaquil and Quito in Ecuador. These lines were laid between 1870 and 1914, to a variety of gauges: standard gauge in Peru, metre gauge in Bolivia, and 3 feet 6 inch gauge in Ecuador. At the time of their construction they helped to bring some political unity to the scattered and diverse population of the countries they served, but their main function was economic and their chief interest freight traffic. They were, and still are, vitally important to the mining industries of Peru, Bolivia and Chile. Passenger traffic has never been more than a troublesome obligation.

Crossing the Andes meant constructing the highest railway in the world, the highest line being that of the Peruvian Central Railway which I was to ride during my stay in that country. Railway construction in such circumstances presented civil engineers with major problems for, in a confined space and short distance, they had to build railways over passes which exceeded Mont Blanc in altitude. The solution they adopted were tight curves, zigzags and rack sections. Operating the lines created further difficulties: steep gradients, lack of local sources of fuel, heavy wear and tear on locomotives and rolling stock, and frequent landslides and washouts. Changing from steam to diesel traction was, initially, a step backwards because diesel units were prone to losing power

in the rarefied air and there were many cases of trains being unable to take the gradients.

Here, then, was another set of railways that had forged a passage through impossible terrain to promise me some adventurous travelling.

My first experience of riding a trans-Andean railway was on the Southern Railway of Peru. Three lines serve the *altiplano*, a grassy windswept plain 12,800 feet above sea level, and one of them is the Southern. Of standard gauge, it runs from Mollendo on the Peruvian coast through the country's second city, Arequipa, to the town of Julaca on the *altiplano*. Here it divides. A short section continues to Lake Titicaca and around its shores to the port of Puno, while a 211-mile line from Julaca runs north to Cuzco, the ancient Inca capital, crossing a summit of 14,154 feet at La Raya. Access to Bolivia was maintained by a steamer service between Puno and the Bolivian port of Guaqui, with another short railway line to link the capital, La Paz. Today, road transportation has taken over many of the passenger services. Actually the Southern Railway of Peru was never a major trans-Andean route but, nevertheless, a very worthwhile ride. The line is single track throughout, and on the Arequipa to Mollendo section the passenger trains had, even then, succumbed to road competition. This necessitated my having to travel from Lima to Arequipa by an overcrowded, smelly abomination of a bus that was delayed for four hours during the intense heat of the midday sun by a nationwide bicycle race.

Arequipa is a depository of old Spanish buildings and churches made of *sillar*, a pearly white volcanic material used almost exclusively for their construction. Though an Inca city, it differs in many ways from Cuzco with few buildings taller than one storey. Earthquakes are the scourge here, the last one being in 1960 when much damage was done.

Travelling on a tight budget, my urban nights were to be spent in the most basic of accommodations, and the pension-cum-dosshouse I located at Arequipa set the standard.

The Puno train was supposed to leave at 08.15 and, in the event, left at 09.15 which, I suppose, is not bad at all in a land where *mañana* doesn't just mean 'tomorrow' but can also mean 'never'.

The early morning scene as we wound up the valley towards Julaca was enchanting. All around were fields of alfalfa and corn and, behind Arequipa, the volcanic peaks of Misti and Chachani. After Crucero Alto, the highest point on the line, the first mountain lakes appeared: Lagunillas and Saracocha, each on either side of the train. My guidebook, ever practical, told me that all water east of Crucero Alto flowed into the Atlantic, thousands of miles away.

I was travelling second – lowest – class, and though the seats were hard my journey was not uncomfortable. The coaches were British-made and ancient, their windows either jammed shut or jammed open. The train was full, but not overcrowded, with cheerful people. I was soon to learn that there is no need to go short of food on an Andean train, for there are vendors both on the trains and at every stop. And Andean trains do a lot of stopping. All sorts of edible oddities were thrust under my nose by large peasant women attired in bowler hats and voluminous multicoloured skirts inflated by layers of petticoats. There was no restaurant car on my train, but that a kitchen existed was plain from the huge roast chicken dishes that none-too-clean waiters brought round to those that ordered them. With the chicken went generous measures of *pisco* brandy which kept everyone in high spirits.

Except for some girls who, to my pleasurable but uncomprehending surprise, all bore a remarkable resemblance to a younger Sophia Loren, my fellow travellers were of Indian extraction. The older womenfolk in their absurd hats and skirts wore their hair in standard greasy black plaits joined together at

the nape of the neck. For most of the day-long journey everybody gorged themselves on chunks of semi-raw meat cut from an obscure joint of an equally obscure animal which was hawked by vendors from bundles of filthy rags. I stuck to the *pisco*, which possibly accounted for my seemingly being in a coach so liberally inhabited by Sophia Lorens. The train was diesel-hauled but so much black smoke issued from the locomotive it could have been a steam engine at our head.

Descending to fertile pampa I saw my first llama, alpaca or vicuna, I don't know which, because the bowler-hatted brigade were each telling me something different, interspersed with gusts of laughter and display of nicotine-stained teeth. Julaca, the junction, involved an interminable delay before the shores of Lake Titicaca came into sight and were slavishly followed by the train for 30 miles to Puno. Weighed down by a heavy rucksack I fought my way off the seething platform.

Another hostel-type hotel – a benevolent description – became my home and in the morning I had a whole day for investigating both Puno and the immediate shores of Titicaca. Neither added up to anything very much in my jaundiced estimation and, though the lake was beautiful from a distance, closer inspection revealed a shoreline befouled with scum, excrement and dead dogs amongst which the locals were contentedly drawing water.

Puno boasted a handsome square, a coldly austere cathedral and a lively market vivid with local colour. But around the small port there was ugly poverty that cannot be disguised by the description 'quaint', an adjective favoured by my guidebook.

While in Puno I developed a touch of altitude sickness, no more than a headache, so was glad of the restful voyage on the good, Newcastle-built, ship *Inca* across the almost ocean-sized lake into Bolivian territory. The *Inca* may have been elderly, but she was far from senile and was spotlessly clean. Brought overland from Lima in pieces, the steamer was reassembled in Puno and had been working ever since. It was an 11-hour crossing and, on the outward

trip, I managed to acquire a bunk bed. At Guaqui, which my guidebook described as 'nondescript', not being able to find anything remotely 'quaint' about the place, we were herded into an equally unquaint train for the run to La Paz.

The train was no more than a rail-car and was capable of containing only about half the passengers from the boat, the rest having to board a bus. First off the steamer got the choice. The little diesel stopped for half an hour at Tiahuanaco to offer a glimpse of the pre-Inca ruins standing on a flat, draughty plateau.

I was particularly pleased to be able to spend a brief period in the highest capital city in the world. The Spaniards chose the site, sunk in a natural canyon, in 1548, both to avoid the chill winds of the plateau and because they found gold in the River Choqueyapu that runs through the canyon. Mount Illimani, with snow-covered peaks, towered over the city. In this topsy-turvy capital the strata of society ran downwards: the poorer Indians lived in the higher terraces below which were the business areas, government offices, main hotels, restaurants and the university. At the bottom resided the wealthy, reaching down to the bed of the valley. Much of La Paz is modern, so that the blossoming skyscrapers broke the traditional patchwork of red tiles and corrugated iron. I was to see more of the capital during a subsequent visit to the country, but that initial short sojourn imprinted a deeper impression in my memory.

Though the fifth largest country in South America, Bolivia possessed a mere 1,400 miles of railway, mostly built by her very many victorious enemies. In the beginning each of the three main routes serving the country encountered obstructions, still not entirely overcome. On the Peruvian line there was Lake Titicaca, where freight as well as passengers had to be trans-shipped. On the Arica line the rack section caused delays. And until 1928, when the Bolivian Railway Board changed the gauge of its Chilean section, all freight on that route had to be trans-shipped at Uyuni as none of the ports at that time had adequate facilities. The major

engineering problem, though, was not the crossing of the Andes, but the descent into the city of La Paz. Lack of finance has always been the vogue in Bolivia and, as a result, many steam engines put out to graze had been reharnessed. I was to see a couple of Henschells pushing wagons around in the La Paz yards.

The intended direction of my travels had always been northwards, so I made haste to return to Peruvian soil and, within the week, was back at Puno ready for the rail run to Cuzco. An added satisfaction for me was that the line roughly followed the route of the southern extension of the old Royal Road to the Inca capital, a historic highway I was later to follow for a quarter of a year on foot.[3]

Departure of the train was in the hands of fate. 'No trains today' vouchsafed the station staff. That there *would* be a train today was the opinion of its potential clients optimistically waiting on the platform. Fate was kind and the clients correct. Again I travelled second class, being low in soles, the Peruvian currency, but the run along Titicaca's contaminated shore offered splendid views of a Titicanan sunrise as a backdrop to the fishermen in tiny reed boats.

Back at Julaca vendors came aboard selling alpaca fur hats that could have fetched a fortune in London. Thereafter the northbound line climbed gradually, reaching its climax at La Raya. The countryside was pure magic with astonishing panoramas of snow-topped peaks, green pastures and woods. With La Raya behind us, the train picked up speed and pounded down the straight to Sicuani, near the ruins of the Inca temple of Viracocha, grandiose and lonely. North of Sicuani the fields were aflame with Californian poppies and lupins prior to giving way to the River Vilcanota which the line accompanied. More stops at small station halts with strange alien names, and dusk saw us in the rugged sierra surrounded by rock cliffs of purple and red. Cacti with long fingers and grey moss hung like tattered veils from alpine shrubs. Scotch broom trees added a more cheerful note of bright yellow

as we emerged out into the valley head populated with gnarled pepper trees. And all this accompanied by music, thanks to the guitar and mouth-organ talents of a blind family and their tuneful rendering of Quechua love ballads. A golden sunset was to climax our entry into Cuzco.

All who go to Peru today eventually find their way to Cuzco. It breathes its Inca history as can no other place throughout the Andean countries. Over the years it has become a shrine to the Incas, the place where the visitor can do the rounds of its museums and memorials. Assuredly there is much to see in this remarkable city that lies in the hollow of a valley at 11,000 feet, with the mountains rising precipitously on three sides and the valley stretching away to distant peaks in the south-east. Sacsahuaman, the massive fortress that guards Cuzco, is the hub of all pilgrimages. This amazing structure, standing high on the plain of Chita beyond the northern suburbs of the city, is a third of a mile long with 60-foot high terraced walls of monolithic blocks, some of which weigh up to a hundred tons and measure 17 feet by 10 feet. And remember, the Inca never possessed the wheel, yet these blocks have been fitted together so perfectly and without the aid of mortar that the blade of a penknife could never pass between them.

During my stay in Cuzco I caught the early morning train to Chaullay which dropped me and others at the legendary Machu Picchu, the 'Lost City of the Incas' which Hiram Bingham stumbled upon in 1911. There are no roads to Machu Picchu, so the train is the only vehicle for attaining this edifice of supreme drama that is outstaged only by the utter magnificence of its surroundings. Today Machu Picchu has become the major tourist attraction in Peru, so I was pleased to look upon it when there were no restrictions placed upon movement around the celebrated ruins.

But with Cuzco my railway dalliances on the tourist beat were, for the time being, over. From now on my wanderings would take me on lesser-known lines.

I was tempted back to the railway at Huancavelica because it was the next point northwards where there *were* trains, though I was forced to reach this mountain-girthed town by road.

A glance at the rail system map of Peru will show how disjointed are the railways of the country; there is no way one can cover it entirely by train. Having 'done' most of the Southern Railway network I now turned my attention to the Central Railway, its route shown as a lop-sided T with Lima at its base, running up to La Oroya at the junction of the crosspiece. The main line runs from Lima through La Oroya to Huancavelica, its terminal on the right. A privately-owned line runs from La Oroya to Cerro de Pasco on the left. This next leg of my journey would take me back to Lima, the Peruvian capital, and the point at which I had arrived in the country.

The Central Railway is regarded as one of the wonders of the Americas and the engineering of the route involved immense problems. The deep Rimac valley between Lima and La Oroya, the only feasible route, narrows to a maximum width of about 656 feet. Within its limits the engineers had to find a way of climbing nearly 13,000 feet within a distance of less than 47 miles, which is the length of the road that runs along the bottom of the valley. The twists and turns needed by the railway to gain height have made the line considerably longer at 73 miles. To keep the gradient down to the necessary 1 in 23, the single-track line has to utilise the whole width of the valley, crossing frequently from one side to the other. Even this would be impossible without the use of the famous zigzags to gain height. Between Chosica and Ticlio, the highest point of the line at 15,693 feet, and there are six double and one single zigzag, 66 tunnels and 59 bridges to negotiate. Construction of the line, which began in 1870,

presented problems in addition to the geographical ones. A mysterious disease killed off many workers and, in 1877, Peru went bankrupt, which effectively held up completion until 1929.

The chief interest of the Central Railway had always been freight, particularly since 1897 when the La Oroya copper mines opened. However, the incredible journey still remains attainable to the traveller. Except for those unfortunates who suffer from altitude sickness and have to be given oxygen by the attendants on the train, all will marvel, as I did, at the ingenuity of the men who built this railway amidst some of the most rugged landscapes on Earth.

Between Huancavelica and Huancayo, midway to La Oroya, the line is metre gauge and meets no substantial physical obstacles. I travelled in a crowded rail-car which whizzed along merrily before it broke down. A normally three-hour trip turned disconcertingly to one of ten hours. At least I was lucky to get a seat, though I paid dearly for it by having a perpetually howling baby next to me dribbling over my trousers.

The delay, most of us spending it outside on the track, resulted for me in a night on the tiles at Huancayo, an old market town that I could have found quite pleasant at any time but two o'clock in the morning. The night was bitterly cold and I blessed a kindly bunch of vendors for allowing me to warm myself around their brazier. The nightlife of Huancayo is not without incident, to judge from some of the prostitutes and shady characters who likewise came to warm themselves by the fire. The town finally redeemed itself in my eyes by displaying in the sidings some ancient models of working steam locomotives surely not much younger than Robert Stephenson.

The 07.00 to Lima was the *Tren de Sierra*, and of more substance to that of the previous day's rail-car. En route towards La Oroya the hilly scenery reminded me of North Wales, and the industrial town into which we drew carried overtones of Port Talbot. La Oroya station was the usual jumble of humanity with everybody

selling everything to everybody else. A wizened old man sitting with a basket of fruit between his knees caught my gaze. The fruits were about the size of oranges but a yellowish-green colour; I think they were *chirimoya*. I went over and entered into negotiations to buy some. Seeing my interest in buying, every vendor on the platform homed in on me and I found myself ringed by eager, beaming Indian faces. My poor old man was edged out of proceedings, so I pushed my way through the throng and made my purchase from him. For this I received a bonus of a great smile and a hug, which made my day. Despite an over-abundance of pips, the *chirimoya* made good eating; a sweet, rather fleshy fruit with a distinctive flavour. While I was sampling it, spitting pips out like a consumptive machine gun, the engine driver came over, tapped me on the shoulder and said, 'El Inglesh, we go.' It was one of the few times in Peru I was given a title other than 'Gringo'.

All the way from Huancayo we had been climbing steadily, though the gradients were not noticeable. Now the name of a station, Ticlio, came into view with its altitude (4,782 metres) prominently displayed on a board. Nobody in my compartment appeared to be affected by the height, though oxygen-bearing medics haunted the corridors in readiness to help those that were. The line reaches its highest point in the tunnel between Ticlio and Galera and, thereafter, the train was off the leash on the downhill leg of the run. Opposite me a German breathed raspingly, as I suppose I did too. In addition to their pale faces, foreigners on the train were distinguishable by their heavy breathing. However, there were few gringos in evidence on my train.

The Andes are great humblers of men. They stretch the length of South America, forming a crenellated wall 4,500 miles long, draped with vegetation at the northern end and with ice and snow at the southern end. And down the length of this range, and on its slopes, lie untamed regions of snow, ice and fire, of dripping jungle and seared desert, of cloud cover and merciless sun, of intense heat and killing cold. This is the barrier that railway

builders had to contend with when they planned and constructed the lateral lines that wind inland from the tropical coastline. As the pace of the *Tren de Sierra* slackened with the application of the brakes, a feeling of awe descended upon the whole train, almost tangible in its intensity. As we began the descent I could see, far below, what seemed to be low hills that gradually flattened into the distant haze. The cruel immensity of the terrain is almost beyond imagination.

The Remac Valley is not beautiful; it is savage, bleak and remorseless. The huge walls and escarpments hem in the fragile track forcing it to curve, wind and dodge in a kind of desperate progress that is more like an attempted escape. Where rock buttresses bar the way the line doubles back on itself, forcing the limping train to grind to a halt up against the canyon wall and reverse downwards the moment the hand-operated points have been switched by the guard. Forwards, backwards, forwards, backwards, slowly we spiralled down the valley. We all chatted inanely as the coaches traversed delicate lattice bridges over bottomless chasms and crept along the edge of sheer precipices on narrow ledges hacked from enormous cliffs of granite. To the north there came a dramatic surge of colour in the morning sky that illuminated a line of smoky blue peaks in gold and crimson; the whole vast contorted landscape abruptly drenched in rose-pink brilliance.

Nine hours after leaving Huancayo the valley flattened out and we entered upon a warm, tropical expanse of green countryside that had pushed aside the mountains to substitute terraced cultivation and urban development. Ahead lay the sea with Lima shimmering in the heat haze of mid-afternoon.

The city in late April is hot and humid. My ensuing urban wanderings were effected by bus, tram and on foot, but mainly on foot for the city is a warren of back streets. It also lacks in scenic splendour while its pavements, let there be no doubt, are unkempt, hard and crowded. The citizens sigh for the sun at this

time. Lima has a strange climate which precipitates, through the winter months, an overcast sky when fog and humidity make it feel colder than it is. My visit coincided with the onset of winter though the local mist, for which the city is known, had not yet materialised.

Nobody in Peru imagines that her Indian heritage could be greater than that of her Spanish conquerors, and most certainly Lima feels herself to be a Spanish city continuing to honour her Spanish founder who, legend has it, was suckled by a sow. The remains of Francisco Pizarro lie in a chapel of the twin-towered cathedral in the Plaza de Armas. The Incas completed their conquest of Peru and Ecuador in about 1450, after centuries of fighting, but Pizarro, helped by his own treachery and a civil war simmering between his enemies, managed *his* subsequent conquest in less than a year after landing on the coast at Tumbes in May 1532 and working his way south to effect the capture of Cuzco, the Inca capital. But an inland capital high in the mountains was useless to the sea-going Spaniards and in 1535 Lima, close to the ocean, was founded, by Pizarro, on a site that had once held Rimac, city of the pre-Inca Chimus. It is said that the Indians suggested the site to the hated Spanish occupiers as being particularly suitable for building their capital, merely because they thought they would all be bound to die in its miserable climate.

The city's power was at its zenith during the eighteenth century; it held some of the best colonial buildings in South America, and there were few cities in the old world which could rival the wealth of its men or the luxury of its women. Today its influence has waned, and Lima has become just another South American metropolis of shabby opulence amidst vibrant slums.

But I had not quite finished with the Central Railway for, a while later, I was unable to resists a part return ride as far as La Oroya. On this journey I travelled first class in a fit of extravagance to lunch on soup, salad, chicken and pudding for less than a pound

while we dragged up the gigantic valley. At La Oroya I changed to the non-state-owned line to Cerro de Pasco on a crowded local full of friendly peasants and their livestock. With a bulging rucksack I was as loaded as they were and managed to share a seat with a substantial lady, each of us supporting one buttock on the wooden slats. The three-hour jolt, costing the equivalent of 15 pence, had us scurrying across the bucking countryside, the line surreptitiously climbing another thousand feet in the process of attaining the wet and mournful Junin Pampa, one of the world's largest high-altitude plains, from the Montaro river valley.

The landscape wore a prehistoric look: simple, terrible hills and gullies; thorn bushes and rocks; and everything smoothed by the wind, for all the world looking as if a great flood had denuded it and washed it of all its particular features. It was only I who was awed by all this drama; other passengers on the train seldom looked out of the mostly-glassless windows, except at the stations, and then only in the hope of buying something to eat. In the gathering dusk, bringing with it fierce icy draughts through the windows, I glimpsed the eastern shore of Lake Junin, an elongated mass of grey-green water, before the view was eclipsed by an abrupt nightfall.

The oil-fired engine appeared to have bronchial trouble, respiring in great gasps and wheezes. The track was narrow gauge and badly laid so that the whole train bucked, swayed and creaked while, when moving fast – which was seldom – it made such a racket of jarring couplings and groaning timber that I had the distinct impression that everything was on the verge of falling apart.

Cerro showed itself to be a mining town of considerable squalor built around a gigantic open-cast zinc mine that is the sole reason for the town's existence. Visitors were plainly rare, with the result that I got the full treatment of the 'Why are you here?' variety. I took refuge in a decrepit café to devour a clutch of fried eggs that arrived unheralded. With me in the darkened room was a group

of men well into the second stages of intoxication from the contents of a big flagon of red wine, which they passed to me at ever-increasing intervals. Much later, in almost as happy a state as them, I staggered from this den of iniquity to search for a bed, which actually I found in the very same establishment.

My closest acquaintance on the train back to Lima next day was a mammoth hangover.

Except for a few short stretches of mainly industrial lines running inland from the coast there was no further worthwhile railway riding to be had in Peru. Many hundreds of miles of daunting, spectacular territory separate the Peruvian Central Railway from the Ecuadorian seaport of Guayaquil, the southern terminal of the Ecuadorian State Railway further, much further, north.

Guayaquil had the most unsavoury reputation of any town in Ecuador, I was told with a certain glee. But having unwittingly passed unscathed through the domain of the infamous *Sendero Luminoso* ('Shining Path') terrorist organisation of which Peru was beginning to be afflicted, I could raise no great fear of the muggers of Guayaquil.

The chief component of the Ecuadorian State Railway is the Guayaquil and Quito Line (misleadingly nicknamed the 'Good and the Quick') which connects the two major cities of the country; the former on the coast, and the latter 9,000 feet up in the mountains. Construction work began in 1871, but it was not until 1908 that the contractors completed the rare 3 feet 6 inch gauge line. To traverse the 288 miles and 11,840-foot altitude tight curves and zigzags are again incorporated. It has never been a commercial success and its resulting near-bankruptcy has given it a dreadful reputation for chaotic administration, breakdowns and derailments. Its rolling stock is antique and the fact that the railway continues to operate, albeit less comprehensively so far as passenger carrying is concerned since I last rode its lines, is probably more amazing than the fact that it was ever built. But

for anyone interested in travelling incorrigible railways, who is not put off by an uncomfortable ride punctuated by possible disasters, the 'G&Q' is a prize experience. 'The world's mightiest roller coaster' it has sometimes been called.

Guayaquil itself, Ecuador's second city though larger in terms of population than Quito, is something of a garden metropolis, though its prosperity derived from the industry it encompassed. The odd thing is that the railway fails to enter the city, the terminus being at Duran on the east bank of the Guayas River, though I should have thought the perfectly good road bridge linking Guayaquil with Duran could have been adapted to carry the single line too.

At Guayaquil I made the mistake of catching the more expensive *autoferro* – a clapped-out rail-car – which, amazingly, was the luxury vehicle of the line and the only sort to go right through to Quito. I ought to have boarded the cheaper and unreliable *tren mixto* that went no further than Riobamba, and then caught the *autoferro*. As it was, my train held only Ecuadorian businessmen engrossed in their paperwork.

Leaving Duran we sped across the broad fertile Guayas valley chequered by fields of sugar cane and rice interwoven with split cane houses built high on stilts, overlooking waterways speckled with thousands of water birds and big dugouts piled high with produce. After Huigra and the River Chanchan the line began its zigzagging course within a narrow gorge and, past Sibambe, climbed the famous Nariz del Diablo ('Devil's Nose'): a perpendicular ridge rising in the gorge to a height of 10,600 feet. Another engineering challenge, this almost insurmountable obstacle was finally conquered by the building of a series of switchbacks on a five and a half per cent grade. First one way and then the other, the train zigzagged higher and higher to gain an altitude of 11,840 feet at Urbina.

This small town lies at the foot of the snow-capped Chimborazo, a dormant volcano once thought to be the highest

mountain in the world at nearly 22,000 feet. I was later to climb this considerable peak, lose my way and, but for the grace of God, end up as dead meat on its flank, an ascent narrated in one of my earlier books.[4] The line now led me down the sensational valley of the volcanoes, the views of which from the train are possibly the most spectacular to be seen from a railway anywhere in the world. One by one the towering volcanic summits of Carihuairazo, Altar, Tungurahua, the burning head of Sangay, and Catopaxi appeared in the clear atmosphere.

But I was not to go right through to Quito on this occasion; as an afterthought, I broke my journey at Sibambe where I rode the branch line to Cuenca, Ecuador's third largest city. Here is a gracious town that had preserved its colonial air with cobblestone streets and picturesque old buildings. I stayed a couple of days in the city, the climax of my sojourn being a long immersion in the warm but eye-stinging sulphur baths at nearby Baños.

Riobamba, the headquarters city of the Ecuadorian State Railway administration, was another destination. A town prone to earthquakes, it held ageing, vaguely impressive buildings which ostensibly allowed it the inaccurate description of 'Sultan of the Andes'. Ambato, likewise on the railway to Quito, I also managed to investigate, though anything that might once have been of architectural merit there had been destroyed in the 1949 earthquake.

What Riobamba and Ambato might have lacked in charm was made up for in full by Quito. Few cities have a setting to match the Ecuadorian capital. Although nearly three kilometres high – it is the second highest capital in Latin America – the mountains that circle it are higher still. Modern Quito extends northwards into a luxuriant plain; it has wide avenues, fine private residences, parks, embassies and villas. But the city's attraction lies in the old south-western section where cobbled streets are steep and winding, and the houses are mostly Indian-made adobe brick with

low red roof tiles, or whitened stone. Quito's heart is the Plaza Independencia, dominated by the usual grim-looking cathedral, this one sporting grey stone porticoes and green cupolas. The government palace was an equally severe colonial structure made a little less gaunt by palace guards in fairytale uniforms.

Quito, of course, is an Inca city if refounded by Sebastian de Benalcazar in 1534 so that the architectural talents of both Inca and Spanish civilisations have, across the years, contributed to the magnificence of this capital. Of the two small Spanish armies that advanced northwards to take this prize of conquest it was Benalcazar's troops that finally entered the city, beating his rival Alvarado and his men. Another army that advanced upon Quito was the Inca force of Quisquis nearing the end of their year-long withdrawal from Cuzco and now retreating from its recent chosen battleground of Teocajas. Had Quisquis arrived earlier and established contact with Ruminavi and his Quito defenders, the former's defeat could still have ended in an Inca triumph with the Spanish invasion forestalled at the gates of the capital. As it was, his men, weary and disheartened, mutinied, disposed of their leader and dispersed to their homes. A determined counter-attack by Ruminavi's Army nearly succeeded, but was eventually repulsed by the city's new occupiers and his soldiers forced to flee. In ruins, its treasures carried away by the withdrawing Inca, Quito became irrefutably Spanish.

Ironically it was not in the old historic city but the modern part of town, and in the posh embassy sector, that I again fell victim to a pickpocket gang, this time on a crowded bus. I managed to retain my passport but lost my air ticket, credit cards and most of my money. Realising I'd been robbed seconds after the event, I made myself extremely unpopular by yelling to the driver to stop, denying exit to all those wishing to alight and dragging aboard a reluctant policeman on point duty. This worthy felt impelled to line everyone up against the bus side with their hands above their heads while they were searched. Meanwhile the villains, who had

escaped before the hullabaloo, simply melted into the horrifying traffic pandemonium that resulted from the now uncontrolled intersection.

Lack of funds forced me to cut short my intended stay in Quito while thereafter the onward journey to Bogotá, point of my homeward departure, was going to be ruled by my deficiency of funds. My remaining cash supply would just about cover basic feeding, but not hotel accommodation and transportation. Fortunately the incident had occurred towards the end of my term in South America, so I was reluctant to put myself at the mercy of the British Embassy who have an unendearing sarcastic manner of responding to such entreaties from victims of crime, or at least that has been my perception. Instead I resolved to go it alone; for me another challenge loomed.

The first thing to do was to get out of Quito; the cost of living in capital cities is invariably higher than elsewhere. But first I was to pay a visit to the local office of ENFE, the Ecuadorian Railway from whom I successfully prized a rail pass from their public relations department on the strength of my profession as a travel writer. The pass was valid for transportation on lines between the capital and the northern border, thus giving me free travel from Quito to Ibarra, the direct route towards Bogotá, and, if I wanted, on the line between Ibarra and the coastal township of San Lorenzo. I had a whole fortnight to kill before I needed to be in the Colombian capital for my scheduled flight home, though I would have to arrive a day or two earlier to arrange for a replacement air ticket.

Before I left Quito to progress northwards I visited the markets of Otavalo. It would be a huge mistake to miss the markets of Otavalo, it was impressed upon me. I could hardly afford to buy anything, but at least a little 'window-shopping' would do no harm. And since a kind man offered me a lift there in his car this clinched it.

The region of Otavalo has a serene atmosphere, almost tangible, from the moment of a visitor's arrival. And the Indians of Otavalo are unique. Their skin is lighter than that of their brothers and here the youngsters run after you in the street not to show contempt or lewd curiosity, but for the mere pleasure of being able to talk to a foreigner. Even the smallest children waddle out of doors of white thatched houses to lisp, '*Donde va?*'

I found this out very soon after I had strolled down the first row of stalls in the Plaza Bolivar. The male vendors wore their hair long and plaited under a broad-brimmed hat; the women were attired in colourful costumes and multicoloured beads. There were actually three different markets. The central streets of the town were crammed with stalls, many selling fine homespuns weaved by families living in the surrounding streets.

There being only one train a day between Quito and Ibarra, I spent the night in Otavalo though aware that I could probably have got back to Quito, even if it meant walking, as it was only some ten miles distant. But what held me to this pleasant little market town was the invitation to stay with a family. Their adobe house was simple in the extreme as was the bean stew they insisted I share with them, but for sleep I had the benefit of one of those massive homespun creations that I had seen in the markets into which to snuggle. I could, as they well knew, offer no payment but pressed upon the lady of the house a three-colour ballpoint pen the family plainly coveted.

I returned to Quito by way of a ride on a lorry and a bullock cart, plus a mile or two on my own feet. Neither of my copies of the *South American Handbook*[5] or *Thomas Cook's Overseas Timetable* could vouchsafe any information or timings of the Quito–Ibarra–San Lorenzo trains, so I took it upon myself to find out since the only timetable that the Quito office of ENFE could produce was one dated 1925. Even the station could not be certain of the timings, but *thought* it might be in the afternoon.

The train that eventually bore me away was another of those little rail-cars, nippy but noisy. The *South American Handbook* pointed out that the rail journey to Ibarra takes over twice as long as does the road journey and 'cannot be recommended for comfort or scenic beauty'. The speed of the train was of little consequence and since the road too ran through some of the driest, dustiest, most barren land in the Ecuadorian Andes before attaining the rich irrigated farmlands beyond, the choice was marginal. There was a brief stop at Cayambe and I momentarily played with the idea of making an excursion to the Inca ruins of Rumicucho at San Antonio, but this was a two-hour drive from Cayambe and impractical for a destitute gringo.

I found Ibarra to be a friendly town neatly ringed by a mountain range, a volcano and a lake where Atahualpa, the Inca chief, is supposed to have drowned his captives. Here I spent the first of two nights on the floor of the station-master's office, with strident bells and telephones ringing unanswered all around though there was but one scheduled train a day passing through the station. In the morning the staff arrived, stepped over my prostrate form wrapped in a sleeping bag, and commenced their duties as if stray Englishmen sleeping on their floor was the most natural thing in the world. One wonders what would have been the reaction in the station-master's office at, say, Temple Meads. For breakfast I was to consume half a pint of rum donated by the staff and, subsequently, half a loaf contributed by a local grocer who was a fervent Jehovah's Witness. I had gone into his shop to enquire of the price of biscuits whereupon, surrounded by succulent goodies, I was forced to listen to his rantings. The loaf had been the reward, but even my pretended biblical enthusiasm failed to produce the seven fishes of the parable.

Aware that my usage of the Ibarra railway facilities as a dosshouse might eventually be construed as an inconvenience if I dallied there a third night, I took to the trains again. But any notions I might have harboured of sleeping cars and plush first-

class compartments were eclipsed by first sight of Ecuadorian Rail's little monster of an *autocarril* that was reserved for this lesser section of their network. Basically, it was a vehicle that had started life as a common-or-garden lorry or bus, to end it on flanged wheels and a fixed course. Depending upon whether the particular vehicle was a one-time bus or lorry went the variation in comfort – or discomfort – and since the distance to San Lorenzo is nearly 200 kilometres this distinction was not without importance.

My train was a Ford and, for the first half of the journey, was of the lorry variety. Though my ticket, obtained free on submission of my pass, stipulated a reserved seat, there weren't any seats. The *autocarril* bulged with humanity, chickens, bags of flour and a nanny-goat. We were classed as 'mixed goods' and the definition was accurate. In a tunnel the train ran out of petrol and the nanny-goat was sick over my sandals.

A seething brown torrent of a river, the Mira, cut the line in two – literally – by the simple expedient of having swept away the bridge. This necessitated us all alighting from the vehicle to walk, four passengers at a time, across a temporary rope structure that swayed and creaked ominously, to the second 'train' that waited on the other side.

This new mode of conveyance was an old British Leyland bus and a slight improvement on the lorry by virtue of having seats. At least it did for some: for me only one buttock benefited. We moved like a bat out of hell along the badly-laid and worn track, swaying from side to side in hair-raising fashion, while the driver talked animatedly to a girl with him in the cab. Several hours later we came to the stock joke of the run: a waterfall that descends directly upon the track. All those in the know had quietly closed their windows, but of course I hadn't and so received a powerful deluge of cold water to huge guffaws of mirth. With the Mira Gorge, a brown cleft in the rocky terrain, behind us we hurtled through a steamy jungle and swept into San Lorenzo.

The seven-hour ride had installed a dream of prolonged immersion in the cool clear water of the Pacific, but the soft beaches of my fevered imagination turned out to be fetid mangrove swamps, while the balmy night disintegrated into a tropical downpour. Rarely have I come across so awful a place as San Lorenzo, a township of wooden shacks and a bazaar rotting in its own sweat. Not even my guidebook dared to call it 'quaint'.

I spent a miserable night on the concrete floor of the tin-roofed ticket-office in the station being eaten alive by mosquitoes. My morning alarm clock – as if I needed one – was the arrival of the first passengers queuing for tickets over my sleeping bag (with me in it) and I was delighted to return to even such an abomination of a train so long as it went anywhere but San Lorenzo. And I obtained a whole seat to myself.

Again the driver was a speed maniac. Not once did he slacken speed for the most excruciating of bends. Around one of them, with his foot hard down on the accelerator, the driver ran over a yellow triangle placed on the track – the one piece of signalling apparatus on the entire line – and ploughed straight into a sea of mud obliterating the metals. As with my Baluchistan line run in Pakistan, a little passenger participation was expected to rectify matters.

In pouring rain we emerged from our cosy bus to be issued with shovels and put to work in company with the driver and, when it eventually arrived, a regular clearance crew to clear the tracks from the sticky soil and boulders that had slid down from the steep hillside. Nobody appeared the slightest put out by being so enlisted, and by the time we ran into the second landslide some hours later we were all old hands at the job.

The waterfall never caught me napping the second time round and, back across the Mira river obstacle where our lorry 'connection' awaited us, I returned without too much regret to Ibarra. It was to be my penultimate railway ride in South America.

The only method of reaching Bogotá was by road, so I made my way to the Ecuadorian–Colombian border by toting for lifts on any vehicle going my way. A cooperative police detachment put me up for a night in their so-called honeymoon suite – the cleanest cell – in the police station, and a village restaurant was persuaded to let me extend my simple and inexpensive one-course meal, and the only meal of the day, into an all-night sitting on the floor. At the border Ecuadorian customs forgot to ask me for the compulsory exit tax of 50 sucres thus, since I had no intention of reminding them, winning myself a modest blow-out at the last restaurant in the country.

Inside Colombian territory I was asked for proof of my solvency and a valid ticket for anywhere outside Colombia, a request that could have stopped me in my tracks. However, an ambassadorial letter well decorated with impressive seals and stamps that I held from 'our man in Peru' – now two countries past – dazzled the immigration authorities to the extent of them letting me continue on my way.

Hitch-hiking in Colombia, they told me, was a dangerous game. Kidnapping, robbery and murder, it appeared, were all too prevalent. But the bus-fares were beyond my means, so I risked the hell and damnation of the open road. My modes of transportation varied from a truck of manure and a lorry load of schoolchildren to a smart Toyota Land Cruiser of the Colombian Water Corporation. Respective drivers were cooperative, sympathetic and charming, and one took me home for a guinea pig high tea. I lived to tell the tale.

In Popayán, learning that an English artist was living there, I hunted him down. The man who came to the door seemed very un-English to me. He gave me a meal nevertheless, and it was only when I enquired about his paintings that I discovered I had called at the wrong house. Peter's was next door. Reoriented, I

ran Peter the painter to earth to subsequently remain with him and his Colombian wife, Nana, for three days.

Peter Walton lived in a bare house on the edge of the town, which is the provincial capital of the district of Cauca. Popayán, founded by Benalcazar in 1536, is to Colombia what Weimer is to Germany, or Burgos is to Spain; a place of monasteries, cloisters of pure Spanish architecture and clean wide streets shaded from an oppressive sun by handsome white buildings. At least that is how I found it before the cruel earthquake struck the town in 1983.

There were two reasons for the bareness of the house: one was that Peter was as bankrupt as I was; the other because, were it even modestly furnished, the neighbours would steal everything. He was nevertheless popular with his neighbours, though well aware that many were nothing less than *banditos*. And that's how it was then in Colombia, even in such a respectable community as Popayán where many an aristocratic family had their roots.

Peter was a mine of stories of the perpetual if undeclared war that was going on in the country which, all too often, boiled over into full-scale civil conflict. Violence and infant mortality, it seemed, were the main scourges of Colombia with drugs, of course, the cause of the former affliction.

Popayán boasted a railway station of sorts though, with Peter's help with the lingo, I was to learn that no passenger services were operating. We found the station-master – again of sorts – drinking coffee in a poky office wreathed in acrid tobacco smoke, and it was he who provided this information. But I had my eyes on a line of freight wagons being shunted on the sidings the far side of the station building.

'Surely one of those will be going to Cali sometime,' we suggested, pushing things a little. The city of Cali lay on my route to Bogotá.

'Yes,' agreed the man, showing signs of a not-inexcusable impatience, 'no doubt so but that's not to say . . .'

I placed the ambassadorial letter under his nose while Peter poured out a story involving the vital importance of my reaching Cali without delay. The exchange ended with me being 'invited' to utilise a wagon in which I could hide myself that night when it was due to be hauled to Colombia's third largest city. What finally clinched the deal, which the station-master insisted never took place in his presence, was the offer of one of Peter's paintings. I would have never imagined that the gruff individual before us was an art-lover, though more likely he had in mind its sale value.

Late that evening I bade farewell to my kind hosts and installed myself in the empty and unlocked wagon, being careful to ensure that nobody saw me entering it. My latest bedchamber was hardly wagon-lit, but bare boards were no strangers to me and, to my relief, the train jerked into motion in the early hours of next morning. Through heavily-louvered window slits I obtained glimpses of a lush countryside interspersed by semi-tropical forest.

I was aware that I was taking a considerable risk doing what I was doing, but probably no more so than that of thumbing lifts on the road. Though it seldom halted, the train moved at a painfully slow pace and, in spite of the thick sandwich that Nana had made me, hunger became my chief source of discomfort.

It was broad daylight when we rolled into a large conurbation that could only have been Cali, a fact confirmed when I glimpsed its name on a factory hoarding. The train finally stopped in another siding and I hurriedly disembarked from the wagon; slipping away after ensuring that no railway workers were in sight. A few moments later I was through the freight yard and amongst people in the street outside.

Such had been the frugality of my living that I had managed to save enough money to take a bus to Bogotá. The bus was full, but I still obtained a seat amongst a clientele of hairy men and women who eyed my person with a disconcerting relish. Colombia's reputation had been thoroughly implanted in my mind so that I held on to my remaining belongings like grim death.

The World Commuter

The journey to the Colombian capital lasted more than ten hours, following which I was pitched out into the bus station; invariably a notorious establishment in violence-prone cities, and Bogotá in particular. My hunger abated slightly by a limp cheese roll acquired at a stall, I made my way, with eyes alert for ambushes and gentlemen with flick-knives, towards the city centre along poverty-stricken back streets. I noticed elderly women squatting in the gutters and wondered why they should be doing so until I saw the stream of urine issuing from beneath their voluminous skirts.

Bogotá, another product of the Spanish conquest, is a capital of nearly six million at a height of 8,661 feet, which puts it fourth in the capital city altitude stakes. Unlike Quito it has no pretence to beauty or illusion about its far from satisfactory climate. A contributor to the *South American Handbook* effuses thus: '. . . shrouded often in the clouds of the high plateau, drenched often in rain, cursed with a climate that has no seasons, it is scarcely an exhilarating spot.' But though a big brute of a city sprouting skyscrapers and spawning asphyxiating traffic fumes, it is saved from downright ugliness by a backdrop of mountains, green with trees, rising almost straight from the eastern section of the town.

Perhaps both the *Handbook* and I are being unfair to Bogotá; certainly my initial opinion was coloured by exhaustion and an entry to the city not made under the happiest of circumstances. However, its notoriety was not to be ignored. 'Armed attacks on pedestrians are common,' warns the *Handbook*. 'Gangs of up to six or eight men with knives frequently attack groups of tourists and do not hesitate to use their weapons for even small amounts of money. Under state-of-siege legislation police may shoot and kill a suspect during any narcotics operation, and it will be automatically classified as self-defence.' Though I had virtually no money I was aware of being a tourist 'group' of only one. Can you wonder at my wariness?

My immediate destination, once in the safer confines of the city centre, was the office of British Caledonian Airways, the then airline that had issued my flight ticket. My explanations concerning the theft of my ticket produced a certain degree of sarcasm, but with telex messages to Gatwick Airport put in hand I turned to leave, and ran straight into an acquaintance of mine.

Captain Adrian Goldsack, attired in perfectly creased service dress complete with a brilliantly polished Sam Browne, stood rooted to the spot as he gazed at the bedraggled apparition before him that appeared to be claiming acquaintanceship. To be honest I did not know him well, but I perceived in his presence the answer to a maiden's prayer since I still had three days to survive before the departure of my flight.

It materialised that Adrian was deputy-leader of the British Amazonas Expedition, recently arrived in Bogotá prior to the undertaking of an ecological, archaeological and medical survey of the Amazon Basin. Furthermore, and more to the point, he was in charge of their base accommodation in a sumptuous district of the city. The unfortunate chap saw how my mind was working the moment he released this information and attempted to wriggle out of offering me hospitality (even though I promised to repay, once I had returned home, the expedition coffers for any expenses I incurred), but I clung to him like a leech. Eventually, and with no great fervour, he relented and in fairness it must be said that I had put him in a difficult position since the expedition funds were, understandably, limited.

Not wishing to take advantage of this lucky turn of events, I delayed until the evening before setting off to locate the house. Once there I came under the kindly jurisdiction of the gracious Bridget Saunders, wife of the expedition leader, Captain John Saunders, who wholeheartedly and unreservedly made me welcome.

Thus, sleeping on sofas that to me offered the pinnacle of luxury, and sharing military rations described as dull by some

standards but certainly not by mine, I marked time in the city. My air ticket was replaced and it became simply a case of waiting for the scheduled departure.

I cannot say that I enjoyed those last days in Bogotá. Not only was I a gatecrasher into someone else's expedition, but I would have given much to have joined it. It was a melancholy state of affairs and quite time I went home.

I still was worth a dollar as I turned into my front door.

Trains Galore

Not all my railway wanderings about the world have involved high drama, adventure and strange, or sometimes disastrous, occurrences. Others have been made in more normal circumstances on rail routes in countries as far apart as Scotland and South Africa.

What follows, therefore, is what might be termed a pot-pourri of mostly, but not always, shorter journeys which provided me with no more than the simple pleasure of riding trains through picturesque scenery with pauses at interesting locations.

Scottish By-lines

Some four score years ago, when its existence was threatened by economic closure, it did not seem as though the railway line from Inverness to Wick, in the far north of Scotland, would survive its centenary. It was on 28 July 1874 that the final section of the line from Helmsdale northwards was opened for traffic, and today, with a current four or five passenger services daily, the most northerly rail route in Britain is still in business. But for how long? The closure threat never quite goes away. So far, however, it has been the unexpected resistance to the shutting down of many of the Highland lines by the public that has kept the tracks open.

To all intents and purposes the main line to northern Britain ends at Inverness. Thereafter, all lines, including those due north of Glasgow except that which feeds Inverness and Aberdeen, could be described as branch lines. But what they lack in traffic density they make up in scenic splendour and historical allure.

They declared a national holiday in Inverness that day in 1860 when they cut the first turf for the northbound railway line to

Wick. In July 1874 the task was completed, though a deficiency of funds had to be nobly made up by the Duke of Sutherland. The distance between Inverness and Wick, where a line linking it to Thursoe on the north coast had already been constructed, was a mere 80 miles as the crow flies but a rugged 161 miles as the track had to go in obedience to the hilly landscape.

Cutting across the head of Black Isle, which actually is neither black nor an island, the line reaches the Muir of Ord where it skirts the rounded bulk of 3,433-foot Ben Wyvis, the highest summit in Easter Ross, and at Dingwall is the junction of another famed line, that of the Kyle of Lochalsh. Foulis Castle, nearby, stands on the site of an older edifice where Macbeth was born. Beyond Invergordon – famed for a naval mutiny in 1931 and named after a gentleman called Sir William Gordon who, given a baronetcy in 1704, celebrated by insisting the town be called after him – are the oil rigs in Nigg Bay.

At Fean the railway makes the first of its inland detours to skirt an indented coastline thus leading the trains due west to Tain, the ancient Royal Burgh on the Durnoch Firth. Not until Lairg does the line begin to revert to its northerly alignment and, with Lairg, we have a township that is virtually the off-centre hub of the scattered communities of Sutherland, surely the last real wilderness in Britain. Distances mean little in such parts. I had a friend whose address included the designation 'By Lairg', though her home was more than 60 miles distant; a distance I covered by hitch-hiking, my first lift offered by the Lord Lieutenant of Sutherland in person. And it was at Golspie, where the line returns to the coast, that I once found myself, a complete stranger to the district, riding a local bus with a lady driver as ignorant of the route as I was. However, with the aid of my map and conflicting directions from other passengers, we found our way to each hidden village bus stop without stranding anyone.

At Hemsdale the track turns inland again to skirt the high land of the Ord of Caithness and enter the Strath of Kildonan, the

scene of Scotland's Klondyke-type gold rush in 1868. Abruptly one obtains a foretaste of the evocative loneliness of Britain's northernmost counties, here rich in prehistoric remains, and at Halkirk the line splits for the short north and east routes to Wick and Thursoe.

Such a journey on the far north line makes for a highly pleasurable experience for the casual traveller – providing time is not the essence – as well as for the railway buff. Although the route lacks the dramatic splendour of the neighbouring Kyle line, it has its own unique character stemming from the variety of the landscape it crosses and from the fact that it takes one almost to mainland Britain's north-eastern extremity.

And it is the Kyle line to which we come next. Again this starts from Inverness and, oft threatened by closure, is a treasure of our island's heritage. Since 1890 trains have traversed the Highlands between the Cromarty Firth and the Atlantic waters of Loch Carron, but establishing this 82 miles of railway was no easy task. The original intention was to drive it all the way to the Kyle of Lochalsh but, once more, the money ran out and there was no benefactor here to step in with the wherewithal. But when the West Highlands Railway Company decided to extend its line from Fort William to Mallaig, no more than a short sail from the Isle of Skye, a crisis of competition arose. Somehow the finance was found and Victorian engineers blasted and hewed their way through uncompromising rock, sometimes to a depth of nearly 90 feet, to Kyle.

I have twice travelled this line; once way back in 1974, and again more recently when snow lay on the tracks. The journey can be divided, someone wrote, like a piece of music, into three distinct parts, or movements. The first, reflecting the quiescent landscape of woods and meadows, through which the line starts, is elegiac and pastoral; the next, set in the towering, misty perspective of the Highland glens, is majestic and slow; and the

final one, celebrating a lovely stretch of coast washed by the balmy waters of the Gulf Steam, is vibrant and joyous, full of exuberance.

Dingwall is the junction where the line branches off from the far north route, and it is ahead of Dingwall that Strathpeffer is located though not fed by the railway. Once a fashionable spa, it was the local gentry who refused permission for the tracks to cross their estates, thereby necessitating a costly and difficult detour to be made. Thus Straffpeffer paid the price by obscurity.

Onwards and upwards now, climbing steeply to spectacular Raven Rock, where, descending through a forest so dense that it can almost be classed as tropical and where, in summer, its perimeter birch leaves catch the sun to glint like new coins, the terrain becomes sterner, less gentle. Across the Blackwater, a dark, shadowy stream stealing through the trees, and along the southern shore of Loch Garve ('The Rough Loch') the line curves upwards again, beyond the treeline, on the slopes of Little Wyvis to attain Strath Bran. All around are the timeless, wide horizons of the Scottish Highlands, the mountain scenery brightly flushed with heather; an aspect that accompanies the line to Achnasheen, translated as 'Field of Rain' and the halfway point.

Beyond and westwards lie the Torridon peaks, amongst the oldest on Earth. And in the deer-haunted Achnasheen Forest, thick with spruce, willow, birch and oak, the track skirts hills still studded with boulders scattered like giant's playthings though the bleak landscape is, once more, softening. Loch Carron and the sea opens up on the right and trains follow the shore, almost dipping their wheels into the cold, clear waters. Groves of rhododendrons and ancient firs hug the line, and perched upon a crag sits Duncraig Castle, once the residence of the Duchess of Somerset. The Duncraig halt, and the stretch of coast on which it sits, has the ordered elegance of a Japanese garden with small islands, standing offshore, likewise sprouting firs and looking as though they belong in a formal Oriental lake. Snug in the shelter of low green hills on a little promontory is Plockton village, unreal

in its exquisiteness; a haunt of artists and photographers, and perhaps the finest jewel in the necklace of the Kyle line. Then, abruptly emerging from a red rock cutting, comes the quay at Kyle, the terminus, with the misty Isle of Skye beckoning across its narrow strait.

The 164-mile line between Glasgow and Mallaig, with a spur to Oban from the junction at Crianlarich, is known as the West Highlands Line. Its history is another story of engineering skill and human endeavour. On 23 October 1889 the first sod was cut, work commencing simultaneously at Helensburgh, Arrochar, Crianlarich and Tyndrum. The railway between Glasgow and Fort William was completed on 3 August 1894, the onward Mallaig section opening five years later. The technical achievements of driving a line through the most tortuous terrain in Britain were numerous; the rigours of working amongst the mountains far from human habitation while exposed to the vicious Highland winter, immense.

The journey out of Glasgow commences by following a river, the busy Clyde, crossing another river, the Leven, and continuing on to the lochs: a watery introduction. First comes Gareloch, then Loch Long and Loch Lomond. Twenty miles out and the countryside takes on a grander look as the line enters the West Highlands proper with, across Loch Lomond, the hills once roamed by Rob Roy, legendary warrior, robber and folk-hero. At Crianlarich it is beset by mountains: Ben More (3,845 ft), Ben Oss (3,374 ft), Ben Dhu Craig (3,024 ft) and Ben Lui (3,708 ft) then, beyond Tyndrum, crosses the watershed where the rivers flow to the Atlantic instead of to the North Sea. The famed horseshoe bend and its double viaducts follow, with more peaks soaring in the east, and at Rannoch Moor, a 20-mile by 20-mile desolation of peat bogs, tarns, streams and tiny lochs, the line takes to a 'floating mattress'. The moor possesses a strange beauty, especially when sunlight glitters on the countless pools and when

summer colouring blazes in the heather to illuminate an exquisite landscape vivid with wild flowers.

How the track was laid across this treacherous wilderness makes for another story of engineering ingenuity. Unable to find a solid foundation amongst the bogs and marshy ground, the builders of the line 'floated' the track on a mattress of tree-roots and stumps, brushwood and thousands of tons of soil. As a result, trains passing over this sodden terrain are subjected to a slight bouncing effect.

The highest point of the line, 1,350 feet, is attained at Corrour summit where the only snow shed in Britain protects trains from winter snow drifting on to the track. Descending almost to water level, the railway changes direction to follow the gradually broadening valley to Fort William, the chief town of the region, and its adjoining Loch Linnhe opening up to the sea.

Fort William heads an area called Lochaber which embraces rugged mountain grandeur including massive Ben Nevis, the highest peak in Britain, and sensationally beautiful glens with long freshwater lochs and sparkling rivers lying alongside. There are deep sea lochs too, and a savage, indented coastline, an abundance of wildlife and a richness of heritage unsurpassed elsewhere in Scotland. To the north and west are those romantic districts of Knoydart, Morar, Moidart, Ardnamurchan, Morvern, Sunart and Ardgour. One of the many historical events connected with them, and the most widely known, is the second Jacobite rising of 1745, and it was amongst their craggy hills and secret glens that Prince Charlie raised his standard to rally the clans in support of his ill-fated quest for the crown; a venture finally and bloodily crushed at Culloden the following year.

At Fort William a subsidiary line runs to Mallaig. Built as a means of transportation of herring to market for the fishing industry of the Atlantic coast, it underwent a number of changes of route and destination as infuriated landowners refused it passage before the line was finally established. Today it provides what is probably the peak of rail travel spectacle in Britain; witness the

graceful curve of Glenfinnman Viaduct and the views of wild hills as remote now as when Bonnie Prince Charlie hid in the heather. Jacobite history blends with the eternity of Scotland as you ride this astounding line to emerge, unforgettably, upon the panorama of the Sound of Sleat with the craggy ramparts of the distant Cuilins of Skye and the isles of Rum, Eigg and Canna.

On my last journey to Mallaig my train was hauled by a steam locomotive, the LMS Class 5, 4–6–0 *George Stephenson*, steam traction being an innovation for some services in the summer months. The heady smell of train smoke and the symphony of the panting locomotive combined perfectly with the magnificence of Loch Eilt, dotted with tiny islands each bearing tall silver trees as if decked out for just such an event as this.

Yet another evocative line to the Atlantic coast is that between Crianlarich and Oban, the seaside resort almost landlocked in its picturesque bay. Beyond Dalmally the ruins of Kilchurch Castle, ancient stronghold of the Clan Campbell, guards the head of Loch Awe before the line sweeps round it to enter the famous Pass of Brander – which means 'ambush' in Gaelic, and well-named since it was here that Robert the Bruce put the MacDougalls to the sword in 1308 – to join the River Awe, taking advantage of its cutting through the base of Ben Cruachan (3,689 ft) linking with Loch Etive. Rail buffs will be eager to point out the unique fencing mechanism that is a safeguard against rockfalls or landslides, such occurrences actuating a series of signals to set them at danger.

The track crosses the river on the Bridge of Awe, the setting for Sir Walter Scott's romance *The Highland Widow,* and, via the village of Taynuilt, keeps company with the elongated shores of Loch Etive through a bush-like landscape before winding down from Glen Cruitten summit to enter Oban.

Narrow roads and increased traffic in summer give to the railways of Scotland's north the edge on other methods of transportation through this idyllic land. Yet it is the car that is slowly strangling these inspired lines.

'We have built a railway here,' said Sir George MacPherson Grant of the West Highlands Railway Company at the opening of the Kyle Line in 1897. 'Will you people of the West take advantage of it?'

He was asking the locals, but his words are ones we all should heed.

Going Irish

I have visited the Emerald Isle countless times to cycle its leafy lanes, drive its much-vaunted but not always so traffic-free roads, and explore its towns and verdant countryside. But the Irish railways have virtually escaped my attentions. Came the first week of September 2000 and the opportunity to rectify the omission and sample the trains, even though the Republic's network was partially on strike. My timing is not always as it should be.

Since my son, Paul, had spent two years in the Army on anti-terrorist duty in Northern Ireland, I wanted him to accompany me so as to observe the pleasanter side of the country, both North and South. Thus I planned to cover as much of the networks as possible inside of a week.

Aer Lingus flew us with panache to Dublin, there to spend our first night at the city's youth hostel, not one of the organisation's more modern establishments but a fine accommodation bargain at IRE£13 including breakfast, which is not much more than £12 sterling. And, much to our relief, the rail strike came to an end the day before we arrived, though some services remained restricted.

It is said that Dublin is a place that can be evoked but rarely summed up; a solid harmony of granite, warm brickwork, harsh concrete, and a blending of trees, canals, wrought iron, cobblestones, bright sunlight and misty rain. The setting is superb; to the east the broad sweep of Dublin Bay and to the south-west the purple Wicklow Mountains. The Irish capital has moved into

the twentieth century with a grace that few other cities can equal, maintaining an air of elegance in spite of new development. The River Liffey flows nonchalantly through an unpompous heart to a port which almost reaches the main thoroughfare, O'Connell Street, one of the broadest city thoroughfares in Europe.

The architecture is a workaday mix. Superficially it is Georgian with smart eighteenth- century houses about which people still move and talk with a Georgian politeness. Further out is Victorian Dublin of a century later; possibly the last Victorian city in the British Isles replete with street markets, derelict warehouses, old-fashioned nameplates of redundant but still active clubs, corner shops and hole-in-the-wall pubs where the serious business of conversation is held over pints of the 'Black Stuff' (Guinness).

In the morning we made our way to Connell Station, one of three main termini in the capital, the others being Pearse and Heuston, all perfectly adequate for the size of railway they serve. In a rural and not prosperous country there was not the same opportunity for intense railway development as there was in Britain. Trunk routes were undertaken from Dublin to Cork, to Galway, to Wicklow and Wexford, and to Belfast. This latter route, the Great Northern, had the distinction of becoming an international main line, operating in both Eire and Northern Ireland after the partition in 1922. The cross-country connections were also important, serving Waterford and Limerick, while in the north, the Belfast to Londonderry – or Derry, as some prefer to call it – line was a busy and prosperous concern, later taken over by the English Midland Railway. In 1925 the railways of Eire were grouped. The Great Northern, because of its international character, remained untouchable, but all other lines were merged into a new Great Southern system, still under private ownership. In 1945 it was nationalised as Coras Iompair Eireann which, in 1958, took over that portion of the former Great Northern Railway situated in Eire. Today the state railway of the Irish Republic is titled Iarnrod Eireann – but don't ask me to

pronounce it – the rail division of CIE. The network covers some 1,180 route miles to which, inclusive of that of Northern Ireland Railways, must be added a further mileage.

We both held an all-Ireland Emerald bus/rail card that covered the chief Republic and Northern Ireland town, country and intercity road and rail services; ours being valid for 8 days' travel out of 30 consecutive days (there are other such good value cards available for a longer period, and also some of a more restrictive nature). Such cards are valid for every grade of train; there's no nonsense regarding paying supplements for super expresses, though Ireland's only top-grade expresses are the Dublin–Belfast cross-border Enterprise and the Dublin–Cork City Gold services. And it was the former Enterprise Express that we boarded for the two-hour journey to Ireland's second capital.

The train gives a bird's-eye view of the Republic's town of Drogheda as it passes high over the Boyne River and, a short while later, evocative glimpses of the Mountains of Mourne rolling down to the sea; the sea in this instance being the head of Carlingford Lough over which the line passes to enter Northern Ireland. These wild, steep-sided granite hills present an unforgettable aspect when seen from the Republic as they rise out of the lough. Paul's military base lay the further side of the Mournes, a convenient distance from Belfast, his battalion's main theatre of operations.

Few people unfamiliar with the city will immediately warm to the prospect of a stay there. Sectarian violence and high-profile security measures have, in the past, given the impression to outsiders that Northern Ireland's capital is a war zone. Like many things in Ireland, however, the reality is a pleasant surprise. Security checks are currently far less stringent than they used to be and, even then, they were endured with the stoicism that prevailed during the Second World War when the bombing of Belfast's dockyards caused high civilian casualties.

A walk around the centre provides a good introduction to the city with the splendid white Portland stone façade of the city hall

as its hub. To me the city held an air of being distinctly more prosperous than the existing economic outlook suggested it should be, and with no sign whatsoever of any terrorist bomb damage or even major agitation. We did meet a patrol of wary Royal Marines as we entered the southern suburbs, and I managed a chat with one of its members who confirmed that the political climate, in spite of renewed inter-Loyalist strife, was far less fraught than had been the case in earlier years.

And it was to the districts of Ballymurphy, the Falls and Shankill that Paul most wanted to venture. Here was his former 'battleground' and, like all ex-servicemen, he wished to rekindle old memories. Thus we came upon the visible signs of agitation, both past and present, with lurid graffiti and house-high painted murals that have become an art gallery for nosy tourists of the likes of us. We walked the notorious sectarian ghettos of Andersonstown that have given the city its worst reputation, but Paul could recognise little since the overcrowded, run-down districts had, in the meantime, been transformed into new and quite handsome development, the former rows of mean dwellings swept away. He did, however, locate the warehouse, once shrouded in barbed-wire, from whence he had issued forth on street patrols (I recognised it too, for my wife and I had once visited him there), while in the Loyalist sectors the red, white and blue painted pavement curbs and arrays of union flags indicated their patriotism, but one that could only inflame the present mood amongst the populace. We partook of a fish and chips lunch wrapped in a Sinn Fein newspaper and returned to more orthodox city sightseeing.

In 1859 the UK's largest shipyards were established in Belfast by the Yorkshire engineer Edward Harland and a young marine draughtsman from Hamburg, Gustav Wilhelm Wolff. A vast yellow crane gantry with the initials H&W painted on it looms up behind the Albert Memorial clock tower to dominate the dockland skyline as powerfully as any cathedral. Alas, it represents

little more than what had once been, for the part-closure of these mighty shipyards has brought them low.

We spent a night in the homely Greenwood Guest House in Park Road, overlooking one of Belfast's abundant parks, prior to a return to the station for onward progress to Northern Ireland's second city and the northern end of the main east coast line. The two and a half hour run takes a route through pleasant agricultural countryside, but it only becomes dramatically exciting over the last 20 miles beyond Coleraine which, rumour has it, might soon be the line's terminus through lack of support for the onward portion to Londonderry. If so it will be a crying shame, since those 20 miles are a climactic sightseeing delight of empty seashore beaches backed by perpendicular crags with the shores of the Foyle Estuary slowly drawing together with the approach to the city.

I had briefly visited Londonderry years before, but what I looked upon now was a brighter, more colourful and bustling town than my memory had conjured up. The place stands on a hill at the head of Lough Foyle, the station separated from the main town by an iron bridge spanning the river. The city's popular name, Derry, derives from the Gaelic *doire* which means 'a place of oaks', though few trees could I discern within sight of even the upper town which holds a wealth of eighteenth-century buildings and memorials to a long, tumultuous past. These, together with the soft-spoken, wry and friendly people, well aware of Londonderry's reputation as a Northern Ireland trouble spot, give the town an interesting and heart-warming dimension which a visitor will not encounter to such a degree elsewhere in the province.

Paul, of course, was all for making a beeline for Londonderry's notorious Bogside district that has seen much unrest, for it is here that Catholic–Protestant tribalism is most sharply polarised. On a section of wall that once separated the two factions are the profound words announcing that 'You are now entering Free Derry,' a phrase adopted from Governor Wallace's response to an

offer of terms from the besiegers during the famous 105-day siege in 1680.

Again Paul enthusiastically led me along once-hostile streets of compacted houses, their gable ends still daubed with garish IRA and Bobby Sands 'artistry', the scene of 'Bloody Sunday' when 13 Catholic civilians died in 1972 during a civil rights march. We ended our tour with a pint of Guinness amongst amicable company in the infamous Bogside pub, once strictly out of bounds to British soldiery.

For all its political ill-feelings, Londonderry is an absorbing city retaining intact the seventeenth-century walls, never breached by an enemy, that have played such a significant part in its history. They are evocatively walkable and take one past the five cannons that defended the city during its siege, the Protestant cathedral of St Columb and a typically Ulster square known as the Diamond which, Irish-like, is neither square nor diamond-shaped so far as I could make out.

Our base here was the comely Georgian guest house, one of a pair of such establishments owned and run by Dr and Mrs Pyne, in Queen Street and neighbouring Great James Street. Ours was the domain of the redoubtable Mrs Pyne who resides there while husband Peter is king of the castle in Saddlers House round the corner.

One disadvantage about riding the trains in Ireland is that there's little of the network that allows any form of circuit. Thus Paul and I had to retrace the tracks to Dublin for the next phase of our journey. From its most northerly point the main line runs down the eastern side of the country to its southernmost terminal at Cork. However, there are a quartet of lateral lines, three splaying out from Dublin, terminating at Sligo, Ballina and Westport, Galway, Ennis and Tralee. The Galway service was, allegedly, still affected by the aftermath of the strike so we chose to embark upon that of Sligo, a town from whence, some years before, Paul

and I had set out by bicycle to follow the indented coast of County Donegal en route to Londonderry. Our launch pad now was Connell station again.

Because of major reconstruction work on this particular line, we were lucky to have chosen a day when passengers were not fobbed off with a bus connection as far as Mullinger, the centre of Westmeath cattle-raising country and one-time stronghold of Anglo-Normans, which was reached in just over an hour out of Dublin. Another station halt was that of Carrick-on-Shannon, Leitrim's quietly busy county town, attractively placed on the banks of Ireland's premier river where it marks the upper limit of navigation.

Rain was falling steadily as we drew into Sligo, a sizeable town that sits astride the Garavogue River. The place was sacked by the Vikings in 807 and, situated as it is on the fringes of Connaught and Ulster, later became a key location for warring clans. 'To Hell or Connaught' was the choice given by Cromwell to the Irish landowners when their lands had been taken from them in the mid-seventeenth century and, for many, Connaught seemed only a marginally preferable destination. The castle here has long gone, but the thirteenth-century Dominican abbey, sacked in 1641, is substantially in place, even though no more than a shell.

Outside the town loomed the domed bulks of Ben Bulben and Knocknarea Mountains; actually hills, but still impressive. Having arrived quite late in the day we searched in vain for a bed amongst Sligo's hotel and B&B resources, but some sort of festival was in progress that had filled every room. So we strode damply out into the countryside to spend a prickly night in a farm haystack being eaten alive by its appreciative inmates. Beforehand, though, we had fortified ourselves with multiple doses of Guinness in a hamlet pub run by a landlord straight out of a James Joyce novel who, while we imbibed, recited all dozen verses of a local ballad for our benefit.

And so back to Dublin once more and continuing from Hewston station on the Dublin–Waterford line to Kilkenny, no mean feat with a severely restricted rail service on an Irish sabbath.

I had never been to Kilkenny, the country's finest medieval town, and was surprised and delighted with what we found in this further considerable-sized urban centre. Again, a river runs through the centre, this one the Nore, guarded by the huge Kilkenny Castle, its walls pink from an early sunset and reflected artistically in the placid waters. Our discovery was a town packed with well-preserved history together with a copious horde of visitors come to drool over it, though in this instance we obtained a simple B&B pad for the night with no difficulty.

The Statutes of Kilkenny, passed in 1366, made for another nail in the English-Irish coffin. This stipulated an assertion of England's authority in Ireland by means of what was essentially a form of apartheid. Intermarriage, social intercourse, Gaelic names and language were all suppressed and the native population forced to live outside the city walls. And when even their religious beliefs were banned the locals rose in revolt to be brutally put down by Cromwell thus, in effect, severing any possibility of an Anglo-Irish integration which, left to itself, might over time have resulted in a harmonious community. We Brits now pay dearly for our past sins.

Apart from the castle, the most striking of a host of striking edifices is St Canice's Cathedral, once used by Cromwell to stable his horses. Rising close to the building, indeed part of it, is a circular factory-like chimney known unimaginatively as the Round Tower. A turning off Dean Street leads to the Black Abbey, the thirteenth-century Dominican friary which likewise suffered the irreverent attentions of the intrusive Cromwell. In fact, every turn of the town's restaurant-packed streets produces something of historical note to catch the eye and divert one's footsteps. Quite a place is Kilkenny.

Wexford was but a short rail hop next day, but our pause here in another expansive town with a historic centre – and a partly-walled one to boot – was of very limited duration; just long enough in fact to discover the rail link to Cork, our most southerly destination, to be far from straightforward and involving a road link over a portion of it. The Wexford–Cork bus service, however, bore no complications and the route is an interesting one taking in Georgian (in parts) Clonmel, Tipperary's county town, and a second but more picturesque Carrick, this one on the Suir, the river that forms the border of Wexford and Tipperary.

'Picturesque' would not be the adjective I would use to describe Cork City, but the traffic-snarled streets are packed with character, the dark green waterway of the Lee River attracting seagulls, swans and freighters to the centre of the town. The Irish name *Corcaigh* means 'a marshy place' and the city grew up on low-lying islands in the river. It had always favoured ousting British rule, becoming known as 'Rebel Cork', and was once a base for the Nationalist Fenian movement in the nineteenth century. But this in no way neutralises the warmth of welcome for English visitors who, very soon after arrival, find streets revealing Cork's mercantile past: tall eighteenth-century bow-fronted houses and handsome warehouses, many under restoration. On foot I saw more of the city than I had on fleeting earlier visits as we looked in on St Finbarre's Cathedral, Elizabeth Fort and Shandon Church, where I once partook of the popular tourist 'fun thing' of attempting to play the carillon on its bells, which must be a pain to local residents though I was assured it wasn't.

Our base in Cork was a step up in accommodation status with the elegant Lancaster Lodge in Western Road providing a luxurious suite for our delectation, but the weather ensured that we were not over-pampered by providing lowering cloud and a damping drizzle for our side-trip on the hourly train service to Cobh

(pronounced 'cove'), a port and coastal resort of which I had long nursed curiosity.

What we beheld there, even under the drizzle, satisfied this modest craving as we initially toured the outstanding Queenstown Heritage Centre formed from the revived Victorian railway station. It tells of the enthralling *Queenstown Story*.

With a sheltered, deepwater harbour, Cobh – once called Queenstown following a visit from Queen Victoria – grew in importance when ocean-going liners became too big to dock in Cork itself, further up the Lee estuary. The first ship carrying convicts to Australia sailed from here in 1791; by the time the practice was stopped decades later, a total of 39,000 convicts had been transported into exile in appalling conditions. Troopships embarked soldiers at Cobh for the Napoleonic, Crimean and Boer Wars, and the port saw the mass departure of emigrants fleeing famines and depressions from the 1840s until well into the twentieth century. For many hundreds of these emigrants the scenic panorama of the colourful houses of Cobh must have been their last glimpse of the Emerald Isle. On the other side of the social structure the harbour berthed some of the great transatlantic luxury liners, including the ill-fated *Titanic* and *Lusitania*, the latter torpedoed offshore on 7 May 1915 with the loss of 1,198 lives.

The hill-flanking town, though fun loving as a coastal resort should be, is touched by a sombre nostalgia; the *Titanic* and *Lusitania* disasters commemorated by plaques and stone memorials in the main square and by a poignant statue depicting an emigrant woman and her two children outside the station. On the steep hill above the harbour, the soaring spire of the massive nineteenth-century Gothic Cathedral of St Colman makes for climactic landmark.

Back to Cork across the mudflats of the Lee estuary and an evening spent imbibing Guinness with the rotund but knowledgeable Andrew Roche, an executive of Irish Railways, who amply demonstrated, with much frustrating circuiting of back

streets, the tribulations of locating parking space in the city. And thanks to him we were furnished with first-class upgrades on the City Gold rail service for our return to Dublin.

This is the principal railway route wholly within the Irish Republic. It was built by the Great Southern & Western Railway Company and, like so many of the major trunk lines in the British Isles, it was a product of the railway mania of the 1840s. Even by the standards of the period, the project was an ambitious one. At 165 miles this line was longer than any comparable scheme in Britain. Given the much less favourable economic conditions in Ireland at the time – construction of the route was undertaken during the dark years of the Great Famine – the fact that the line was completed at all and on schedule was a remarkable achievement.

The present Cork station – plans are afoot for a new one closer to the river – is unique in that it is built on a curve of the tracks. Trains leaving it for Dublin and the North plunge almost immediately into the longest tunnel in Ireland, carrying the line under the north-western sector of the city. The route is relatively level except for sharp gradients at either end and, at Mallow, the line crosses the Blackwater River on a viaduct that replaces the original one destroyed in the Troubles of the 1920s. At a commendable rate of knots, with speeds not far short of 100 miles per hour, our express traversed the Curragh of Kildare, where thoroughbreds were exercising alongside the track, to arrive at the bright and airy Heuston Terminus exactly on schedule.

I am sometimes asked which part of Ireland is my favourite haunt, and I have to say the West, its coast and hinterland running from County Donegal's far northerly Malin Head down to the country's southernmost tip. There's little to compare with the lonely shores of Donegal where the Atlantic has bitten out ragged saw-teeth of peninsulas; the softer terrain of County Sligo that contradicts its legends of savagery and glory; Connemara and its dramatic hill and mountain ranges that soar above tiny sheltered

coastal bays and inland lakes; the further drama of Galway and Clare with the Arran Isles; the strange Burren plateau and the gigantic cliffs of Moher dropping sheer into a boiling ocean. Ireland's West is, quite literally, Europe's last frontier.

However, on this occasion we had no time to cover the lateral lines to the west coast except for that to Sligo town. I do, though, have a favourite county in the east and this is Wicklow, which not only adjoins, and is conveniently attainable from, the urban spread of Dublin but also can be described as Ireland virtually compressed into a nutshell, together with all its amiability, scenery and attractions. Here, beyond the oft-overcrowded seaside resort of Bray, is a coast of wide sandy beaches unspoilt by commercialism; a blessed emptiness even in the high season, backed by wooded dunes and green hills that, further inland, buck themselves into the rugged Wicklow Mountains; round-topped hills sprouting occasional granite peaks. A lonely, awesome countryside of peat bogs, lakes, open moorland, verdant valleys and waterfalls, historic monastic sites and spectacular gardens.

With just 30 hours to spare before our Emerald rail cards expired, we utilised the Irish capital's superb DART suburban rail service that has now been extended southwards beyond Bray to smaller Greystones, there to enjoy a brief reunion with County Wicklow.

The DART extension will no doubt see an expansion of the simple township and fishing harbour, for railways of the world have a habit of opening up the countryside whether for good or bad. But there is plenty more of Wicklow for those who crave solitude and the wonders of nature.

We spent our last night at the friendly Castanea Guest House off Rathdown Road and the following day, Cinderella-like, sped back to Dublin to catch our flight home before our golden railway coach turned into a pumpkin.

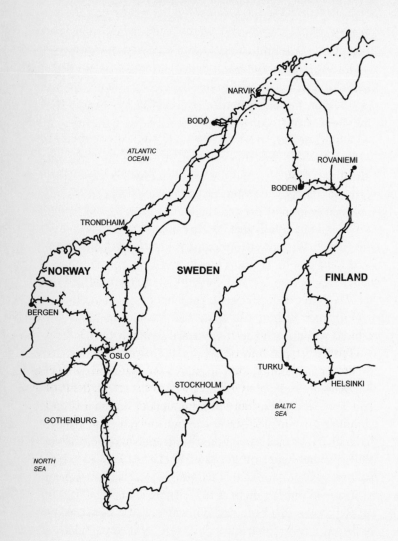

Rails to the Arctic

It was way back in the 1970s that I rode the Scandinavian rail network for the sole purpose of sampling the long-distance public transport systems; their routes and expertise in a quartet of countries with particularly daunting geographical barriers to overcome. The memories of those journeys are fading, but vivid enough to allow brief narration.

All four of these northern nations are railway conscious; three of them have the bonus of magnificent scenery to match, and at the time in Norway and Finland could be found the occasional working steam locomotive.

The Swedish railway system came into being in 1849 with a narrow-gauge line eight kilometres long using horse-drawn trains though the mainline network, and the state-owned system dates from 1856. Today, the Swedish State Railway operates more than 90 per cent of the total traffic, and has a route length of around 12,000 kilometres, much of it electrified.

Norwegian railways, of which the first section was opened in 1854, have the particular fascination of being operated for the most part in exceedingly rugged terrain subject to great extremes of climate. In striking contrast to Sweden, barely six per cent of the total length of about 4,500 kilometres is on gradients of less than 1 in 100, more than three-quarters of the total is on truly mountain gradients of 1 in 40 to 1 in 67 which is extremely high for a railway. In the far north, the line from Narvik to the Swedish border is completely isolated from the rest of the Norwegian State Railway's system; to reach Narvik by rail one has to use the trains of the Swedish State Railway and continue on the north-west to south-west ore-carrying line from Kiruna. This was the route I had to take to attain Narvik following my ferry crossing from Travemünde in Northern Germany to Trelleborg and Malmö on the southern tip of Sweden.

The geographical structure of Denmark, with some of its most important and populous areas on islands, presented special problems when it came to building up an efficient rail network, in spite of the fact that the country is predominately flat. The first section of line was laid in 1847 between Copenhagen and Roskilde, but later extensions involved trains being carried between the main islands on ferries, though the bulk of these are now linked by bridges.

From their inception in 1862, the Finnish State Railway, because of the long eastern border of the country, has been oriented towards the Russian model rather than that of the rest of Europe. Thus the rail gauge is mostly 1,524 millimetres (5 ft), although at Tornio in the far north there existed exchange facilities with the standard-gauge Swedish system. Finland, too, is subject to extremes of climate, yet railways are effectively operated in the depths of the sub-Arctic winters.

Sweden has, by far, the most comprehensive railway system. The country is the largest of the Scandinavian quartet; fourth in size in Europe, and covering an area nearly twice that of the British Isles. Yet the population is only something over eight million. Its network is thickest down in the industrial South but, unlike Norway, continues, unbroken, to its northern extremity. Its trains are a lesson in efficiency, good timing, comfort and standardisation of amenities, the likes of which we have never seen in Britain. And this goes, generally speaking, for all the Scandinavian railways. In spite of the comparative flatness, the terrain offers pleasant and sometimes incredibly beautiful scenery of forests, lakes, rivers, rock and, in the north, the occasional glimpse of mountains towards the Norwegian border (the isolated summit of Kebnekaise, 6,965 feet, in Lapland is Sweden's highest mountain).

But for long narrow countries, Norway holds something of a world record (perhaps shared with Chile). Its population is half that of Sweden but, in area, is not much smaller. Only a fifth of the country is less than 500 feet above sea level, while more than

half is at an elevation of over 2,000 feet. Oddly it is the more attainable South that contains the greatest mountain complexes: those of the Hardangervidda and Jotunheimer being of higher altitude than the northern ranges. This difficult terrain and the sparseness of the population hardly encouraged the promotion of railways, so the scarcity of track is not at all surprising. These facts, together with a long coastline, explain the prominence in the pattern of transportation in Norway of the coastal shipping services. These cooperate closely with the running of the trains and, together with a dense network of railway buses, make up for the sparsity of lines particularly in the difficult north where indents made by rugged fjords bring, the width of the country down to less than 20 miles in places and the bulk of this is pure granite.

My journeying centred mainly on Norway. And it is Norway where the engineering feat of the railway meets the evaluative feat of nature. My Norwegian portion of the journey commenced at Storlien, to whence I was whisked in nine hours by the Jamtlandspilen Express from Stockholm.

The far north was my initial objective. For this I could use the train as far as Bodø and the line that was to take me there was called the Nordland Railway. It is one of the few in the world that pass the Arctic Circle, and was built over a period of many years. A clergyman, Ole Tobias Olsen, was the moving spirit behind its conception, and this remarkable man not only continuously urged the construction of the line but personally undertook much of the preliminary reconnaissance. Olsen died in 1924, but 40 years later the first train entered Bodø over the final stretch completed in 1962. With a total length of 453 miles it is the longest mainline railway in Norway and snakes along the side of many fjords and lakes that fissure this giraffe neck of the country.

Except for the twenty-odd miles of east–west Norwegian track that connects Narvik to the Northern Sweden rail network there is, as yet, still no railway east of Bodø connecting that city, though

Northerners have long been loud in their demands for a Bodø–Narvik rail link. In the meantime, surface transport in that region is represented by the excellent coastal steamer services and those of the lowly bus. And at Bodø commenced the longest scheduled bus route in Europe. It was run by the North Norway Bus Company and covered, inside of four days, the 1,308 kilometres to Kirkenes, close against the Russian border. I made the run in both directions. It took me, in pleasantly relaxing stages, right across the top of Sweden and Finland past and over some of the most stark fjord scenery to be found in all Scandinavia. The route traversed Norwegian Lapland and the vehicle frequently filled with Lapps in their colourful national dress, while herds of reindeer trotted daintily across the road.

To me the most enchanting characteristic of the service was its encroachment into the daily life of the local communities it served. One moment it was a post bus, the next a grocery van, and it would stop on demand at any point along that winding bumpy road to the final reaches of Europe. A few years later I was to make the outward and return voyage together with my wife, from Bergen right round the North Cape to Kirkenes, by one of the sturdy coastal ferries which, like their wheeled associates, carry both passengers and mixed cargo calling in at dozens of community centres en route.

Along the endless road, stopovers were made at small townships including Sorkjosen, close to the dramatic Lyngseidet complex of mountain, fjord and glacier that provides scenery of breathtaking dimensions. Three fjords cut the route and gave reason for a trio of mini-cruises on vehicle ferries that closed the gaps and provided welcome leg stretches and a breath of ultra-fresh and nippy air. Kirkenes, at the end of the road, I found to be a striking town of some 5,000 people in remote countryside bisected by rivers renowned for superb salmon fishing.

A return to Bodø meant yet another bus ride to Narvik, and only then could I get back to the trains. The Ofot Line runs from

this pleasant city, unspoilt even by its vast iron ore- loading plants, to Riksgränsen on the Swedish border. It is only 26 miles long, but renowned not only for the part it plays in bringing Swedish ore to the sea, but also as a magnificent scenic line through precipitous mountain terrain. For many years it was the world's most northerly railway, and even today is probably the most northerly electrified line anywhere. I was told, with righteous pride, that the line carried about half the total quantity of goods transported annually by the whole of the Norwegian State Railway, and was especially built to meet the transport requirements of a single commodity. My informant went on to explain that more than half the output of high quality iron from the mines around Kiruna travels this way yet, even though single track, modern signalling systems allow passenger trains to share the line. The trains cling to the granite walls like flies to a window.

In Sweden again I changed to a series of first Swedish, then Finnish, rail-cars, or buses as they were titled, which ran at considerable speed and verve through the lake and wood-mantled countryside into Finland. It seemed a great shame that these plucky little diesels were being phased out of service by both railway administrations, and today the route is taken over by road transport. A branch line from the Finnish border town of Kemi led me to Rovaniemi, headquarters of one of a trio of Scandinavian Santa Clauses I was to meet, and fortunately this most northerly Finnish passenger-carrying track is still in operation, though the former extension to Kemijärvi has since surrendered to the road.

The country is somewhat larger than Norway, with about the same population and had, then, 5,924 miles of working line, the main physical impediments to construction and running being lakes, not mountains.

My overnight journey to Helsinki was made in one of the old pre-Second World War coaches being phased out and which everyone tried to avoid. But the new coaches with reclining seats

were full to the brim which, fortuitously, left me plenty of space and a whole row of seats in the old coaches on which to doze my way to the Finnish capital. During the hours of daylight I looked upon a countryside wrapped in the great silence of a myriad of Finnish lakes that hold the very stuff of tragedy and heroism in their loneliness and ethereal beauty. Here it is all too easy to appreciate how Sibelius obtained inspiration for his haunting music.

Helsinki is, in the vintage table, as new as the country it heads. Much of the centre is the work of the German architect Carl Ludwig Engel, whose harmonious Senate Square fronting his Lutheran cathedral is, perhaps, the finest square in Northern Europe. What many people regard as the most Finnish edifice in the city is the red granite railway station, so heavy-looking that it gave me the impression of having sunk several feet into the ground.

Another train carried me to the port of Turku, there to embark on one of the numerous and slickly-run ferries bound for Stockholm. Sharing my cabin for the crossing of the Gulf of Finland was a Norwegian who treated me to a non-stop eulogy of the glories of his country. I was hardly in a receptive frame of mind with a sleepless night behind me, but was nevertheless grateful for his companionship. Even his subsequent snores, as we lay in opposite bunks, had a musical Peer Gynt quality about them. In Stockholm I caught a further express back into Norway again with Oslo as the immediate destination; the most unlikely of the Scandinavian capitals. Modern ugly buildings jostle for prominence amongst older and mellower ones, the whole ungainly mixture tempered by an aura of hospitality, charm and fish. But capitals were only a means to an end for me on this journey.

The more bulky southern end of Norway is a rail-traveller's paradise. Possibly the most famous scenic line is that of the Bergen

Railway with its offshoot, the Flåm Line. Across the roof of the country runs a railway through deep forests, by lakes and waterfalls, up narrow valleys and across bare and windswept mountain heaths bearing glaciers and perpetual snow. For 60 miles of its total 300 the track lies above the tree line, and over its full length are 200 tunnels, 18 miles of snow sheds and 300 bridges. The Bergen Railway was opened by King Haakon VII in 1909 to connect eastern and western Norway. It is the most important year-round land route between the country's two chief cities, the capital, Oslo, and Bergen. A masterpiece of engineering, it reaches a climax with the Flåm offshoot, which is just over 12 miles long between Myrdal station at an altitude of almost 3,000 feet and Flåm near sea level, making this branch line one of the world's steepest non-rack-operated railways.

My ride to Flåm was a truly awe-inspiring experience. A near-one hour journey – then taking longer to go down than to go up – the train spent three and a half miles in 20 tunnels including a reverse tunnel whereby the line runs at five levels within a point-to-point distance of 0.6 of a mile. This ensured that, just before the Nali tunnel, the line could be seen at four levels corkscrewing up the steep mountainside while, close by, was the road climbing Mount Myrdalsberget in 21 tortuous hairpin bends. During my journey in both directions suitable music by Edward Grieg was played over the speakers to drown the pumping of my own and fellow passengers' hearts.

Another essentially tourist line operating at the time I was there was the Valdres Railway, which was almost eclipsed by the decision to build the Bergen Line. But the people of Valdres were determined to have their railway and finally got it in the early 1900s. Less dramatic, it was still an impressive ride.

There are two rail links between Oslo and Trondheim, the most picturesque being the Dovre and Røros line opened in 1921 which follows the ancient path linking southern and northern Norway.

It winds past Lake Mjosa, the country's largest and longest lake ending at Lillehammer, to Dombås and the mountain plateau via the 865-yard long Gronbogen double-back tunnel. Superb views of Mount Snöhetta and the peaks of the Trollheimen Mountains can be glimpsed, as well as the Magalaupen falls at Engen.

South of Oslo the perimeter of the huge bulge of Southern Norway is covered by the Sorland line, 372 miles to Stavanger. Regrettably I was not to see the more scenic portion between Kristiansand and Stavanger, as my destination and exit from Scandinavia lay in Sorlands capital, Kristiansand. Within this second portion lay Norway's longest and second-longest tunnels and some rugged terrain known as 'God's Wrath'. Instead my path lay across the not always placid waters of the North Sea.

With a bellyful of rich Scandinavian rail travel beneath my belt, the mountains of *smørbrød* available on board my home-going ferry became wellnigh superfluous. But not quite.

Making Tracks in North-East Europe

Having traversed Poland on two different occasions on foot and by bicycle it seemed a logical step to undertake the far lesser accomplishment of traversing it by train. And to broaden the scope of this undertaking add Lithuania to the itinerary plus, as a further objective, the *oblast* of Kaliningrad, that region of the Russian Federation separated by an independent Lithuania from her main territory. Ever since my son, Paul, and I had cycled through all three Baltic States en route to the Black Sea seven years earlier, we had envisaged the idea of entering this then forbidden Soviet zone now cautiously open to outsiders but seldom visited except by elderly Germans intent upon a glimpse of East Prussia as it once was.

Hence, at the end of July 2000, I left London, courtesy of Eurostar, bound for Paris on that most efficient and swift if, after

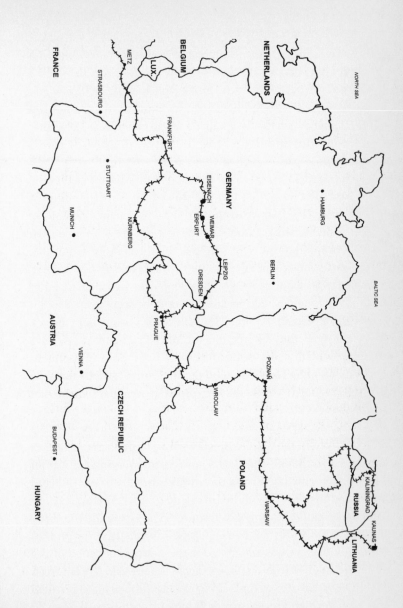

one's first experience of it, ever-so-slightly dull method of negotiating the English Channel. The first leg of the whole journey was to take me to Prague, there to pick up Paul who currently lives and works there. Eurostar's Paris terminal is the Gare de Nord, conveniently neighbouring the Gare de l'Est where my 17.19 Frankfurt-bound EC express commenced its run. Again I was equipped with the huge value interrail pass and, as a weekend coincided with my departure, there was no super-express supplement to pay.

At the Gare de l'Est disaster struck. First into my coach as the train backed into the platform, I stowed my small amount of baggage on the rack above my head and paid momentary attention to a well-dressed man addressing me in rapid French. Unknown to me his colleague was sussing out the most easily removable items of passenger's belongings on the racks and targeted mine. Covered by the confusion of milling people the two men, together with my belongings, disappeared never to be seen again.

'This happens all the time,' I was informed by my neighbours. Now they tell me. Thereafter, the only bright interlude in a journey suddenly gone sour came with an empty compartment between Frankfurt and Pilsen on the subsequent strictly non-EC train to Prague. At least I could lay prostrate for what remained of the night.

I thus arrived in the Czech capital with no more than the clothes on my back, though this was soon remedied following a brief buying spree, the borrowing of various garments from Paul, and the donation of ditto from his girlfriend's father. Fortunately my vital documents and financial resources had reposed around my waist; the only serious consequences of the theft beyond an expensive camera was the bible for the journey, my copy of the current edition of *Thomas Cook's European Timetable*. My enforced shopping spree, needed to re-equip myself with the more personal items of attire, had its moments. It took place in a small town 35

kilometres out of Prague, and just *you* try purchasing male underpants in a largely women's outfitter with barely a smattering of Czech, and with most of the lady assistants of Vietnamese origin! I solved the problem by spreading a pair of girlie black frilly knickers across my lower stomach, which produced a certain amount of levity.

Joined by Paul, we caught the 07.23 non-express from Prague's Central Station next morning with Polish Wroclaw, the former German Breslau, as our initial destination. Here was a city I had last looked upon, albeit briefly and none too pleasurably since it was no more than a vast ruin, in 1944 as a prisoner-of-war en route to slave-labour in a Silesian coalmine. What I beheld now was a remarkably beautiful city, its edifices restored to their former glory. Attempting to find our way from the station to the first hotel of a pre-booked two-hotel sojourn – which, unknown to us, lay five kilometres distant – we asked the way, utilising Paul's considerable linguistic ability, of a knowledgeable-looking Pole about to enter his car.

'Get in and I'll take you there,' was the response in good English.

Consequently we made the acquaintance of George, and he was as good as his word. More to the point, he expressed a desire to return the following day to give us a tour of his city; an invitation we readily accepted.

The Orbis Novohotel was an oasis of comfort, our night there made the more pleasurable by a multi-course dinner offered us by the engaging manager. And in the morning a beaming George, happy to further his English pronunciation, whisked us off for a day's exploration of Wroclaw.

The multinational influences which shaped the city – Bohemian, Austrian and Prussian – are reflected in its architecture; the huge Germanic brick Gothic churches which dominate the skyline are intermingled with Flemish-style Renaissance mansions, palaces and chapels of Viennese Baroque, and boldly utilitarian public buildings of the early nineteenth century. The

tranquillity of the parks, gardens and River Oder offer ready escape from the urban ferment, while the town yields a vibrant cultural scene, its theatre tradition enjoying worldwide renown.

With George we climbed the spiral staircase of one of the twin towers of the cathedral and explored the famed university buildings in which he taught as a professor. With a break for coffee, cake and *lody* (ice cream), we were deposited at our second hotel, the resplendent four-star Park Plaza of ultra-modern design where the manager and his assistant joined us for a further multi-course repast, washed down by copious draughts of beer, wine and vodka. And in the morning, brooking no refusals, the good man, having learnt of my deficiency of clothing, pressed upon me the complete gentleman's outfit insisting that anything surplus to requirements be given or thrown away.

Prior to leaving Wroclaw, Paul and I took a morning stroll along the banks of a tranquil River Oder recollecting the time, three years earlier, when it had catastrophically flooded the city as well as other parts of Poland, the Czech Republic and Germany, causing enormous damage and much human misery. The disaster had taken place the year of our trans-Poland hike, its floodwaters diverting us for many miles.

Driven to the station by the hotel manager and seen off by the ever-attentive George, we headed for Poznan in an oft-stopping and jam-packed post-midday train that providentially emptied at the first sizeable town. The countryside through which we were passing was flat, agricultural and devoid of great interest; the only hills and eye-catching terrain traversed up to then had been that around the Czech town of Náchod on the Czech-Polish border, marred on the Polish side by the ugly scars of redundant coalmines.

Our accommodation star rating dropped to three with the Orbis Mercury Hotel, just ten minutes' walk from the station, but it still provided an adequate base for our weekend exploration of a city I had visited but briefly before. Its most recent flashpoint of fame was the 1953 anti-communist government uprising during

which a sizeable number of citizens were killed, injured and jailed by a brutally repressive police. Though the revolt was put down, it lit a spark that would later burst into a flame to engulf and destroy the Communist regimes of Europe. The grandiose monument near our hotel makes this eloquently clear.

Poznan is essentially a commercial centre, as exemplified by its annual Trade Fair. Many a Central European city has a *Stary Rynek* ('Old Town') and this one is no exception. Numerous weekend activities were taking place in the square, from brass bands to pop groups and high-stepping majorettes to art and photographic displays. A city of great diversity, it encompasses a tranquil cathedral quarter, the animated centre, and a dynamic business district while enjoying a reputation as a rallying point for Polish nationalism.

Our second night at the Mercury Hotel ended before it had properly begun, as we had to catch the 02.00 train to Warsaw for the start of a 14-hour rail journey on a trio of trains that were to convey us to Lithuania. This entailed rising from our beds soon after midnight and making our way through empty, slightly sinister streets to the station. Here we donated an unwanted but well-tailored jacket to a surprised beggar before fighting our way on to a mysteriously packed train, the only space available being the corridor.

Four hours brought us to Warsaw and a terminus likewise devoid of seating so, having been ejected from the wall of the adjoining car park by an unsociable security guard, we devoured a sandwich breakfast on the stone steps of the station concourse. The second train, agreeably half-empty, deposited us close to the Polish-Lithuanian border at Šeštokai, beyond larger Suawaki, a town Paul and I remembered as places where we had paused during our cycling marathon.

The third train was Lithuanian and initially consisted of a single coach, and a first-class one at that, into which we and a handful of other passengers were herded. And because we possessed no

lats (Lithuanian currency) we optimistically tendered our interrail passes, although they were not valid for the railways of the Baltic States. This produced a certain amount of puzzlement as a relay of officials, each one senior in rank, entered the compartment to scrutinise the passes, finally and happily accepting them. We had been perfectly willing to pay the fare in US dollars, British sterling or German marks, or even Polish zloty, but presumed this would only lead to complications.

Though the train was continuing to Vilnius, the Lithuanian capital, we alighted at Kaunas, the second city and one of which we were already acquainted, to be met by the heart-warming Kuprys family with whom we had stayed on our previous sojourn.

In their company again we spent a rewarding three days and nights in the city based at their home in the outer suburbs. Once Lithuania's capital, it was also a prosperous Hanseatic town and a centre for the formation and concentration of Lithuanian intellectuals following liberation from Tsarist Russia. Again swallowed by Russia and, during the Second World War, savagely occupied by Nazi Germany, Lithuania finally gained independence in 1990 when, in company with the other two Baltic States, it threw off the yoke of Soviet repression. The city stands at the confluence of two rivers, the Nemunas and Neris, overlooked by the substantial thirteenth-century castle. The Gothic houses of the Town Hall Square, part of the Old Town, are centred by the ornate white town hall marked by a slender five-layered tower, the edifice being affectionately known as the White Swan.

Sometimes alone, sometimes with Pavilos and wife Rute, together with their teenage offspring, Simon and Julia, we explored the city anew; Paul and I taking ourselves, on one occasion, beyond the city boundary to the remains of one of the series of forts that surround Kaunas. Only four of the forts have survived, the best preserved being number nine which, during the last war, became the site of mass killings by the Nazi occupiers.

Paul being a devotee of aviation, we also footslogged across the airfield we had last seen occupied by Russian military aircraft, today used by the local flying club. A well-presented aviation museum now occupies the administration buildings partly destroyed by the withdrawing Soviet military.

In consequence of our proposed entry into the Russian *oblast* of Kaliningrad a problem had arisen. For various reasons we had been unable to obtain our respective visas from Russian embassies in London and Prague, so my good friend, Neil Taylor, who runs a specialist agency arranging group and individual travel to lesser-known and even controversial regions of the world, came up with a proposal. This involved us in collecting our visas from one of the two road entry points from Lithuania and, for this, it was vital to present ourselves at a specific time on a specific date. Easier said than done, however. Neil's agency had designated for us the most northerly and, from Kaunas, the most distant crossing point. In consequence we had to find our way to Sovetsk, on the Russian side of that crossing point, some 200 kilometres distant. All we possessed in support of our visa acquisition were photocopies of the visas themselves and an assurance that somebody would meet us at the border.

'You haven't a hope of getting in,' opined Pavilos, and he should know, having been a reluctant officer of the Soviet Army and thus well acquainted with the unreliability of Russian authority.

The closest Lithuanian town of any consequence to Sovetsk is Šiauliai, still a long way from the Russian border but at least on the main railway line linking Kaunas to Riga in Latvia, though train services in this neck of the woods are thin on the ground. There did seem to be a once-a-day bus service linking Riga to Kaliningrad, or so *Thomas Cook's European Timetable* had indicated, but no times were available for the intermediate stops. However, the problem was solved by our good hosts who undertook to take the day off, prompted by a national holiday throughout the country, and drive us to the border. Thus we transferred our

allegiance from the railway to the road, stopping off en route to stretch our legs with a hike up an ancient fortification mound overlooking the Nemunas River, a visit to the seventeenth-century Raudone Castle, and partake of coffee and cake at Jurbarskas situated on another confluence of rivers. We arrived at the frontier village of Panemone shortly after 11.00 a.m.; plenty of time, we thought, to keep our 1.00 p.m. appointment the other side of the border.

It was the queue of cars several kilometres long that aroused our initial sense of foreboding. Pavilas drove uneasily past the long line of stationary vehicles to drop us near the head of the queue and then hastily departed. The family had been wonderfully good to us and our sense of loss was palatable as we contemplated likely hassles lying ahead.

On our own again we crossed a bridge over a tributary of the Nemunas River to join a huge queue of pedestrians plus another but shorter line of cars gradually inching forward towards a distant cabin from which one solitary official was unhurriedly perusing and stamping passports of both pedestrians and the occupants of cars. And this formality was solely to leave Lithuania. An untidy conglomeration of stalls selling foodstuff had been set up and were doing a roaring trade from hungry, thirsty, frustrated and, no doubt, many a disillusioned potential transitee who had given up hope of entering Russian territory.

It took us about an hour and a half to reach the no man's land of the Queen Louise Bridge that spanned the main course of the wide Nemunas, only to come upon another great queue that stretched the whole way across the unlovely bridge. At the Russian end of it a gaunt and shrapnel-chipped archway, still adorned with the Soviet emblem, marked the entry into the 'promised land' though the queue continued beyond it. But, processed out of Lithuania, we had reached the point of no return. I wondered why so many people wanted to enter Russia, particularly since

there were few vehicles and pedestrians going the other way. For that matter I had reached the point of wondering why the hell *we* were doing so.

Then it began to rain, and rain hard. To add to my own discomfort I was suffering a dose of the 'runs'. A woman in front of us wore no more than a cotton summer frock and was soaked through in seconds. A further hour and a half went by; our 1.00 p.m. deadline long past. Dismally we inched forward as batches of pedestrians and a few cars were ushered through the hallowed portals, watched with disdain by border guards shouldering machine-pistols and leading German Shepherd dogs straining at their leashes. Below us, rain-drops danced disconcertingly upon the brown waters of the river.

We were within new hope of reaching the portal before nightfall when a blonde woman escorted by a guard appeared, walking alongside the soaked and sullen queue. Something told me the lady might be there to collect us and, glory be, she was. I can never look otherwise than English, and this was again proved when she came straight up and pulled us out of the queue. Propelled forward to its head we had our passport stamped and visas inserted, watched balefully by our erstwhile companions. I felt mortified at having been forced to jump the queue, but was not going to argue.

Splashing through the rutted, pot-holed streets of Sovetsk in the woman's car we were taken to the Hotel Tilsit, named after the former title of the town, and a hostelry of very basic facilities. But the piping hot water that emerged from the shower was a godsend. Told – falsely – that there were no restaurants in the town, we accepted the hotel's overpriced dinner that was at least substantial. We were the only mugs in the dismal and damp dining room.

Sovetsk, it has to be said, is exceedingly awful; as dilapidated a town as I have ever seen, even by the standards of those I had been to in the old Soviet Union. Its saving grace is the river that

flows sullenly by. The square is centred by the pigeon dropping-splashed statue of Lenin, still virtually a compulsory adornment to all Russian urban centres. The only spark of colour in this grey town of drab, plaster-cracked and broken buildings was provided by vivid graffiti, an affliction of capitalism that is repeated with a vengeance all over the former Soviet empire. Beggar children mumbling unintelligible words followed us about unmercifully.

Yet once Tilsit was a town of note and we attempted to dredge up from our combined schooldays knowledge what treaty had been signed here. We finally identified it as one signed by Russia, France and Prussia in 1807, resulting from which the latter country lost nearly half her former territory.

We were not sorry to leave Sovetsk, though the acquisition of a rail ticket at the station (our interrail passes were, of course, not valid in Russia) was a distinct tussle which had us queuing at wrong kiosks where telephone calls by the manning staff appeared to form part of the business of selling a ticket. It was our introduction to repeated performances of a similar nature at other stations along the line.

The oft-stopping slow train of hard wooden-seat coaches we eventually boarded clutching our hard-earned tickets got us in due course to Chernyachovsk, which the Prussians called Insterburg. Here our initial low opinion of Russian urban centres rose a notch or two. The place held a distinct aura of character; its buildings less mournful than those of Sovetsk. I was extremely grateful for Paul's command of basic Russian and its, to me, incomprehensible cyrillic lettering; without him I would be a lost soul. But even he had difficulties in locating Tunnel Street in spite of diverse and oft contradictory directional explanations by passers-by. However, when at last we came upon the Hotel zum Baren we were in for a pleasant surprise. This was a small, privately-run pension of exquisite taste that catered for a mainly German clientele.

The *oblast* of Kaliningrad having been once East Prussia, the only foreigners in evidence here and elsewhere were Germans; many elderly pensioners come to look sadly upon a one-time homeland run to seed and dereliction by war and Communism. From the thirteenth century until as recently as 1943, the Kaliningrad region was undeniably German; part of the core territory of the Teutonic Knights and their successors, the dukes and kings of Prussia. Following the First World War, East Prussia (the northern half of which the region approximated) was separated from the rest of Germany, and Hitler's desire to reunite it was the spark that lit the Second World War. The three-month campaign by which the Red Army took it in 1945 was one of the most savage of the war, with hundreds of thousands of casualties on both sides. Ironically the region is in a similar position to what it was before the war, only this time the 'hinterland' is Russian, not German.

The rest of the day and the one that followed was spent exploring the town, second in importance to Kaliningrad City. Tall brick churches of solid Prussian construction rose from streets of sturdy houses while the shops displayed an assortment of Western goods. The iniquitous central square was climaxed by a statue of the Soviet general after which Chernyachovsk is named, which at least made a change from Lenin. With the aid of Paul's linguistic abilities we elicited the fact that the town boasted a brace of castles but we found only one, a ruin of minimal interest. A morning parade by a detachment of Russian soldiers in the square made a welcome diversion for a couple of hours. This seemed to be for the purpose of marking the anniversary of the Second World War Battle of Smolensk, and a collection of elderly veterans well festooned with medals were in attendance. For us the high spot of the proceedings was provided by a large dog that insisted on taking part and was only persuaded to desist when a volley of shots in salute was fired into the air, whereupon the animal took refuge amongst the ranks of soldiers as they goose-stepped away

from the square. We made ourselves known to the officer in charge of the parade, took photographs of the veterans and, our visit at an end, made our way to the station for our next port of call.

A one and a half hour rail journey brought us to the capital, its station a big barn of a place uncannily barren without advertising hoardings. Our pre-booked accommodation for two nights was vested in the Hotel Kaliningrad laying at the head of the wide, two-mile Lenin Prospect of grandiose aspiration, and our walk there on the warmest day since leaving the UK had us in a muck sweat. The Kaliningrad was a step back into Sovietism; a great barrack of an establishment of bad plumbing, minimal character and zero courtesy. Our room could be rated as adequate if you weren't too fussy about cockroaches. Breakfast in the restaurant was served with more snarl than smile, and *niet*, you can't have cold milk with your cornflakes.

For the best part of three days we slogged around the drab but unquestionably fascinating city. Founded as a Teutonic Order fortress in 1253, Königsberg joined the Hanseatic League in 1310 and for 150 years was the residence of the grand masters of the order and their successors, the first King of Prussia being crowned here in 1701. Bombed to rubble in 1944 by the Allied airforces and destroyed anew in April 1945 following the Red Army assault, many of the surviving Germans were sent to Siberia, their place filled with settlers brought from all over the USSR.

All around were grim 1970s office blocks, some still defiantly bearing a rusting hammer-and-sickle symbol or image of Stalin, the most prominent of them being a gigantic H-shaped high-rise concrete atrocity. Apparently Brezhnev had Königsberg Castle dynamited to make way for the House of the Soviets, which is what this empty and decaying structure was. In the distance, rows of further grey apartment blocks ringed the city like tombstones of Communism. We gawked at the Memorial to the Tank-Driving Heroes, and the Sailor Heroes, and the Burial Ground of the 1,200

Guards, and the Cosmonaut Memorial that pronounces upon the achievement of a local man who made good in space. In Victory Square, formerly Hitlerplatz – and subsequently, probably, Stalinplatz – a statue of you-know-who stands expectantly as if awaiting the Second Coming.

Unlike St Petersburg, Kaliningrad is ice-free throughout the year and is still considered a vital strategic port and naval base, which was the reason for its strict exclusion of foreign tourists until the early 1990s. An obviously obsolete but quite modern submarine at the entrance to the port has been turned into a museum and was plainly a popular weekend draw. In general, we found it hard to conjure the glory days of Königsberg and the only building that reflected a fraction of those times was the lofty cathedral, which is slowly being restored with German funds. But for all its dreary architecture, the city does have a rough-and-ready glamour while its parks, kept immaculate by a multitude of sweepers, are enchanting.

We spent a half-day on a Sunday rail excursion to the nearest coastal resort, that of Zelenogradsk, of forlorn houses, ugly and never-completed concrete bomb shelter-like structures and a myriad of people with nothing to do except stroll the promenade and lick delicious ice cream cornets. But the manicured beach was idyllic and deserved well-planned and sympathetic development. A fortune awaits anyone who can provide it. Further up the coast lay the Curonian Spit, the thin 60-mile strip of dune-laden land that arches around the coast like a bow. Its southern half is Russian, a silent world of woods and farms. But, on the Lithuanian side, there are seaside villas, an abundance of new hotels and a rash of souvenir shops stuffed with amber jewellery. Yet, only very few years ago, Lithuania was also part of the Soviet empire, albeit a reluctant part. It makes you wonder why, if they can raise the initiative to give joy and enrichment to their people, what's stopping the Russians?

Rail-ticket acquisition for our departure and transit back, direct, to Poland became a further prelude to insanity. Now that the locals are permitted to possess passports and to travel outside their country, the authorities appear to make doing so as difficult as possible. It's as if they're taking a perverted revenge for the easing of restrictions forced upon them by the liberalisation of conditions brought about by the collapse of Communism. In addition to the hassle of obtaining a ticket they inflict harsh financial punishment; a ticket to the border village just inside the frontier is cheap, but the cost for one valid for a couple of miles further, across the frontier, is astronomical by comparison and a considerable burden for the average Russian. And it's no more than simple bloody-mindedness that lies behind those long, patient queues at the borders with just one official dealing with thousands of would-be transitees.

If getting into Russian territory had been a trial, it was to be a similar punishment when trying to get out, plus another horrendous wait while Polish officials had their pound of flesh. Expecting the train, classed as international, to be an express of reasonably high standard, we found ourselves in a broken-down abomination of a coach with hard seats hauled by a dirty locomotive that moved no faster than walking pace. On arrival at the Polish border the weather added to the frustration with a downpour of rain, but a saving grace on this occasion was that the passport inspection queues ran down the whole length of the *inside* of the multi-carriage train so at least everyone remained dry. Polish customs had a field day confiscating all the carefully hidden excess cigarettes and vodka (cheaper in Russia than in Poland) from the multitude, so that by the time Paul and I passed through we all but lost ourselves amongst the mountains of cartons and bottles piled high around the inspection tables. With Russians, Poles and Lithuanians hating one another, here, on their respective borders, was a chance to display it. Across the platform lay the waiting, and last, train of the day bound for the Polish town of

Olsztyn, where our final pre-booked hotel awaited us. And just as we alighted from the Russian train, our passports checked at the front carriage exit, the damn thing upped and left.

It was dusk by the time our new and a degree more comfortable Polish train slid out of the station, but not dark enough to hide the barbed-wire fences and watch-towers that marked the boundaries of the two countries. Maybe these fences were not quite of Iron Curtain proportions, but they looked ominous enough to me.

Elblag, another stronghold of the Teutonic Knights, was the nearest we could get to Olsztyn that night. Reduced to dust in the Second World War it has since become a tidy little town marked by two massive Gothic temples rebuilt, brick by brick, since the passing of the tempest. All too many Polish towns and cities have suffered similar fates and their rebuilding has been a labour of intense devotion. With no room available at the inn we took refuge in a Polish disco; hardly a haven of tranquillity. Nor was the station waiting-room where we stretched out on wooden benches to a rhapsody of snores courtesy of its permanent residents, until our early-dawn departure on the milk-run to Olszyn in a bone-shaker of a train, draughty and bare of anything appertaining to comfort.

Our new hotel, the Park, simply *had* to be on the far side of this considerable town; in fact, just outside the urban boundary. This entailed an early-morning trek of quite a number of miles, which at least gave us an initial view of the city sights. Olsztyn has the usual history hereabouts of overlapping successive Prussian and Polish influences, and, likewise, it suffered grievously from the occurrences of the last war. Its *Stary Rynek* today is essentially a post-war creation; a strange blend of old and new, though pleasant enough to behold. After booking in at the Park we returned to see more of the place, including its sizeable castle and cathedral both of the usual red-brick construction. The hotel provided us with a profoundly deep sleep in a lot more edifying surroundings than had been our accommodation lot of late. As a

commercial emporium it raised all the facilities one expects from such a hotel, though the fact of being five kilometres out of town and on an almost non-existent bus route meant that carless clients of the likes of us had to be devotees of walking.

And so back across Poland to Prague on very much a similar route as that we came. A change of trains at Warsaw allowed a leg-stretch circuiting the enormous Soviet-built Palace of Culture before the clicking indicator board at the station announced the arrival of the Prague Express, 20 minutes late. An empty soft-seat compartment gave us a reasonable night in the horizontal position until a deluge of early morning Czech office-workers routed us for the final miles to Prague.

Thus ended our double rail traverse of Poland, and I have to say that it was a darn sight easier than walking and cycling it.

From Prague our way home, via Paris, was not quite the direct one I had undertaken on the outward trip. Discovering that there was a summer months-only direct Prague–Paris through-service detouring round Northern Germany and reaching the French capital at the convenient hour of breakfast-time, led us on a final bout of railway touring. With a few further days to spare and our interrail passes still valid, we proposed a repeat of my earlier North Germany excursion, stopping off at random at some of the cities that had rusticated under Communism. Our nights would be spent in youth hostels which offer incredible accommodation bargains.

Hence, via the rocky fastness of the so-called 'Saxon Switzerland', through which the Elbe forces a majestic passage, and passing through the small riverside spa of Bad Schandau, scene of one of my ill-fated attempts to effect a tryst with my Czech fiancée, we came to our first drop-off point: Dresden.

The capital of Saxony is not a 'pretty-pretty' sort of city by any means, but is dramatic and sombre. It likes to call itself the 'German Florence' and its architecture, made the more enthralling

in the knowledge that 80 per cent of it was destroyed by Allied bombs in 1945, has not yet been fully restored even 55 years after the event. I first set eyes on the superb skyline – the inspiration for Canalletto's famous painting – through the ventilation slit of an eastbound prison train in 1944. I saw it briefly again during the Communist era and, even then, it was difficult to perceive that, between these two sightings, the skyline had been shattered into jagged ruin. Now I was back yet again.

The city is a compact metropolis, easy to explore. With its rococo yellows and greens, interspersed by stark, age- and fire-blackened structures, the effect is overwhelming, and in spite of the vicissitudes of history the place remains one of the architectural and cultural treasures of the civilised world.

On the train again we passed through a resurrected Leipzig. Though the scene of another of my failed trysts, I would never have found any similarities with the skeletal ruins I remembered from my previous sojourn, when I had used the first post-war Trade Fair as cover for one of my nefarious deeds. So we ignored it and continued to Weimar in the neighbouring state of Thuringia, a rich depository of towns that are the stuff of a cultural utopia.

What city could offer stronger magnetism to any cultural-minded visitor than this one of Goethe, Schiller, the Bach family, Liszt, Luther, Cranach and Mann? All have their preserved houses, statues and plaques gracing the elegant town. There is hardly a figure of note throughout Europe who was not born here, lived here or worked here.

Paul and I strolled through the Ilm Park, bisected by the little Ilm River and spread with the summer retreats of Weimars's illustrious citizens. We also took a bus up the hill behind the town where Weimar has its darker side. Never was there more extreme contrast in the abomination that overlooks it from the pleasantly-wooded Etterberg Hill: Buchenwald. Not an extermination camp of the likes of Auschwitz and Dachau, but only a degree less depressing.

Thuringia's capital is Erfurt, to whence our train carried us next. A little less culturally overbearing than Weimar, it was founded by an English monk to become a city of spires plus the celebrated Krammerbrucke – a mini Ponte Vecchio – lined with half-timbered houses. Erfurt's skyline is dominated by the Cathedral and Church of St Severus, an ensemble of church architecture unique in Europe. The great square in front of the cathedral holds a spirited market selling everything under the sun, including tasty sausages that provided our midday meal.

Another short train ride and we were in the third of Thuringia's notable towns, this one Eisenach, lying west of Erfurt and a further history-laden centre that has managed to retain its medieval atmosphere. Today it is hard to imagine that the town held a vital component in the German automobile industry and was the home of the now-shunned Wartburg car. This subjected Eisenach to considerable attention from the Allied airforces but renovation has restored the seventeenth-century look of the place. Johann Sebastian Bach was born here, while a line-up of celebrities including Martin Luther, Richard Wagner, Goethe et al. were frequent visitors to Wartburg Castle on the hill behind the town and for which Eisenach is justly famed. Its thirteenth-century Great Hall is breathtaking; a wonderful venue for concerts, which are regularly held there. We were invited to attend one and felt slightly out of place amongst so smartly attired an audience, but the music, blending with the surroundings, soothed our misgivings.

So back to Paris and, on a stopping-train that not only stopped frequently but interminably, to Calais, the grande finale to our rail odyssey. To stroll the decks of the P&O Stena Line ferry of cruise ship proportions and even to roll along English roads by courtesy of National Express made, by this time, a not entirely disagreeable substitute for train-riding.

And the funny thing was that, though deficient of an expensive camera, I came home with more clothes than I started out with!

Trans-North America

To watch the slender track emerge from the darkness of the easternmost spiral tunnel beyond Field in British Columbia is exciting enough in itself. To see it best you have to be, as I was, in the cab of the leading locomotive of one of the great Trans-Dominion trains of Canada. Here was an experience indeed, and the startling white snow shimmering in the brilliant sunshine gave an ethereal quality to the violent mountain scenery which hit me like a thunderbolt at the tunnel mouth.

The World Commuter

Much water has flowed under many bridges since I rode the tracks of America's Amtrak and Canada's then CP Rail at the invitation of both organisations in 1973, not long after the setting-up of the former. This made it an interesting year to sample the delights of two railway systems which, even then, were slowly dying on their feet and crying out to be travelled before rigor mortis on their more quixotic lines set in.

Amtrak was formed by the United States government to counter the plummeting standards of the various passenger-carrying railroad companies since, before 1970, their passenger services had declined to a point when they could hardly be described as a 'service' at all. In the increasing scramble for the more lucrative freight transportation, human cargo went by the board. If a company was unable to ditch its travelling clientele by fair means, it resorted to methods bordering upon the foul. Overcrowding, inconvenient hours of departure and arrival, ill-timing of schedules, soaring fares; anything, in fact, to prove to the Inter-state Commerce Commission that passenger services were running at an ever-increasing loss and so were fit for abandonment.

With Amtrak was born an organisation whose sole interest was the restitution and efficient running of a nationwide passenger rail service, and it went to work with a will. Its goal became the corporation's slogan: 'To make the trains worth travelling again.' And in this they succeeded brilliantly. Thirteen former passenger-carrying railways were merged to form the country's first integrated system. By 1973 it was operating more than 200 passenger trains daily over 27,000 miles of track connecting 440 cities and towns plus Montreal and Vancouver in neighbouring Canada. Though there were still shortcomings, the improvements were remarkable.

Americans are not railway-minded. In the land of the automobile, multi-lane interstate highways and shuttle service domestic airlines, the train ranks with the lowly bus services of

the likes of Greyhound and Trailways, and even then cannot compete in convenience and speed. Though Amtrak continued to improve in efficiency, its trains were, and are on most routes, slow by European standards and, with many lines single track, infrequent. That they are luxurious by comparison to European trains is a bonus for the pleasure traveller, though this is not enough for the business commuter. This is a sad state of affairs when you remember that American history is threaded through and through by its famous railroads.

Since 1973 and my Amtrak journeying, the passenger train network has been reducing by the year, the lines given over solely to freight-carrying. But there are still plenty of routes available to the traveller wanting to see something of the vast territory of the United States and the high quality of comfort and luxury has been maintained.

I commenced and ended my sampling of the railroads of North America at Montreal. *The Washingtonian* I think my train to New York was called, though today I see from *Thomas Cook's Overseas Timetable* it's something called *Adirondack*, which is hardly an inspiring title for a train in a country that goes in for train-naming in a big way. My *Washingtonian* wasn't the fastest of expresses. Leaving Montreal in the early evening it deposited me at Penn station, New York, 444 miles away in time for breakfast next day. The current *Adirondack*, I note, covers the route during the daylight hours.

They say New York is one of those places you love or you hate. There's no in-between. Until recently I've been in the hate camp, but I'm mellowing, though not too happy with its brash discourtesy. And riding its maze of a subway system still gives me grey hairs. Like our own London Underground, it's a misnomer because a lot of it is above ground. Back in 1973 I found a gobbledegook of IRT, BMT, IND, 6th AVE, BROADWAY, 8th AVE, LEX and more to decipher and choose from, and where

these infuriating independent lines all went I'd yet to discover. Having just left Montreal I was spoilt by the refreshingly straightforward Montreal Metro with its quiet efficiency and trains bouncing along on rubber tyres.

From New York I caught a Metroliner to the United States capital and, by doing so, rode one of the then fastest trains in the world, with more than a dozen departures daily in both directions between New York and Washington, DC. Travellers on the Metroliners were elevated to the calibre of superior beings, qualifying as patrons of a special coffee lounge – with free coffee – at Penn station while waiting for departure. My train was electrically powered and covered the 225 miles in about three hours, as it does today. Its sleek coaches were equipped with comfortable armchairs, jazzy snack and cocktail bars and the exclusive cosiness of what was described as a club car.

The architecture of Washington, DC goes outwards instead of upwards, which may account for the more peaceful way of life compared to most American cities. Being there on a cold November day I might have picked up a false impression, but it cannot be denied that the capital's imposing real estate, its wide lawn-surrounded boulevards and majestic statuary provide a certain calming influence.

Chicago is the clearing house for the four main routes that cross the country. On most of them there is just one train a day, as was the case when I made the crossing. And what trains they were! *The Sunset Limited* ignored Chicago to cover the southerly route via New Orleans to Los Angeles. From Chicago went *The San Francisco Zephyr*, *The Empire Builder*, *North Coast Hiawatha* and *Texas Chief* to various destinations along the West Coast. And then Amtrak's pride and joy, *The Super Chief*, a splendid animal that made the daily run to Los Angeles by way of Kansas City. Although long-distance express coaches compete with the trains that cross America, there is today a new breed of eminent trains with new names.

Great Journeys by Train

I reached Chicago by *The Broadway Limited* in 16 hours over a 907-mile route, and my accommodation was a so-called roomette. This initial leg of my trans-America journey was to give me my first insight into what American long-distance trains could offer, and I have to say at the outset that these inspiringly-named vehicles were an eye-opener to those travellers accustomed to the comparatively short-haul services of Britain and the Continent. My roomette contained an adjustable armchair, washbasin, toilet, wardrobe, radio, a selection of reading lights and various temperature and air-conditioning controls. By pulling a lever the whole bag of tricks turned into a well-sprung bed.

Just down the corridor was the cocktail bar, reading room, upstairs observation lounge in a double-decker coach, and a moderately priced restaurant. In the reading room full-length feature films were shown and pretty girls in red blazers came round to inveigle one into party games. For clients not needing a bed the 'sitting-up' coaches provided very adequate relaxation facilities with reclining seats, adjustable footrests and paper-covered pillows. At the top end of the accommodation scale, bedrooms provided a full suite of rooms for two.

My route from Chicago to Los Angeles took 40 hours and crossed 7 states, a distance of 2,222 miles of flat farmland, high mountains, forests and the semi-desert of the legendary Wild West. I had already passed through Pittsburgh and Cleveland in Pennsylvania and Ohio respectively prior to reaching Chicago; the longer leg now forded the wide Missouri and Mississippi Rivers, crossed the Great Plains of Nebraska and wound through the Rockies and Sierras in a series of twists and turns. Hauled by two, sometimes three, giant 3,000-horsepower diesel locomotives, the silver train offered a sense of event. The ascent into the Sierra Nevada was marked by the strain on the diesels becoming audible by the intensity of the climb, but perhaps the climax of the journey for me was that between the Colorado state line and Salt Lake City, where the train grinds through some of the most desolate

scenery in the western states; colossal rock formations, mauve-coloured canyons, painted deserts and flat-topped blocks of eroding sandstone echoing in its lonely emptiness to the alien screech of the locomotive siren. Here and there amongst the sage-brush and the juniper, abandoned mine-shafts stood witness to a dead industry.

Occasionally we had to wait longer at stations than seemed necessary. The reason for this was that Amtrak does not own the track, but rents it from Southern Pacific whose freight services have priority over the right of way. It was at one of these enforced halts that I got talking to an American attired in a loud suit who was trying to find someone at which to direct his expressions of delight at his surroundings.

'I've never travelled on a train before,' he told me. 'The notion of doing so has never occurred to me. I expect you Brits do it all the time.'

I affirmed that we indeed did so, but more for necessity than simple pleasure.

'It's a great way to travel,' he went on, adding ' If there's the time to spare – something we Americans never seem to have.'

The train was already an hour and a half behind schedule as we crawled through the backyards of the endless Los Angeles suburbia, which accentuated his comment. What a train can cover in four days can be accomplished by an aircraft in less than that number of hours; hence Amtrak's battle to survive.

Los Angeles Union Passenger Terminal – the main station – was, to me, the nicest building in the city and about the only edifice there of any historic significance. Los Angeles, as nowhere else, is a city given over to the excesses of the motor car. To the first-time visitor it is a frightening place, a place with no heart nor even a proper centre. Giant one-way, six-lane carriageways on concrete stilts criss-cross one another in wild abandon; the urban sprawl goes on and on into suffocating eternity with parts of it labelled Pasadena, Hollywood, Long Beach, Glendale, though

it's all Los Angeles. The multi-lane highways spew speeding traffic in all directions, and I shall always remember the time I found myself with a hired Ford of vast proportions equipped with an automatic gearbox, to which I was then unaccustomed, faced with the proposition of getting from Hollywood-Burbank to Pasadena in the rush hour. The gearbox had a fault that caused it to change gear when I didn't want to change gear and, trapped in a middle lane, I must have been halfway to San Diego before I could cut across to the inner lanes to leave that nightmare of an expressway.

The best way to escape this city of suburbs and automobilism is that offered by the train. I did so by courtesy of the *Coast Starlight* which then began its run at San Diego on the Mexican border and now, as then, continues via San Francisco to Seattle. It went on to terminate at Canada's Vancouver. The whole of the 1,700 miles of the Pacific coastline is covered by this line, skirting the seashore in many places to offer passengers striking views.

Every American, it is said, has two home towns: his own, and San Francisco. It is enchantingly beautiful with a humorous, rakish, slightly zany air. Railways and freeways steer clear of the city; its internal public transportation vested in buses, trolleybuses, the famous old cable-cars, and BART. And with BART (Bay Area Rapid Transit) you have the ultimate in subway systems. Smoothly, silently, effortlessly, its silver trains accelerate to nearly 100 miles per hour between stations, or at least they did when I was last there. The system was suffering teething troubles and, somewhat disconcertingly, the doors kept automatically opening in the tunnels and refusing to budge upon arrival at stations.

The station serving San Francisco is at Oakland, across San Francisco Bay and connected by the great Bay Bridge. And from Oakland Amtrak took me right into Vancouver, Canada's third and, arguably, loveliest city that is ablaze with gardens and bordered by beaches, the whole backed by the awesome bulwark of the Rockies. If I had to live anywhere outside of my own country I think it would be there.

In 1973 there were two principal Canadian railway-operating concerns: the state-owned Canadian National and the company-owned Canadian Pacific while, for a portion of the coast-to-coast route across this vast land, there were two passenger-carrying lines. Today there is only one.

The story of transportation to the west coast of Canada could be said to have started with the great canoe journey of Alexander MacKenzie who, on 22 July 1793, first reached the Pacific coast. Other travellers, mostly of the fur trade, followed MacKenzies's lead so that by the early years of the nineteenth century links were already being forged between the fur settlers in the west and the well-established colonies in the east.

Gradually the idea of a transcontinental railway took hold and obsessed the dreamers of railway conception. Surveys were made, money raised and companies formed until finally, on 16 February 1881, the construction of the Canadian Pacific Railway Company received the green light.

So began one of the great railway-building epics of all time. Distance was just one of the problems ahead; the great mountain barrier of the far west presented another, and the climate provided a third with its extreme temperatures ranging from 20 degrees centigrade below zero to 40 degrees above. As if these problems weren't enough, the company faced continuous financial difficulties with sustained opposition not only in Canada but also in Britain, and the start in 1882 was delayed by one of the worst spring floods ever on the Red River.

Men, supplies and horses were poured in to keep the work going at top speed. Winnipeg was the main supply point, receiving rails from England that were shipped to New Orleans and up the Mississippi River, lumber from Minnesota and ties from eastern Canada. By the end of the first year, 417 miles of mainline track were completed, a truly phenomenal achievement. Over 5,000 men were now directly involved, night shifts were put on bridge

construction, and with the summer of 1883 the line from the east reached the summit of the Rockies at Kicking Horse Pass.

Meanwhile, work on the difficult section west of Lake Superior started, and here some 12,000 men and 5,000 horses were employed. As during the construction of the Trans-Siberian Railway in Russia, strife interfered with the project and the uncompleted line became a weapon. The second Riel Rebellion broke out in the prairies and for its suppression troops were transported to Fort Qu'Appelle over the unfinished track, a most uncomfortable ride for the soldiers who had repeatedly to disembark at rail-less sections and untested bridges.

In 1885 a regular passenger service was inaugurated between Winnipeg and Moose Jaw, followed by that of the lower Northwest Territories, now the province of Saskatchewan. Further track-laying continued in isolated sections until the whole project was brought to triumphant fruition, the final meeting of the rails taking place on 7 November 1885, just four and a half years after building work began.

Completion of the unbroken rail link of 2,893 miles between Montreal and the Pacific coast was far more than merely the end of a stupendous construction job. In a very real sense it gave life to the concept of the Dominion. Almost immediately, settlement along the track began spreading on both sides. Additionally it led to the building of competitive lines that ran roughly parallel to the Canadian line.

My train was CP's *Canadian*. It was diesel-hauled and, with me ensconced comfortably in the cab, we left Vancouver at 17.45. I had obtained special permission from senior authority to be allowed to ride in the locomotive for much of those 2,893 miles and, because they thought I would have my wife with me, two soft chairs had been installed for our well-being. Ahead, the slender track breasted the mountain ramparts of the Coast Range, the Monashees, the Selkirks, the towering Rockies and the long, steady slopes eastwards across the Great Plains, all of which my

train would take three days and nights to negotiate. In the wellnigh incredible adventures that the pioneers had in finding any sort of route at all through this maelstrom of mountain peaks, densely forested slopes and swift flowing rivers; in the magnificent engineering embodied in building the line; and in the never-ceasing challenge its curves, gradients and tunnels make to the locomotive men past and present, it must remain a route without parallel on the world's railways.

The two drivers in the cab of the front locomotive were salt of the earth CPR men. Their lives were wrapped up in their railway and the big diesel units were more nursed than driven. The fact that Canadians were deserting their trains for their cars bordered upon treachery. Their bitterness was something you could feel.

For me the most fascinating portion of that journey, both from a geographical and constructional sense, was that of the 'Big Hill' where the line descended to Field after Kicking Horse Pass. Dangerous in descent, the 'Big Hill' was a major operating problem for the eastbound trains that had to climb it, each train having to be split and taken up in sections by small locomotives of the day working to the limit of their capacity. The problem was solved by the construction of two spiral tunnels, now world-famous. The first, under Cathedral Mountain, is 3,206 feet long and turns through 234 degrees in its descent of 48 feet between portals. The second tunnel correspondingly drops 45 feet in its length of 2,890 feet and turns through 232 degrees. Emerging from the second tunnel it is an odd sight to see part of one's own train travelling in the opposite direction to that of its leading coaches on the short level stretch between the adjacent portals of the two tunnels.

An equally important improvement had been the Connaught Tunnel. Sixty miles west of Field the line turned south and commenced another great climb up the west side of a valley of the Beaver River in order to reach Roger's Pass, climbing nearly 2,000 feet in 17 miles with gradients of 2.2 per cent most of the

way. The route through the pass had many curves, and from the start of operations it was plagued during the winter months by avalanches. The Connaught Tunnel, built to take a double track, is just over five miles long. My train still had to undertake the long haul up from Beavermouth to the eastern portal of the tunnel, but the summit elevation was 552 feet lower than the summit of the pass; four and a third miles were saved in distance travelled, and no less than the equivalent of seven complete circles of curvature eliminated.

All this and more was explained to me in some detail by my driver companions and so pleased were they at my interest in the affairs of the railway that, bursting with pride, they repeatedly slowed the train as we passed through the Rockies so that I could take photographs of particularly scenic spots. Because of this we were late arriving at Calgary – then on the CPR line – which probably irked a number of passengers.

The route of the *Canadian* across the country varied in its scenic and historical interest. Before Banff (likewise no longer on the line) at a place called Stephen, a mile above sea level and the highest point of the railway, is the Continental Divide where the rivers flow into the Atlantic instead of the Pacific. Banff itself, penned in by mountains, owes its existence to the discovery, in 1885, of some hot sulphur springs, hitherto sacred to the Indians who established a reserve there and which has since become the well-known Banff National Park.

Apart from the tremendous spectacle of the Rockies, one of the most beautiful stretches occurred when the train made its way along the northern shores of Lake Superior. It was a terrible section to build, since it was necessary to cut a ledge in the towering walls of rock that rose sheer from the waters of the lake. 'Two hundred miles of engineering impossibility,' said William van Horne, who built the line. The lake was like a grey sea and appeared to contain no sign of life; I saw not a boat, nor even a bird. After all this I found the Great Plains, though dramatic, ever

so slightly dull and monotonous; rolling downs of sand-coloured stubble, occasional undulating prairie, and huge fertile strips of landscape broken by isolated farm buildings and grain storage tanks.

We drew into Montreal almost on time, having made up for time lost by cutting short the pause at Calgary. I was given bear hugs by my drivers who implored me to send more Britishers to make the journey.

'Why don't you Brits flock to our aid?' they asked with a kind of desperation. 'It's your railway too. Why, why don't you come in your thousands and keep it alive?'

Why indeed.

Four years later an Amtrak-type operation was mounted to revitalise the lagging rail passenger business and reduce the financial burden carried by the government to maintain these services. Thus it was that VIA Rail came into being which, in June 1977, took over the passenger marketing function for both railways. It was, I felt, a sad climax to the inspiring history of Canadian railways.

I returned to Canada again in 1979 and on several subsequent occasions to drive the full length and more of the Alaska Highway, footslog for weeks on end across the Yukon and Northwest Territories, fly in plucky little Islander aircraft between Innuit settlements in Northern Alaska, and explore the little-known marvels of Newfoundland. But never for the specific purpose of railway riding. However, opportunities sometimes presented themselves and whenever they did I found myself on a train.

Though not Canada, Alaska offered me one such chance. Anchorage, the largest Alaskan city, is not, as one might expect, the terminus of the Alaska Railroad. This is reserved for the smaller town of Whittier on the coast. Northbound, the train winds through the farmsteads of the Matanuska Valley passing historic gold towns like Talkeetna, over the Susitna River, across

Hurricane Gulch and along the eastern edge of Denali State Park (in which stands Mount McKinley, the highest mountain in the United States) to the end of the line at Fairbanks.

I travelled in an air-conditioned blue and gold coach called *AuRoRa* (after the Northland's aurora borealis) offering Amtrak-style comfort and observation facilities. The Alaska Railroad relies predominantly upon tourists, and today most of the few services are run by rail-cars.

Only two trains a day cover the whole length of the line; most run between Whittier and Anchorage. You won't find quaint wooden houses and tobacco-chewing cowboys shuffling along dusty streets in this latter city. Instead it is what might be described as the standard American metropolis with a grid street system and high-rise blocks à la Chicago and elsewhere in the 'lower States'. As cities go – even American cities – Anchorage is practically newborn. Old-timers, called 'pioneers' or 'sourdoughs' in Alaska, can recall the day when there wasn't a paved street in town, nor a two-storey building standing. The first residents, in fact, lived in tents, these being the construction workers for the railway.

Most visitors from the Gulf of Alaska cruise ships calling at Whittier will want to spend their Alaska hours at Denali National Park (formerly Mount McKinley National Park). Here is an immense 3,030 square mile wilderness, more a reserve than a park, containing towering mountains, alpine glaciers and gently rolling grasslands traversed by wide rivers. Denali, or 'The Great One', was the name given by the Indians to 17,000-foot Mount McKinley rising impressively above the grasslands, its peak sheathed in eternal snow. The park is home to caribou, Dall sheep, moose and grizzly bears amongst the more common wildlife, while golden eagles soar overhead. I spent just one day in this road-veined wilderness (the roads carry no more than park-touring buses) and was lucky to spot a distant grizzly when, sometimes, one can go a whole week without seeing one.

Fairbanks, at the end of the line, is very different from Anchorage. Situated in the heart of the Tanana valley, with the gold-bearing hills rising in the north, it is still, in spirit, a frontier town. Here I walked the streets side by side with miners, Indians, Innuit and pioneers, if not tobacco-chewing cowboys with or without snow-shoes. To use the well-worn cliché, it is a city of contrasts with old (by American standards) timber buildings mixing with the modern façades of department stores and office buildings. Fairbanks was born in July 1902, when an Italian miner, Felix Pedro, discovered gold 'in them thar hills.' The resulting rush brought the prospectors who, in turn, brought their families, and so the town sprouted. Gold, of course, is what Alaska was all about and old mines and mechanical equipment still lie, collapsed and rusting, about the huge territory.

There is, in fact, much of the frontier too about the far north of North America, and this includes Canada's Yukon and Northwest Territories. It is a land of airstrips, of cold lakes bordered by seaplanes, and flat vistas merging into the mists. It is also a land of startling beauty. Alaska throws up unique obstacles to Man, and he in turn invariably finds novel ways of surmounting them. Farmers and builders must compress their year's work into brief summers, nearly all provisions must be shipped in from the 'lower' United States, and the Alaskans live with the threat of earthquakes such as the one that struck on Good Friday 1964. They also fly over roadless terrain; take to their boats despite bone-chilling water and rugged coastlines, and exist in temperatures that we in lukewarm Britain can barely imagine. It is, above all, a land of challenge holding beneath the surface of its permafrost and waters the vast wealth which first attracted the scruffy hot-eyed miners in 1896.

Further south, and sharing its route with both Alaska and the Yukon, runs the White Pass and Yukon Railway. Riding this down-to-earth line is one of Northern Canada's great experiences, and

its history is an integral part of the story of this exciting land, just as much as that of the Canadian Pacific. I was shocked to read in *Thomas Cook's Overseas Timetable* that the passenger-carrying service of the line was to close in mid-2000. Yet another superb passenger line was sacrificed in deference to road transportation, I thought, but I now learn that it has remained open over half the previous length. At least I have had the joy of riding its full length.

The 110-mile narrow-gauge railway connects Yukon's Whitehorse to the Alaskan port of Skagway and the coastal ferries that call there. It was constructed to transport the thousands of gold seekers and their supplies from Skagway through the coastal mountains to the beginning of the river route to the Klondike gold fields. Started in May 1898, the railway's last spike was driven at Carcross on 29 July 1900, the conclusion of 26 months of the blasting, chipping, shovelling and hardships of construction crews whose number fluctuated from 700 to 2,000. A stone inscription beside the track is a mute reminder of the trudging steps of the thousands of men and women who believed in gold at the rainbow's end.

The Gold Rush died away, the Yukon population dwindled, and during the dark days of the 1930s the trains operated only once a week, but the steam locomotives and the rotary ploughs kept the line open. Until mid-2000 it was used only by tourists, and for them the journey is truly a spectacular one. Some of the parlour cars in which I travelled were built as early as 1883, but their ancient silhouette and interiors made strange bedfellows with the heavy steel mineral wagons and multiple diesel electric locomotives that formed the rest of the train.

Probably no tunnel in the world was bored under greater difficulties than the one that penetrated a perpendicular barrier of rock which juts out of the mountainside like a giant flying buttress some ten miles north of Skagway. A short distance from the summit of the pass, a deep canyon is spanned by a steel cantilever bridge, 215 feet from the creek's bed. Below, in Dead

Horse Gulch, winds the old White Pass Trail, worn into the native rock by thousands of sourdoughs. To improve the grade and curvature of the railway, both bridge and tunnel were replaced in 1969, but the originals still stand. From sea level at Skagway, the line climbs to the summit of the pass, 2,885 feet, in 21 miles. The highest point is Log Cabin, actually just inside British Columbia, at an altitude of 2,916 feet.

From terminal to terminal the journey took about eight hours and the views of mountains and lakes were fine indeed. Forty miles east of Skagway is a rambling frame building called 'Bennet Eating House' where the trains from both directions met and passengers descended to sit down to a hearty prospector's lunch (included in the fare) of stew, sourdough bread and the tastiest apple pie.

I rode the line in both directions, spending the intervening night at a Skagway hostel, there being no other accommodation available, even if I'd wanted it, in the little town hardly changed since the days of '78. Snow was falling as we crawled back into Bennet the next day, adding to the hazards of a rickety line that is all heart and not over-endowed with safety features. May it rest in peace.

Further south still and, at Prince Rupert, I took to the tracks once more. They belonged to the British Columbia Railway. Many railways in the world contend for the title of the most scenic, the most beautiful, the most thrilling, but assuredly the British Columbian Railway is high on the list for sustained enjoyment from a visual point of view.

Prince Rupert to Vancouver by train meant a ride of some 1,000 miles though, at the time I was there, regular passenger services were in operation only between Prince George and North Vancouver, the most spectacular portion of the line. My train was called the *Caribou Dayliner*, and I note it is running today.

The British Columbian Railway was formerly the Pacific Great Eastern Railway, a title that is more nostalgic than geographical, and perhaps fitting in a region full of regal princes! When construction began in 1911, it was by men recruited from the Great Eastern Railway of England who came to Canada to build a line intended to open up the rugged and remote caribou country beyond Squamish, 40 miles north of Vancouver. After immense difficulties and major engineering problems, the Pacific Great Eastern was pushed 580 miles up-country to expire at the township of Quesnel on the Fraser River, where the stream was navigable. This rugged section was opened to traffic in 1921, but it was not until 1949 that work commenced on the 80-mile extension northwards to Prince George, completed early in 1953. At the southern end of the line the eagerly awaited extension to Vancouver was opened only as recently as 1956.

The Fraser River provides travellers with some grand spectacles. But these are less astonishing than is the first sighting of the Fraser River when descending from Williams Lake to Lillooet. This is a route of amazing scenic variety, ranging from an almost pastoral Scottish strath quality between Prince George and Williams Lake, and finishing alongside Howe Sound, in fjord-like surroundings, from Squamish into Vancouver. This last section now has the compelling added attraction of a vintage steam-run, regularly-scheduled and worked by one of the magnificent Royal Hudson 4–6–4 locomotives.

So ended my rail wanderings in North America to date. With their interstates and freeways choked with speeding cars, their drivers hell-bent on a single objective of putting distance behind them, those who linger along the byways of history and saunter past the wonders of nature aboard a train, turn travel into a rich reward.

On the *Viceroy Special* in Sri Lanka

It was a plume of smoke that put the *Viceroy Special* on the rails. One Clifford Jones, tour operator extraordinary of Manchester, was in Sri Lanka on tour-agency business, and one day happened to ask his Sri Lankan associate whether steam engines were operating in the country. 'We have no such locomotives on Sri Lankan Government Railways,' he was emphatically told. But Cliff was not to be put off and persisted in seeing for himself. His curiosity led him to the rail yards in Colombo, the capital, where, amongst a collection of rusting Garratts he came upon an ancient specimen of a locomotive with a banana tree growing out of its long-defunct stack. Cliff was ecstatic. 'You're sitting on a gold mine here,' he told his startled host; a view repeated to the Minister of State and Minister of Transport he was subsequently to meet.

The upshot of this incident was the birth of a tourist train that was to be titled the *Viceroy Special*, a steam-hauled train of informal elegance and homely comfort that was to herald the short-lived re-emergence of steam traction on the Sri Lankan Railway. Sadly, hostilities on the island have since suspended operation of this sensational little train and, with the civil war still raging in the north, no one can say when, or even if, it will ever run again. But such an initiative that brought the project into being deserves recognition in my narrative of railway journeys.

Once Cliff had the bit between his teeth there was no stopping him. His pleas to be allowed to go ahead and contribute something to the benefit of tourism in Sri Lanka from the rotting treasure that lay neglected in the sidings even reached the Prime Minister. He was given the go-ahead.

Cliff's invitation to me and a colleague, the late Ken Westcott-Jones, railway-fanatic supreme, to ride the train was enthusiastically accepted. We formed part of a group of 16 clients, who had elected to participate in the inaugural tour of the island, that flew into Colombo's Katunayake airport. They were mostly an independently-minded bunch as ever I've seen with a single interest in common. Trains. Speaking for myself, I had a second reason for wanting to come to the country, resulting from my forced deflection from it some years earlier.

Sri Lanka is not a new name for the island as most folk imagine. The Romans knew it as Taprobane, Arab traders called it Serendib, the Portuguese named it Ceilao while, backwards in time, Stone Age civilisations bequeathed cave markings relating the legends of the ancient Hindu sagas telling of a 'Splendid Land, the Grey, Green and Glorious Lanka that is like the Garden of the Sky'. Roughly 270 miles long and 140 wide – about the size of Ireland – the pear-shaped country came to be known as Ceilao or Ceylon only in the sixteenth century.

The constant association with nearby India is inevitable, but it would be wrong to think of the island as no more than an extension of its larger neighbour. In the process of wresting itself from India, Sri Lanka has developed a distinctive personality. Sinhala is a language unique to the island, as is the Sinhalese culture. Buddhism flourishes too, having been supplanted by Hinduism in India. The very fact of the island's proximity to that country, however, results in constant conflict with the Tamils, a Hindu minority of Indian origin rebelling against discrimination by the dominant Sinhalese, a fact all too well-known today.

Our four-coach train, to which we were introduced the day after our arrival, made a handsome sight. It was headed by *Sir Thomas Maitland*, a 4–6–4 BIA class, side-tank and tender engine, number 251, built by Robert Stephenson & Hawthorne in 1926 – or so I was assured by Ken, who was a walking encyclopaedia of things railway – and though I have looked upon much larger and

more dramatic-looking steam locomotives, this one wore a sprightly air, with couplets of national flags and the emblem 'Viceroy Special' emblazoned across her front. All four coaches were painted in the bright red livery of the former Ceylon Government Railway and, outlined in gold, the CGR crest prominently displayed. A larger engine, *Lord Mountbatten*, No. 213, would be taking over the train at Kandy, and this was a unique B28 side-tanker, built by Vulcan Foundry at Newton-le-Willows in 1916.

Of the two observation cars, the one at the rear of the train was to become the most popular by virtue of giving an unimpeded view of the track and scenery behind it. And with the petering out of the Colombo suburbs, there unwound a lushly voluptuous land. All life was on display in a countryside liberally endowed with villages, coconut groves, paddy-fields and buffalo herds. The track, as in India, was used as a pedestrian thoroughfare, with the locals stepping off the rails only long enough to let the train go by, there to wave enthusiastically at our receding rear.

At Polgahawela, the junction for the Kandy line, we took on water and I transferred to the locomotive, having been the first to apply to do so. The cab was singularly crowded, due to the presence there of the driver, a learner driver, fireman and learner fireman, and an inspector. With the reintroduction of a steam train on the system, the railway authorities were conscious of the need for younger driving staff and those experienced in steam operation, hence the swollen footplate population. Reflecting the Indian model, the small station bore the unmistakable stamp of a pre-Second World War station in Britain with its pots of geraniums, class-graduated waiting rooms and, alongside, the old-fashioned semaphore signalling.

It was good to be back on the footplate, imbibing smoke and soot. On this occasion, however, I was no more than a tourist to be indulged, though had there been space to move I would have been happy to earn my keep.

Another watering operation was deemed necessary at Maho Junction, where an overflow of water flooded the tender to immerse my sandalled feet in liquid coal dust as soon as the hose had been inserted into the tank. There is a famed story of the station-master at Maho being unable to set the points because of the presence of a persistent and unsociable leopard which took up residence for some days close to the operating lever, an event that brought the whole CGR system to a standstill. But no such incident enlivened our brief stopover here.

On a gradient beyond Maho, we ran out of puff. This caused a degree of consternation and a prolonged delay while we built up a new head of steam. Everyone – members of the group and the locals on the station – gathered round to gawk and advise as the *Viceroy Special* blocked the tracks. The cause of the mishap was a ruptured air-line and, with its repair, all eyes were on the steam pressure gauge as the indicator arrow steadily rose to the point where we could move off again.

By mid-afternoon we reached Anuradhapura, the holy city. This was as far north as we were permitted to go, for it is well on way to Jaffna and the Tamil-inspired turmoil in the north. Already the state had decreed that no trains were to operate after nightfall as a measure to reduce the risk of an 'incident'.

The *Mahavamsa*, Sri Lanka's Chronicle of Buddhism, records that Anuradhapura was founded in 380 BC by King Pandukabbaya, though it was not until after the conversion of King Devanampiya by Mahinda in 289 BC at Mihintale, seven miles east of Anuradhapura, that his capital also became a holy city. Whatever the historical details, nothing can detract from the remarkable quality of the excavated ruins visible today; the timeless palaces, royal gardens, ritual bathing ponds and huge domed shrines, dazzlingly whitewashed or covered over with grass and vegetation of centuries past.

Our next objective was Habarana on the Trincomalee and Batticaloa line. This involved a return to Maho, and progressing

east on what was originally the BTLR (Batticaloa-Trincomalee Light Railway) but which became the main line after 1955 when heavier track was laid in order to take the increased traffic. At one wayside station we waited for an interminable period while the *Hijra* ('Pilgrim's') *Express* lumbered by in a cloud of diesel smoke. According to the meticulous Ken, it was 19 minutes behind schedule.

At Aukana there was a halt for the purpose of observing the 40-foot high standing Buddha, sculptured during the reign of Dhatusena in the fifth century. Aukana means 'sun-eating' and dawn is the best time to see it, when the sun's first rays illuminate the huge but finely-carved statue's features. Unfortunately we had arrived at midday, the hottest hour, which, together with the ugly brick shelter constructed to protect the image, detracted from the allure of the enormous figure.

Lunch on the train was a popular event and, invariably, there was a rush for the first sitting in the restaurant-cum-observation car. Invariably too, I was beaten to it by a couple that had booked to come on the tour in the mistaken belief that it did not involve rail travel! The female partner was a town councillor with an inflated sense of her own importance who, if not approving of trains, appeared to thrive on train-served food. The good lady was to raise universal ire amongst the group with a daily appearance over-dressed in pink frilly creations and voluminous hats more suited to Ascot than to Sri Lankan rail travel. In this regalia she was wont to sweep majestically along station platforms, making quite a hit with the astonished local populace. I once came upon the offending headgear lying unattended in the observation car and had to resist a mounting temptation to plant it atop *Sir Thomas Maitland*'s smokestack.

A short train ride out of Habarana the next day brought us to Polonnaruwa, also once a capital of Sri Lanka. Though a thousand years old it is still much younger than Anuradhapura but its relics in a lesser state of repair. A walk through the crumbling, age-

blackened structures of this medieval city is a very different experience to that of Anuradhapura. Rescued from centuries of jungle overgrowth its silent stones, even under squalls of rain, gave me more contemplative backtracking into Sri Lankan history with no modern restorations to jar the mood.

Some 20 miles from Polonnaruwa is Sigiriya, the 'Lion Rock', undoubtedly the most spectacular monument in the country. The massive fortress perched atop a granite mountain was the work of King Kasyapa to defend himself against the wrath and attack of his half-brother, Moggallana. But when the long-expected attack finally came 18 years later, Kasyapa spiritedly but unwisely rode out with his troops to meet it, only to lose himself and expire in a bog.

So the 'Lion Rock' became a folly, a folly of immense proportions, rising sheer and mysterious from the surrounding jungle and ringed by a moat and a rampart. At one time, a gigantic brickwork lion sat at the summit and the final ascent to the top commenced with a stairway that led between the lion's paws and into its mouth. Today this once-sheltered stairway has totally disappeared apart from the first few steps, and to reach the top means clambering across a series of grooves cut into the rock face.

The road transcends the railway when it comes to a journey between Polonnaruwa and Kandy, yet another Sri Lankan capital. By road, the journey takes two hours; by train, ten. Thus, with reluctance, we took to a motor coach to continue through bucking hills, thickening forests, rubber plantations and the ubiquitous paddy-fields. There were tea plantations too, and fluffy balls of kapok hanging from telephone wires, all of which indicated the extravagant abundance of the land. We rumbled on through the spice gardens of Matale and across the wide Mahaweli River on the Katugastota Bridge, delighting in the spectacle of working elephants bathing in the river with their keepers, or *mahouts*, soaping the great beasts as if they were recalcitrant children. For

the last few miles we followed the spurned railway line into the city.

When the British conquered Kandy, the hill capital of the last Sinhalese kings, they terminated a monarchy that had ruled for more than 23 centuries. Kandy's citizens consider themselves apart from other Sinhalese; until the British came they had remained relatively unaffected by colonial influence, courageously resisting the armed might of the Portuguese, the Dutch and, for a time, the British, preserving the nation's identity while the rest of the country collaborated with the colonial invaders.

It is the Temple of the Tooth that takes pride of place in Kandy. The historic stronghold, set amongst quite astounding beauty, is a place of pilgrimage for Sri Lankans who come to venerate the sacred tooth relic of the Buddha, knowing that they will not see it but are content to be in its presence.

I, too, made my way to the temple, crossing over the moat to enter to the sound of drums and wailing flutes. Babbling humanity swirled around me as I joined the queue to process by the shrine. All around me were brown-skinned people, young and old, with respectful yet cheerful faces; there was none of the hushed tones and morose expressions we Christians are wont to exhibit when entering a European cathedral.

Hidden within the surprisingly unadorned shrine, sheltered by bulletproof glass, reposes the tooth. It lies in a golden casket beneath seven other caskets, or so I was told for there's little to see. Guardian monks looked on impassively as worshippers offered flowers and money.

Kandy is but the latest resting place of the tooth. Far older Sinhalese kingdoms have harboured it, and the relic has been plundered many times over the ages. The temple itself is something of an anticlimax, an unspectacular, nondescript building, but the wailing flutes, clashing cymbals, slow-moving processions of white-clad pilgrims carrying pink lotus blossoms

plus the ever-pervasive scent of joss sticks give the place an undeniable mysticism.

The town today preserves its distinctive architecture characterised by gently sloping tiled roofs. But, above all, Kandy is an atmosphere, a spirit set apart from the rest of the island. Situated at an altitude of a thousand feet, its temperate climate and astounding setting amongst hills, forest and the lake that is the centrepiece of the town, gives to it a highly individual personality. In the suburb of Peradeniya are the most beautiful botanical gardens I have ever seen; 150 acres of parkland containing thousands of trees and plants of every hue, scent and type. The orchids alone are breathtaking.

Back aboard the *Viceroy Special* at Kandy's solid British-built station, the reunion between train staff and clients was as fervid as if we had been apart a year rather than a couple of days. And the journey we were about to make was to constitute a high spot of the tour.

At Peradeniya, where Lord Mountbatten, as Commander-in-Chief of the Second World War's Far East forces, had his headquarters, I was to join his namesake locomotive for another spell on the footplate. This time I was in distinguished company; the cab containing the divisional inspector and chief locomotive foreman, who between them related to me a few facts about the rail history of the island.

Sri Lanka's first line opened in 1865 to the Indian 1,676 millimetre gauge, though it was not until 1856 that a provisional agreement was signed by the government and the Ceylon Railway Company to construct a railway between Colombo and Kandy. Unable to meet the costs, the company's assets and liabilities were taken over by the government, and so work began on what was probably the first nationalised railway in the world: the CGR. The Colombo–Kandy link was completed in 1867 and, a century on, the total mileage of the CGR was 914 miles, of which 90 miles was narrow gauge, the remainder broad gauge.

I must have had a jinx on me for at Hatton we ran out of steam again, and this time *Lord Mountbatten* virtually lost its fire as well. We were now deep into the central highlands – 'hill-country' our empire-building forbears used to call it – and the air had turned cool, while grey-blue mist hung in the terraced mountains around us. Tea-pickers made blobs of colour amongst the grid-lines of the plantations on the emerald slopes and the views across the distant blue ranges were magnificent. While we waited for our locomotive to gain its second wind, we climbed a viewpoint to gaze at the 8,000-foot high Adam's Peak, a superbly shaped, violet-tipped mountain revered by pilgrims.

A blast of newly-raised steam sent us scurrying back to our train, I struggling for a toehold in the crowded cab. We rattled and swayed through the early evening with a golden sunset of epic proportions turning everything, this time, an unnatural maroon. At Nanu Oya, at 6,000 feet, we reached the end of the line, a line that is the steepest broad-gauge in all Asia.

Once a narrow-gauge spur line ran a further six miles northwards to Nuwara Eliya, but today the road has taken over. For more than a century Nuwara Eliya served as an outpost of Empire, a home-from-home for British planters. They built themselves houses with gable roofs and bow windows, set out yews, evergreens and hedges, and attended services in a proper Anglican church. In 1886, to make life complete, they founded a golf club, still in use when I was there by Sri Lankans who were not at all adverse to following some of our quainter customs.

We were delivered to the century-old Hill Club, a fragment of 'olde' England that could hardly have been maintained better in its British heyday. A huge fireplace dominated one end of the spacious lounge with stags' heads glaring, glassy-eyed, from the walls. Immaculate in a uniform as white as the napery in the dining room, barefoot servants came forward to serve us.

In my bedroom, a hot-water bottle had been laid in my bed, and a discreet notice informed male guests that the Club expected

'gentlemen to wear jacket and tie after sundown'. My heart missed a beat. The only gesture I had made to gracious living was to bring a safari suit needing neither shirt nor tie. But the good Ken came to the rescue with a selection of ties and assorted suitings, the former representing most of the railway companies of the world. So, attired in the colours of the Deutsche Bundesbahn and an old-fashioned jacket and trousers several sizes too large, I descended to dinner, willing the trousers not to slip down to my ankles.

Over the next couple of days we explored Nuwara Eliya and district. Somebody described the little town as the Chislehurst of Ceylon, and one could see why. It was the British who discovered the charms of this Sinhalese Shangri-La and turned it into a hill resort. Although the faded Georgian and mock-Tudor houses must sadden any expatriate ghost still haunting Sri Lanka, the 'Englishness' of the atmosphere remained. The gardens had immaculate lawns, tinted with rose bushes and herbaceous borders surrounded by privet hedges; the moss-covered gravestones in the churchyard were worthy of Thomas Gray's Elegy. The post office boasted an indisputably English clock tower and there were familiar red pillar boxes about the town.

Out in the tea plantations Tamil women worked amongst the bushes, picking the new leaves and tossing them over their shoulders into baskets on their backs. I took myself to a processing plant – most were open to visitors – and was shown around the tea-grading facilities. I learnt that the flavour of tea depends on altitude, soil and rainfall; the higher the altitude, the better the quality of the tea. The tender new shoots and buds are allowed to dry until brown and wrinkled, then crushed and dried further to produce what we know as tea leaves. The residue is fit only for tea bags, I was told disdainfully.

Sri Lanka is the world's largest exporter of tea, and it is tea that is the cornerstone of the Sri Lankan economy. Yet tea only came to the island as an emergency substitute for coffee when disease

wiped out the original coffee plantations. Unfortunately, and it is the same in India, the Sri Lankans may grow very fine tea but they were not very good at making a decent pot of it. The British introduced them to adding milk and, as far as I know, this custom remains.

I left Nuwara Elliya with a pang of regret but the Horton Plains, a hiker's delight, cheered me up. A cliff called World's End, one of the scenic wonders of the island, drops down 5,000 feet providing a prodigious panorama over the southern coastal lowlands.

It was but a full day's journey back to Colombo. At Peradeniya Junction we joined the line from Kandy and continued downhill all the way. For *Lord Mountbatten* it was virtually freewheeling home.

Riding the Luxury Trains of South Africa

On the quartet of visits I have so far made to South Africa I have managed to undertake a trio of railway journeys, though not, perhaps, in the correct order of comfort and resplendence. Way back in the mid-1980s I was invited to make the run from Johannesburg to Cape Town on the world-renowned *Blue Train*. Some ten years later, having to pay my own way, I made the return journey Jo'burg–Durban–Jo'burg, second class, on an ordinary scheduled service, one optimistically titled *Trans-Natal Express*. And, at the end of November 2000, another invitation sent me helter-skelter back to Durban for no other purpose than to experience the affluent offerings of Rovos Rail's three-day 'safari' excursion from Durban, via Swaziland, to Pretoria, run by the *Pride of Africa*, billed as 'The Most Luxurious Train in the World'. 'You *must* take the *Blue Train*,' gushed everyone I spoke to about my intention of riding South African trains. 'It's the most luxurious train in the world.'

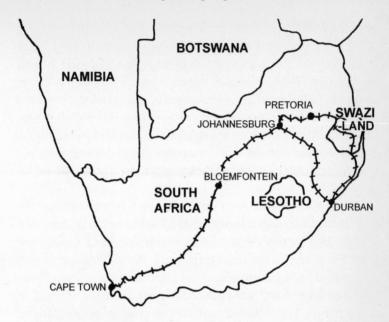

This criterion had never struck me as a reason to travel as readers may have noticed; quite the opposite, in fact. But I must put things right on one point; it *is* the most luxurious *scheduled* train in the world. And since South Africa is a land of the most violent contrasts it seemed to me to be an appropriate method of introducing myself gently to that country.

Railways came comparatively late to the African continent. A variety of motives prompted the building of them, especially mineral exploitation but also strategic and political factors. The penetration, annexation, and opening up of Africa by the white man occurred during the full flush of the railway era, and railway construction was given great stimulus by the rapid occupation of territory. Cecil Rhodes suggested the longitudinal Cape Town to Cairo line, and this caught the popular fancy. However, as the railhead pushed north from Cape Town, so the mineral fields successively drew individual lines and effort away from the

proposed spinal route. Thus the Cape to Cairo line remains a dream, and throughout the continent there is no rail network as we know it in Europe except, to some extent, in North Africa, the Egyptian Delta and South Africa.

Particularly South Africa. Here there is a route mileage in excess of 14,000 miles sustaining a railway system comparable with any in the world. It grew from a simple two-mile stretch of track near Durban, opened in 1860, to a complex organisation employing the most modern rolling stock, signalling, track and other equipment.

A number of named trains came into being, as they do whenever there are great distances involved and a rail link to cover them. Amongst them were, and are to this day, the *Orange Express* between Cape Town and Durban, the *Trans-Natal* overnight express between Johannesburg and Durban, and the *Trans-Karoo* between Cape Town and Pretoria, this last the route of the *Blue Train* which, undoubtedly, remains the pride of South African Railways.

Its legendary romantic aura can be said to have materialised at the turn of the last century. In 1901 a train de luxe was built for Rhodesia Railways by Metropolitan-Cammell and was used between Cape Town and Bulawayo, and also for special excursions from Cape Town to Victoria Falls. The sleeping cars each had four compartments comprising coupés, washrooms, showers and toilets. The smoking room, buffet and dining cars sported oak panelling together with settees and chairs upholstered in dark red leather. A card room was provided as well as a small library.

In 1910 the various operating railway companies were brought together to form South African Railways & Harbours, and when a new and prestigious train was introduced in 1923 the result was named the *Union Limited* running from Johannesburg to Cape Town, and the *Union Express* which ran in the opposite direction.

The original standard passenger coaches were replaced in 1927 by special articulated saloons imported from Britain that were

fitted with hitherto undreamed of luxuries. Their livery was blue and cream and the trains came to be known as 'those blue trains'. A decade later these were replaced, again by Metropolitan Cammell, by fully air-conditioned sleeping coaches and all-steel, air-conditioned lounge and dining cars with blue leather upholstered seats, loose cushions and writing tables with headed notepaper. At the rear of the trains was an observation car. The *Blue Train* was officially named in 1946 following the suspension of its operation during the Second World War.

Two to three times a week – only twice when I rode it – the train runs the thousand or so miles from Petoria to Cape Town. In the old days it used to meet the Union Castle liners, and still preserves that vanished air of pre-war gentility – it ignores the outside world. At a sedate 40 miles per hour it transports its pampered passengers smoothly and soundlessly behind windows tinted with pure gold to keep out the glare. The saloons include private suites with lounge and bathroom, a bar and, on my train, a pince-nezed maître d'hôtel whose fastidious regard would do credit to Claridges. This, in short, is a vehicle on which travel itself is the destination.

Unlike any other train I know, the *Blue Train* is virtually noiseless and vibration-free when on the move, the ultra-comfortable ride made possible by air-sprung bogies. My train comprised 16 coaches permanently coupled, and was hauled between Pretoria and Kimberley and Beaufort West and Cape Town by electric locomotives, and between Kimberley and Beaufort West, by diesel units. The steam locomotives used on this section, not so long ago, have been withdrawn.

My journey from Johannesburg to Cape Town was without incident. This was strange for me because, as readers may have noticed, invariably on my trans-global rail expeditions *something*, usually disastrous, happens. But incidents and the *Blue Train* are incompatible; the very idea! Twenty-six hours of serene gliding across South Africa is the order of the day. In a manner of speaking

I was moving in the wrong direction by leaving from Jo'burg. Had Cape Town been my departure point I would have followed the historic route by which the whites penetrated the interior, first by ox-carts through a precipitous and almost trackless mountain terrain, later by the railway tracks which were laid up the Hex River in the late 1870s, rising from the orchards of Worcester to the top of the pass at nearly 3,600 feet. As it was the fertile, temperate plains of Cape Province with their vineyards and oak trees in the lee of the grandiose spurs and peaks of the Drakensberg Mountains were my viewing treat towards the end of the ride.

I felt out of touch with South Africa on the train, with all life having to be viewed through those gold windows. The tinted glass hindered the taking of photographs, so I retreated to the observation car where I could snap away to my heart's content through about the only openable window on board.

Eating on a train is, for many of us, one of life's small joys. Eating on the *Blue Train* is more joyous still. The dining car on my train sat 46 people, and one could choose from a menu of international or traditional South African cuisine of the highest standard. A wide selection of South African and imported wines was available, but who would want the imported stuff when there was the classic nectar of Paarl and Stellenbosch on tap?

Unfortunately, Kimberley was reached at night. The town bears few signs of its diamond rush today. Except for the Big Hole, the site of the largest pit ever dug by Man (though I had obtained the notion that the one I had looked upon in Manchuria bore this distinction) and now a monument, there's nothing left to see of Kimberley's diamond mining heritage. I was told by a fellow traveller that when the pit was closed in 1914, it had yielded 28 million tons of gravel and mud as well as three tons of diamonds. Except for this amazing accomplishment, history has passed the town by. But 50 miles south is De Aar. And here it was easy to see why steam had survived so long in South Africa with, visible

through those golden windows, rows of steam locomotives lined up as if for inspection by a passing general. De Aar is not a town one would visit for fun. Central junction of the republic, like Crewe in Britain, it is an out-and-out railway colony standing in the middle of nowhere, its rail yards all smoke, grime and coaldust; the sort of place I rather like.

The morning of my second day saw us climbing the Hex River Pass by an extraordinary series of curves so that at one point, as in the Canadian Rockies, the front and rear of the train ran parallel but in opposite directions. And with the dawn, I looked out upon a wilderness like nowhere else on Earth; the Great Karoo Desert over which the Afrikaners made their Great Trek in the 1830s. This immense tract, nearly a third of South Africa's area, was once a swamp, though today its burnt landscape makes this hard to believe. Personally I have an affection for deserts, finding the awesome desolation and limitless space to be evocative and exciting.

With the petering out of the Great Karoo, the line passes through a land of small flat-topped hills, sparsely punctured by windpumps and remote red-roofed farmsteads shaded by sentinels of cypress trees. An 'end of the journey' feeling began to permeate us denizens of the coaches.

Arrival at Cape Town was at the civilised hour of 11.00 a.m., and I could see the familiar shape of Table Mountain long before we got there. I never thought I'd be sorry to leave a train of such overwhelming luxury, but I was.

For my second sojourn in South Africa I found a country freed from apartheid, though racial attitudes seemed to have changed little beyond the most visible and superficial manifestations of segregation. This was in March 1998, when I had come to stay with friends outside Johannesburg. But whereas I had considered apartheid to be obnoxious, I was to find the inevitable backlash of

violence and what was looked upon as the 'black menace' equally disquieting.

Johannesburg city centre had, since my last visit, become virtually a 'no-go' zone, particularly after dark; even in daytime muggings and murder were not uncommon. Much of the white populace now go about their business with automatic pistols in their belts and in the more affluent suburbs the homes of the white occupants had become, literally, well-guarded fortresses. The 'City of Gold', as Jo'burg is called, is by far the largest urban complex in Africa south of Cairo with an official population exceeding three million though, in reality, probably double that figure. Brash, gritty, fast growing, ugly, are adjectives that can be applied to the place though, hand in hand, goes a metropolis of great wealth and energy blessed by a beautiful climate. Side by side with this wealth lies an eye-searing poverty all too visible in the squatter's camps and black townships that ring the centre.

It was in this unsettling atmosphere that I made my second trans-South Africa train ride, this one between Jo'burg and Durban on the express known as the *Trans-Natal*. Eleven years before, I had spent a night in Jo'burg's top central hotel, the Carlton, and had felt no qualms about walking the streets at any hour. What little walking I undertook there now I did with a sense of foreboding, made worse by firm advice from the railway staff to remain within the station while awaiting the 18.30 departure of my train.

The *Trans-Natal* may be classed as an express, but it holds not the slightest aspiration to approach the distinction of the *Blue Train*, as one might expect. And as if to emphasise this it left more than half an hour late. My second-class compartment (there are three classes on South African railways) was designed to hold a maximum of six in daytime and four at night when it transformed into four berths, and was entirely adequate. We were only four in the compartment for the whole journey of nearly a thousand miles,

our skin colours ranging through the full spectrum of the human race: black, brown, yellow and white.

The black African opposite me was a rotund, eternally-smiling individual who straightway introduced himself to trigger a round of introductions. Beside me was a lugubrious Pakistani and opposite him a soft-spoken Oriental gentleman from Thailand. Our conversation – when not attempting sleep – ranged, as they say, from popsies to politics which, with occasional sorties to the restaurant car, agreeably passed the daylight hours. Bedding was available if wanted.

I think there might have been technical problems at the time, but our train not only failed to make up for the late departure but dawdled and stopped at the slightest excuse. The route itinerary included Germiston, Heidelberg, Balfour North, Standerton, Volksrust, coal- and steel-producing Newcastle, the Orange Free State town of Kroonstad (supposedly named after a settler's horse), Ladysmith (famed for its siege by Boer forces during the Anglo–Boer War) and Pietermaritzburg, capital of Natal Province and another wartime town of note, though this time of the Anglo–Zulu War. Morning daylight illuminated a countryside bucking into hills and, between Pietermaritzburg and Durban, a region known as 'The Valley of a Thousand Hills' endowed with rocky gorges, spectacular waterfalls and exuberant vegetation.

We drew into Durban's uninspiring and dingy station a good two hours behind schedule and, needing exercise, I walked to the city centre. Its historic heart is the small Francis Farewell Square sprouting as many statues as trees and encircled by solid nineteenth-century buildings, the replica Belfast City Hall, the Natural History Museum and, across the road, the Old Railway Station since cut into sections to comprise the Workshop Shopping Mall.

Mohandas Gandhi spent his early life in Durban; the city is home to more Indians than any other outside India, and my walk

down Warwick Street with its Indian markets and mosques held distinct undertones of Bombay or Calcutta.

It is, however, the magnificent beaches that give to the city the appellation of resort and its wide flowerbed-bedecked promenade holds every entertainment facility imaginable. Heavy rollers offer fine surfing, though frequently these are of a size prohibiting safe bathing, the red warning flags being out just at the time I wanted a dip in the ocean to cool off in the abruptly warm and humid atmosphere.

This, my first visit to Durban, was disappointingly brief; its purpose no more than a sampling of a 'normal' South African train. And though, as previously mentioned, there might have been valid reasons for the delays, my return journey to Jo'burg was afflicted with more of the same. Worse, in fact; the train left Durban an hour late and arrived at its destination *three* hours behind schedule.

So to my third and latest South African rail journey in November 2000. And since some of my earlier observations in these pages have been about travel on rock-bottom trains it is fitting to end on a sky-high note of super luxury. This paragon of transportation is, of course, *The Pride of Africa*, run by Rovos Rail as an elite excursion train of exquisite perfection, possibly outdoing in extravagance even the *Blue Train*. I have to say the notion of riding it filled me with awe.

This, my fourth sojourn in South Africa, was to last no more than the inside of a week, but what a classy week it was! It started with a flight, courtesy of South African Airways who entered into the spirit of things by flying me from London to Johannesburg business class which, with its wide, near-horizontally-reclining seats, commodious legroom and faultless cuisine, began the pampering the moment of take-off. Actually, I have flown SAA before, though in less-exalted circumstances to find even economy class to be more than ample. As we descended towards

Johannesburg I watched a sunrise of majestic proportions confound the Southern African night.

From Jo'burg it was only a 50-minute hop to Durban from whence *The Pride of Africa* was to commence its run. And with a whole day and a night based at the old-established five-star Royal, the city's top hotel, I made the most of it with the abruptly sultry 28-degree temperature and warm sunshine mocking the windswept, rain-soaked Britain I had left barely 12 hours earlier.

Following a mighty breakfast I was driven in style to the Durban terminus of Rovos Rail, a mile or so beyond the city's shabby station that is unrepresentative of so flamboyant a resort-cum-maritime metropolis. And there, in a redundant freight yard of much more allure than the main station (and soon to be renovated by Rovos Rail to match its chief terminus at Pretoria), a champagne reception greeted the arriving guests – on *this* train we were classed as guests, not mere passengers – as the long and elegant train backed into the platform.

I should explain at this point that *The Pride of Africa* runs a number of routes throughout Southern Africa of from one to ten days' duration. As well as South Africa itself these cover Swaziland, Namibia, Mozambique, Zimbabwe, Botswana, Zambia, Tanzania and more, all utilising numerous halts for off-train excursions, safari drives and sightseeing trips. Mine was the three-day tour traversing Swaziland and ending at Pretoria.

Rovos Rail operates two such classic trains of superbly restored coaches, half of which date back to the 1920s. These coaches, as with India's *Palace on Wheels*, were rescued from dereliction in remote sidings all over the country, and then painstakingly transformed into conveyances of ornateness and grandeur. The use of traditional furnishings and period decor, with high-class craftsmanship evident in the fine wood panelling, ensured an atmosphere far in excess of the original embellishment. Each coach, from kitchen and restaurant cars to sleeper coaches, lounge coaches and guard's vans, has its own story to tell. A few, dating

back to 1911, were constructed in Europe and shipped to South Africa in the first half of the twentieth century while, again like the *Palace on Wheels*, some have carried royalty; others served as restaurants, but most ended their early existence mouldering under the African sun. Today, all are now cherished members of the Rovos Rail fleet of 60 coaches.

There's a story, too, behind each of the Rovos Rail steam locomotives used on short sections of the routes. Each is named after members of owner Rohan Vos' family. The first acquisition was No. 2702 *Bianca*, a Class 19D locomotive built by Borsig in 1938. The second was No. 2701 *Brenda*, another Class 19D found in a scrapyard in 1989. Rohan Vos had his eye on No. 3360 *Shaun* ever since he spotted it standing on the scrap line at Witbank in 1986, while *Tiffany*, No. 439, a Class 6 locomotive, was one of 40 constructed by Dubbs & Co in Glasgow. The latest is *Marjorie*, a 25NC locomotive that has been converted from coal to oil-fired traction. For the greater part of the routes diesel and electric locomotives, hired from South African Railways, are used, but for the first and last 50-odd miles in and out of the Rovos Rail home base of Pretoria one of the celebrated steam locomotives heads the train.

Though each 20-coach train can carry up to 72 passengers in unrivalled spaciousness, my group of fellow guests numbered just 26, distributed in three suites per coach including a Royal Suite equipped with a full-scale *en suite* bathroom. My de luxe suite contained a double bed, lounge area with bar fridge (its contents free of charge), toilet and shower, all air-conditioned and provided with windows that could be shuttered. Towards the front of the train was the restaurant, an exquisitely pillared car of Victorian aura, one of several though, in our case, one was adequate. The last coach was the lounge car fully equipped with armchairs and sofas, writing desk and bar. At its end was an outdoor observation platform overlooking the track.

This, then, was to be my home and domain over the next two nights and three days, interspersed with a trio of three to four-hour game safaris in both South Africa and Swaziland. My initial sense of awe began to subside and I felt that, maybe, I could cope after all with a few further days of pampering. At times luxury can be contagious!

My fellow guests were a mixed bag. The bulk of them were well-heeled Afrikaans-speaking Boers, but a few youngish European couples – German and Danish, an English lady from the Channel Islands, and an Australian journalist – provided variety. The staff, mostly white in our case, almost outnumbered the guests.

We left on time at 09.00, backing into the main station to join the Durban–Maputo line northwards. Until 1998, this line had not seen regular, long-distance passenger trains for decades, but the need for greater free movement between Swaziland, Mozambique and South Africa gave rise to the daily Trans-Lubombo Express. Though currently suspended – according to my end-of-2000 edition of *Thomas Cook's Overseas Timetable* – this train covers the 640 kilometres between Durban and Maputo in 20 hours. *The Pride of Africa* bypasses Maputo but would be riding the same line through Swaziland and close to the Mozambique border.

The first town reached was Stanger, a sugar-processing centre. It is also a town of significance to the Zulu people since Shaka, the great Zulu warrior-king and founder of the Zulu nation, is buried here. With the suburbs of Durban petering out, the landscape had become one of blue-green meadows bounded by timber and wattle plantations together with cane fields and rolling hills, the very same hills I had passed through on my earlier, more north-westerly but less exalted rail journey between Jo'burg and Durban several years earlier. Here, close to the coast, we were within shelling distance of the Anglo–Boer War battlefields of

Estowe, Elandslaagte and Dundee amongst others that once scarred the face of what is now called Kwa Zulu-Natal.

Following 'elevenses' at ten o'clock – a delicious snack comprising tea or coffee, fresh fruit juice and pastries – the first full meal of the trip was lunch at 12.30 p.m. in the restaurant car, a longish hike along gently-swaying corridors which was to provide virtually the only exercise on offer throughout the journey. And that first lunch was to set the standard of cuisine over the whole three days. How the chefs produced the superb meals served aboard *The Pride of Africa* under the conditions they worked was nothing short of miraculous. I visited the tiny and cramped kitchen, stiflingly hot, and this on top of the humid temperatures outside. The accent of the three-course meals was on local and traditional dishes, with vegetarian ones also available. And the choice was almost as wide as that of the selection of gorgeous South African wines.

The first prolonged halt took place at the Hluhluwe-Umfolozi Game Reserve, once the hunting ground of Zulu kings. I am not a fan of safari drives, my wife and I having sampled a few in Kenya and Tanzania which we found repetitious; though more to the point, I, having spent a week, unarmed, trekking through the East African bush on equal terms and at the mercy of its big game inhabitants, the heavily-controlled motor safari becomes, to me, anticlimactic in the extreme.

However, in the comparatively small Hluhluwe-Umfolozi the game is highly concentrated, and, within minutes of passing through the park gates, our vehicle was half-surrounded by elephants, some with young, one great tusker blocking our path. A little further on half a dozen rhinos dozed by the roadside, so close I felt like tickling their ribs. During the four-hour drive through undulating savannah we saw buffalo, wildebeest, zebra, giraffe, elephant, rhino, hyena and an assortment of antelope, many at close quarters and in considerable numbers, before dusk

sent us back to the train for our 8.00 p.m. dinner, the one repast where a jacket and tie was the order of the day.

During the meal the train continued northwards, crossing the border into Swaziland at Golela. We were entering the smallest country in the southern hemisphere and one of its few remaining African monarchies. In company with an independent Lesotho it is bounded entirely by South Africa, except for its eastern border with Mozambique. The land has long been inhabited, though the Swazi people did not arrive until relatively recently, gaining independence from the Zulus early in the nineteenth century. This independence was recognised by the British in 1881 and by the Boers three years later and, since the Swazi sided with the British in the Boer War, their territory was made a British protectorate under the High Commission for South Africa prior to gaining full independence and admission to the United Nations in 1968.

From midnight until late the following morning the train was supposed to have remained stationary though, in our case, being slightly behind schedule it carried on into the small hours. This was unfortunate because, not only was an early rise scheduled for another game drive, but such was the shaking and creaking of the old coaches that, for the majority of us, sleep was impossible. In this respect the *Blue Train* scored with its shake-reducing suspension.

This second drive was centred upon Mkhaya, Swaziland's refuge for endangered species, and, at 5.00 a.m., 26 bleary-eyed guests emerged from the train to clamber aboard a fleet of open-topped Land Rovers. The reserve takes its name from the Mkhaya tree which abounds here, its fruits used by the Swazis for the production of beer. Lying close to the hamlet of Phuzamoya, the park is privately owned and encompasses no more than 24 square miles.

Our three-hour drive allowed us to observe most of its full range of endangered species which included white and black rhino,

elephant, buffalo, roan and sable antelope as well as a variety of colourful birds that find the rich pastures and fruit-laden trees of great benefit. The drive ended at a very civilised encampment beneath the enfolding foliage of a giant so-called sausage tree where the ritual of 'elevenses' took place.

Back on the train, brunch was served in the dining car as the journey continued across Swaziland's endlessly forested countryside to the border township of Komatipoort, a border of both Mozambique and South Africa, the former marked by foothills of the Lebombo Mountain range.

Almost at once *The Pride of Africa* entered the Kruger National Park, proclaimed a conservation area by President Kruger a little over a century ago, and at Malelane, a fair-sized township, we disembarked again for our third and final game drive.

The Kruger is the largest and oldest National Park in South Africa, internationally renowned as one of the world's most important game reserves. It extends 220 miles from north to south with a maximum breadth of 55 miles and a total area of 7,523 square miles. It is bounded in the north by the wide Limpopo River, in the south by the Crocodile River (over which we were to drive), in the east by the Mozambique frontier and in the west by a 1,100-mile impregnable fence that protects humans from animals and animals from humans.

These vital statistics were reeled off to us as we assembled prior to boarding the high-sided specially constructed vehicles that made for the only traffic on the tarmac and dirt roads veining this section of the park. For the first hour of the three-hour drive we saw no game whatsoever; that is, unless you count as 'game' a large black dung-beetle rolling a cricket-sized ball of elephant excrement, together with his mate clinging to it, across the road. It certainly intrigued our group as we stopped to watch, with admiration, the insect's Herculean exertions.

Straightway it became apparent that, unlike most of the parks in Southern Africa, the Kruger fails to offer a true wilderness

experience. Its infrastructure is too highly developed and organised; I felt I was in no more than an inflated Whipsnade Zoo lacking animals. But the last couple of hours produced our reward.

Except for lion and leopard, we were to come upon an abundance of the three remaining 'big five' animal category: elephant, buffalo and rhino, as well as giraffe, hippo and a large variety of antelope in addition to smaller beasts including a pack of wild dogs and a litter of young hyenas looking so innocent and cuddly at that age.

With the dusk our meanderings ended at a scarcely native *boma* – the Swahili name for a fenced tribal enclosure – where an outdoor buffet of a scope and quality that could hardly have been bettered by a royal banquet awaited us before, slightly the worse for an excess of wine, we were returned to the train and a night of blessed immobility.

On the move once more, the train ascended from the Lowveld to the comparatively stark grassland of the Highveld, its progress accompanied by a dramatic change of scenery. The climb to the escarpment between the two townships situated at the bottom and top of the wall is but 6 kilometres, but the line has to cover 14 kilometres to enable trains to make the grade. Traversing this escarpment was not always an easy task and, at first, trains were assisted up the gradients utilising a ratchet between the rails. While breakfasting, those who had risen early enough were awarded the sight of the impressive waterfall that climaxes the train's slow grind through the high cliffs that hem in the line, occasionally giving way to allow magnificent views over a tortured landscape.

And then, all of a sudden, everything flattened out and we were rumbling through townships with homely names like Belfast and Middelburg to one called Witbank which holds a special significance for Anglophiles. It was here that a young Winston Churchill, as an escaping prisoner-of-war of the Boers, took refuge

in a mine-shaft to subsequently jump a freight train, on the same line upon which we were travelling, to make good his escape.

A final and exquisite lunch, a last free drink at the bar, and everyone trooped out of the train to watch the steam locomotive *Brenda* take her place at the head of our line of coaches for the final 50-mile run to Pretoria. I was lucky enough to be in the right place at the right moment to climb into the cab prior to the locomotive performing its shunting movements to attain the right line to couple to the train. I was the envy of other guests who were slower on the uptake.

We arrived at Rovos Rail's private terminus at Pretoria's capital Park on the stroke of 15.00. Originally used by South African Railways as a maintenance depot, the complex was totally rebuilt in 1999 and is now the departure and arrival station for all *The Pride of Africa* rail excursions.

I have visited Pretoria only once before, and that but briefly. However, it was long enough to discern that, though only 60 kilometres from crime-ridden, razor-wire-bounded Jo'burg, the two cities could scarcely be more different. The administrative capital of South Africa and seat of government for half the year, alternating with Cape Town, Pretoria is a city of comely parks and gardens, trim residential districts and dignified government buildings. On the heights at the edge of the city stands the brooding Voortrekker Monument that commemorates the Great Trek. Surrounded by a carved laager of ox-wagons, it eloquently expresses the stubbornness and beliefs that powered the Boer's journey across South Africa.

But I was to see even less of Pretoria on this occasion. To give a grand finale to my week of luxurious living I was met at the station by a crown prince and his entourage, or at least his bodyguard and driver.

And here I must explain that my Jo'burg friends happen to be the exiled royal family of Albania, who it has been my good fortune to know for many years and with whom I stay whenever

circumstances find me in South Africa. With them, this time, I spent no more than a couple of days before flying home to a sodden and abruptly down-to-earth Britain.

Epilogue

As I finish writing this book our UK railways are, this first year of the new millennium, gradually emerging from a crisis resulting from a series of fatal derailments and disasters which entailed the replacement of large sections of track throughout the country. Trains have been reduced to speeds of 20 miles per hour in many cases, resulting in massive disruption and huge inconvenience to the travelling public who, in desperation, turned to alternative methods of conveyance. But Britain's congested highways and overburdened airways, unable to sustain further growth, make a poor substitute. Future expansion of mass transportation assuredly lies with the railways.

A spark of this hoped-for prospect was ignited in the historic Belgian city of Bruges when, in December 2000, at a special ceremony that I was privileged to attend, Sir Richard Branson and his Virgin Rail launched a £1 billion fleet of diesel-engined, sloping-nosed trains capable of speeds of 125 miles per hour. These trains, it is expected, will speed rail travel out of the inertia into which it has fallen. The new air-conditioned coaches, complete with airline-style audio entertainment and other refinements, should not only offer improved comfort and speeds but a vastly increased frequency of services across the network.

Following decades of under-investment, a new railway age may be dawning in Britain at last. We can only wait and see.

But this, though exciting, is of only passing relevance to the subject of this book. For a willing traveller, a voyage by rail, wherever in the world, in this modern age can be a journey inward and backward; an invitation to unwind, ruminate and enjoy.

That, at least, is one man's observation and perhaps a somewhat highfalutin one. On a more basic level there's much to be said about railway journeying, and if my own experiences have awoken the realisation of what trains can offer the enjoyment- or adventure-seeking traveller, then my chronicle will not have been in vain.

References

1. Kennedy, Ludovic *Railway Journeys* (1980, Cassell)

2. Portway, Christopher *Pedal for your Life* (1996, Lutterworth Press) and *A Good Pair of Legs* (1999, Rambler's Association)

3. Portway, Christopher *Journey Along the Andes* (1993, Impact Books)

4. ibid.

5. Box, Ben *South American Handbook* (1999, Footprint Handbooks)

RAMBLING
ON THE ROAD TO
ROME

Peter Francis Browne

summersdale *travel*

Donna Carrère

MONKEYS
IN THE RAIN

TRAVELS, TRIALS AND TRIBULATIONS
IN SOUTH EAST ASIA

summersdale *travel*

John Wassner

espresso with the

HEADHUNTERS

A JOURNEY THROUGH THE JUNGLES OF BORNEO

summersdale *travel*

TOM CUNLIFFE

good
vibrations

COAST TO COAST BY HARLEY

'A PITHY THROBBER OF A BOOK' CHRIS STEWART

summersdale *travel*

some like it cold

NEVILLE SHULMAN

ARCTIC
AND
ANTARCTIC
ADVENTURES

FOREWORDS BY
SIR RANULPH FIENNES
& DAVID HEMPLEMAN-ADAMS

summersdale *travel*

two feet,
four paws

walking the dog 4,500 miles

Spud Talbot-Ponsonby

Foreword by Ffyona Campbell

summersdale *travel*

For a current publishing catalogue
and full listing of
Summersdale travel books,
visit our website:

www.summersdale.com